921

Library of
Davidson College

NAVARRA

BOOKS IN THE BASQUE SERIES

A Book of the Basques
by Rodney Gallop

In a Hundred Graves: A Basque Portrait
by Robert Laxalt

Basque Nationalism
by Stanley G. Payne

Amerikanuak: Basques in the New World
by William A. Douglass and Jon Bilbao

Beltran: Basque Sheepman of the American West
by Beltran Paris, as told to William Douglass

The Basques: The Franco Years and Beyond
by Robert P. Clark

The Witches' Advocate: Basque Witchcraft
and the Spanish Inquisition (1609–1614)
by Gustav Henningsen

Navarra: The Durable Kingdom
by Rachel Bard

THE BASQUE SERIES

NAVARRA

The Durable Kingdom

RACHEL BARD

UNIVERSITY OF NEVADA PRESS
RENO, NEVADA
1982

Basque Series Editor: William A. Douglass

University of Nevada Press, Reno, Nevada 89557 USA
© Rachel Bard 1982. All rights reserved
Printed in the United States of America

Library of Congress Cataloging in Publication Data
Bard, Rachel, 1921–
　Navarra, the durable kingdom

　(The Basque series)
　Bibliography: p.
　Includes index.
　1. Navarre (Spain)—History. I. Title. II. Series
DP302.N27B37　1982　　946'.52　　82–8660
ISBN 0–87417–073–7　　　　AACR2

CONTENTS

Introduction		xi
I.	Prehistory: The Mystery of the Basques	1
II.	From Celts to Romans	6
III.	Four "Conquests"	10
IV.	The Young Kingdom, 824 to 1004	19
V.	The Pivotal Reign of Sancho the Great	29
VI.	The Foral Base	41
VII.	In the French Orbit	59
VIII.	Dynastic Decline, 1349 to 1517	70
IX.	Ten-Year Transition	84
X.	Navarra Under the Hapsburgs	98
XI.	Less War, More Government	104
XII.	The Kingdom Within a Kingdom	123
XIII.	Cautious Progress	138
XIV.	Continuity in Crisis	149
XV.	The Long Adjustment: From Kingdom to Foral Province	172
XVI.	Into the Twentieth Century	189
XVII.	The Durable Province	199
Appendices		212
Notes		215
Bibliography		230
Index		241

ACKNOWLEDGMENTS

Research for this book was carried forth in Pamplona, Madrid, Bayonne, San Sebastián, Pau, Paris, London, New York, San Francisco, Seattle and Reno. To the many, many persons who helped along the way, my sincere gratitude.

My first thanks, for encouragement during the long years of preparation, go to William A. Douglass and Jon Bilbao of the Basque Studies Program at the University of Nevada, Reno. Their patience and constructive suggestions spurred me on, just as the example of their scholarship illuminated my efforts. The resources of the Basque Collection at the University of Nevada Library were of inestimable help, and I also appreciated the cheerful assistance of Virginia Jacobsen, Jill Berner and Linda White of the Basque library staff.

Many other libraries and librarians have earned my fervent gratitude, especially the British Library and the Biblioteca General in Pamplona—from which I still treasure my Tarjeta de Lector N° 41.

I wish, also, to acknowledge the debt I owe to those persons who read portions of the manuscript, or who permitted me to interview them and draw on their wisdom and knowledge: in particular, Jaime del Burgo, Florencio Idoate, José María Lacarra, Idoia Estornés Zubizarreta and especially Javier Zabalo Zabalegui, who generously read and commented on an early draft of the entire manuscript.

My researches in Spain were greatly facilitated by the hospitality and refuge afforded by my Basque landlady and friend in Pamplona, Francisca Zubeldía.

Finally, my deepest thanks to Joan Connelly Ullman of the University of Washington, whose impeccable standards for academic writing have been my constant if seldom attained examplar. Without her impetus the book might never have been written: during research on my thesis, I complained about the lack of a history of Navarre. "Why don't you write one?" she said. So I did.

March 1982   Rachel Bard

INTRODUCTION

When Navarra, after seven hundred years of independence, capitulated to Ferdinand II of Aragon, in 1512, Spain was at last complete, ready to bid a tardy goodbye to the Middle Ages and adjust to its new role as not only a European but also a world power.

But the century that was a turning point for Spain was only a way point in the thousand-year history of the Kingdom of Navarra. Despite their nominal loss of independence, the Navarrese were determined to maintain their right to govern themselves. They insisted that their new king respect their rights and liberties, embodied in their fueros—their customary laws.

Since the year 824 every king of Navarra had sworn to abide by the fueros. Ferdinand could do no less. Navarra was absorbed into Spain on its own terms, its governmental system virtually intact. And for three hundred years more, Navarra, and only Navarra among the components of the new Spain, continued to enjoy the designation and the autonomy of a kingdom.

What can explain the unique durability of this small, seemingly vulnerable state?

Geography is part of the answer. Navarra is one of the seven provinces that constitute the "Basque Country," along with Vizcaya, Guipúzcoa and Alava in Spain and, in southwest France, Basse Navarre, Labourd and Soule. But unlike the other three Spanish Basque provinces, Navarra is squarely on the border between the Iberian Peninsula and the rest of Europe. Loyalty of such a strategically located people could be insured by respecting its tradition of self-government.

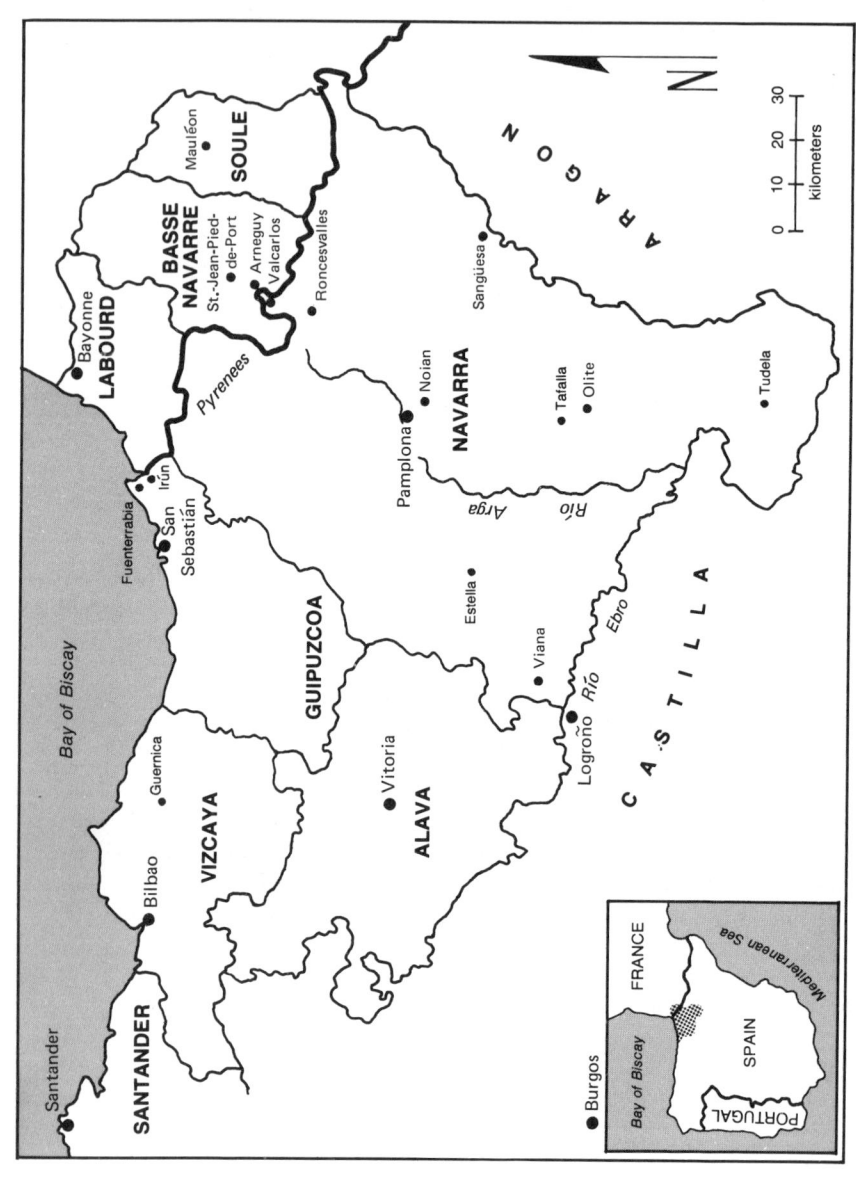

The Basque Country.

INTRODUCTION   xiii

"Basqueness" is also part of the answer, though Navarra's ethnic base is not so solidly Basque as is Vizcaya's, Guipúzcoa's and Alava's, because Navarra has been more subject to racial admixtures of invaders, settlers and passers-through from north and south. (Hence the frequent references to "Navarra and the Basque Provinces" or to "Vasconavarra," the convenient term that includes all four.) Still, in Navarra as throughout the Basque Country, a lively and combative sense of a national identity has prevailed for many centuries—and, as is dramatically evident, still prevails.

Finally, there is the devotion of the people of Navarra to their foral tradition (to adopt the Spanish adjective). This concept of the fueros as an unwritten but binding guarantee of rights and liberties was not unique to Navarra. But nowhere else did the fueros remain in full force so long—persisting until the kingdom became a province, in the nineteenth century. Even today, much survives, nourishing the considerable degree of self-government the province has managed to retain.

To borrow from Rodney Gallop, in his *Book of the Basques:*

> Basque history . . . is the history of the independence of the Basque provinces, and of their gradual submission, not so much to the countries to which they offered allegiance, as to the irresistible forces of time and progress. It resolves itself into the history of the *fueros,* . . . the traditional inheritance of the Basques from the Dark Ages and the warrant of their national independence, to which they clung for nearly a thousand years.

Without fail, as we trace the history of the Kingdom of Navarra, we find the foral tradition the interwoven thread of continuity.

I

Prehistory: The Mystery of the Basques

THE STORY OF NAVARRA STARTS WITH the tantalizingly incomplete story of the Basques, key to the kingdom's character.

The Basque homeland is a compact area straddling the western Pyrenees, including four present-day provinces of Spain (Navarra, Guipúzcoa, Vizcaya and Alava, known collectively as Vasconavarra) and three of southwest France (Labourd, Basse Navarre and Soule). It is easy to define geographically but impossible to account for historically.

Few ethnic origins are as cloaked in mystery. Theories abound as to where the Basques came from, and when. The Caucasus, Siberia, Finland and cradles of such ancient Mediterranean civilizations as the Phoenician have been proposed as points of origin. An early medieval traveler from France held that the Basques must be of the same derivation as the Scots, because of the many similarities, even to the men's short skirts.[1] A later and only slightly more reasonable hypothesis was that the Basques as well as the inhabitants of the Canary Islands (who have similar cranial structure) are descendants of the people of lost Atlantis.[2]

Nevertheless there is now general agreement on two facts: that the area known as the Basque Country has been inhabited for tens of thousands of years, certainly since the Upper Paleolithic Age; and that its present occupants, descended from races established there since pre-Celtic times, have maintained a unique ethnic identity over more centuries than has any other European people.

But whether the persons who lived there forty thousand years ago were direct precursors of present-day Basques may never be known. In spite of centuries of archeological, anthropological, linguistic—and recently, biological[3]—research, we still do not know exactly when the history of today's Basques began. Julio Caro Baroja, the contemporary ethnologist, speculates that present-day Basque culture may be considered the result of a series of cultural cycles that began with the Franco-Cantabrian cycle of hunters and wild-food gatherers of the Upper Paleolithic Age.[4]

But not until the end of this era—which lasted from about 35,000 to 10,000 B.C.—do we find concrete evidence of a people who could possibly be the ancestors of the Basques of historic times.

Toward the close of the Upper Paleolithic Age, about 15,000 to 10,000 B.C., the Magdalenian culture flowered in an area that curved around the Bay of Biscay, from Cantabria in Spain, through the Basque Country, and to the Dordogne River in France. The people of this era sought shelter in natural caves near rivers or other water sources. Deep in many of these caves they left startlingly realistic animal paintings, including many species still to be found in the area and others now extinct.[5]

Two of these caves, one at either end of the area the Magdalenian culture embraced, are particularly significant because of the variety and excellent preservation of their painted bisons, bulls, boars, oxen, deer and horses. These are the Cave of Altamira near Santander in Spain, one of the first to be discovered (1868), and Lascaux near the Dordogne, discovered in 1940, both subsequently closed to the public to prevent deterioration of the paintings.

Not much evidence of the cave cultures has been found yet within the Basque Country, which Altamira and Lascaux bracket. But recent explorations promise the substantiation of a link between the Upper Paleolithic people in what is now the Basque Country and the French and Cantabrian cave dwellers. Two examples are the caves of Santimamine (studied since

1917) and Ekaín, both in Vizcaya. At Ekaín, discovered only in 1969, and where exploratory work is still in its early stages, some sixty drawings have been documented, including fish (rare in Paleolithic art) and thirty-three horses showing great similarity to the present-day Pyrenean horse.[6]

Whether the cave paintings were created as celebration of the hunt or propitiation of the gods or simply as exuberant self-expression we shall probably never know. But the fact that so many similar paintings are found within a rather precisely limited area does give support to the theory that within that area there was a community of thought, traditions, perhaps even language.[7]

For the succeeding Mesolithic and Neolithic Ages (to about 2500 B.C.) we have no such striking evidence of what the enigmatic ancestors of the Basques were up to. But we do know that at least toward the end of this period they were no longer cave dwellers and had begun to build shelters for themselves and their dead.

The Basque Country offers growing evidence of inhabited localities dating from the late Neolithic Age, when megalithic constructions proliferated. These constructions were dolmens: funerary shelters with upright stones for walls, topped by horizontal stone slabs for a roof.

During the late Neolithic Age (from about 2000 B.C.) the practice of dolmen building and its funerary cult spread northward through Spain and on into western Europe and Scandinavia, possibly disseminated by "missionaries." Whoever introduced the practice seems to have found many converts among the Basques. Remains of more than four hundred dolmens and other burial structures, mostly on high ground, have been documented in the Basque Country.[8] Some of the burial structures, however, may belong to a later culture.

In spite of plundering and natural deterioration over the millenia, these dolmens, during the past three-quarters of a century, have yielded revealing clues to the culture of their builders: not only human remains, but also human possessions. These include enough copper and bronze objects to indicate that the age of metals had reached the Basque Country.[9]

There is still no way to prove that the dolmen builders were a continuation of the race or races that lived in the caves. But the anthropological evidence shows no appreciable difference between the two, and both have characteristics typical of present-day western Pyrenean Basques.[10]

Animal husbandry began sometime toward the end of the Neolithic Age. By then, men of the northern Iberian Peninsula had learned to tame and breed, at least to some extent, the sheep, cow, horse, pig and goat. With this began a practice that had an enormous effect on Navarra's (and Spain's) history: transhumance—the twice-a-year movement of grazing animals between summer and winter pastures.

Geography was at the root of it. From the Pyrenees to the central plains, northern Navarra, cradle of the future kingdom, is a conglomeration of ridges and valleys formed by the rivers that feed the Ega, the Arga and the Aragon. To make the most of what nature had presented them with, the early Basques grazed their animals on the lowlands and plains in winter, and led them to mountain pastures in spring and summer. The result was increased opportunity for cultural interchange. Shepherds transmitted new customs, transported new tools and materials. In their wake came commercial travelers. Consequently, throughout the land where the pastoral life prevailed, we find similar megalithic constructions, ceramics, weapons and metal objects. This was an area embracing all the Pyrenees and their adjacent lowlands from the Ebro Valley to Aquitaine.[11]

At about the same time as they domesticated the beast, the protohistoric Basques learned to sow and reap. Primitive agriculture began in the valleys and lowlands. These two quite different activities—grazing and crop growing—were then, as so often throughout history, sometimes incompatible. The issues that divided the mountain dwellers from the valley dwellers during the second millenium B.C. revolved around the very basic question of landownership. The shepherds had adopted communal use, sharing pasturage and shelters. Plains dwellers, individually responsible for success or failure of their sowing, cultivating and harvesting, were drawn to private landownership.[12]

Thus began a divergence in interests and objectives of the inhabitants of the future Navarra that still obtains to some degree. The *montaña* is still sometimes at odds with the *ribera*. Today, the terms differentiate between the northern, predominantly Basque Country, close to the Pyrenees, and the southern plains and the broad valley of the Ebro.

THE AGE OF METALS

In spite of plenty of evidence of very early temporary habitations in the Basque Country, especially the high-country shelters of the pastoral itinerants, no remains have been found of what might have been permanent population centers until the end of the Bronze Age. During this period (until about 1000 B.C.) we can only presume that the same races were living and progressing toward what we call civilization in these mountains, valleys and high plains; cultivating some grains and nurturing flocks. No remains have yet been found of their activities in the interval.

But with the introduction of iron, around 1000 B.C., which implies more highly developed tools and a more settled existence, we find foundations of what were permanent population centers. The valleys of this mountainous region provided natural defensive sites where human beings could live with security and find the essentials of existence. So we find evidence of habitation on hillsides and near rivers. One such well-known site is at Echauri in mid-Navarra; others, in neighboring Alava, near Vitoria and La Guardia; others in Vizcaya.[13]

Based on the evidence at these sites and from excavations of burial sites, the inhabitants of the Basque Country of this era were mainly engaged in agriculture, pasturage and hunting. They knew how to work in metal and ceramics. They had weapons that could be used in hunting or for battle. And it was well for them that they were armed, for during this last pre-Christian millenium they were threatened for the first time by major invasions from the north.

II

From Celts to Romans

WE ARE NOW IN THE LAST THOUSAND years of the prehistoric period of the Basques. This millenium saw many foreign incursions into the Iberian Peninsula, but most of them apparently had stronger impact on other peoples than they did on the Basques. Documentation and evidence of these influences, though actively sought by linguists, archeologists and ethnologists, is still scanty.

Starting about 900 B.C., Indo-Europeans came down through the Pyrenees, entered Catalonia and eventually moved into the Basque Country. Other Germanic tribes, including the Celts, followed in waves, meeting the Iberian civilization that was well established in the east and south. These invaders infiltrated much of the Basque Country, sometimes encountering fierce resistance if they tried to settle there rather than pass through.

The Celts brought at least two innovations: their skill in metalworking and their custom of cremation. The second, unfortunately, destroyed most of the evidence of their culture, because worldly possessions were burned along with the deceased.

The Celts were not the only newcomers to the peninsula in the first millenium B.C., but they were the only ones, until the Romans, to penetrate deeply into this rugged northern area. Neither the Phoenicians nor the Greeks advanced beyond their

FROM CELTS TO ROMANS 7

geographically shallow colonizing and trading areas along the Iberian Peninsula's east and south coasts. The Phoenicians had been visiting Spain's shores since perhaps 1100 B.C. They were followed by the Greeks from about 600 to 300 B.C. Both peoples traded and founded cities, and certainly had a powerful cultural and economic impact on the coastal Iberian inhabitants, but none that has been ascertained on the northern interior.

The Carthaginians come closer. During their third-century B.C. penetration of the peninsula they reached the foothills of the Pyrenees, but did not try to conquer or colonize. Their relations with the Basques seem to have been good. The Carthaginians admired the Basques' warlike nature (a product of centuries of tribal conflicts) and readiness to serve as mercenaries—provided they were well paid and permitted to plunder. In fact Basques may have joined Hannibal's expedition to Italy in 216 B.C.

LIFE IN PREHISTORIC NAVARRA

When we reach the third century before the Christian era, we begin to perceive a portrait of the inhabitants of what was to become Navarra. We can describe, if imperfectly and incompletely, their society and their culture.

They no longer lived in tiny, separate, mutually suspicious groups, but in established communities. These were small and at high altitudes in the north, but larger and on flatter land in the central and southern regions. They were governed by councils of elders, and were led by their war chiefs. Women were in a position of power: inheritance of lands and honors was through the female line. But the distinction was earned, for women were responsible for the farming while the men rode off on horseback to hunt or engage in tribal brigandage. The Basques had learned how to make shoes of leather and garments of woven fiber, and how to brew a fermented drink like beer. They preserved and passed on their warrior epics through poetry and song.[1] They were speaking either the unique Basque language, or a close ancestor, but did not write it.[2]

Judging from the legends and folklore that have been passed on, their gods took many forms, mostly animallike or associated with such natural features as springs, trees, mountains and rocks—as well as the sun and the moon. Inasmuch as the Basque dwelling places were set apart geographically from each other by mountain ranges, each little valley would be likely to have its distinctive local deities. And there were different names for similar divinities.

Gods of human form were mostly feminine. One exception was Basajaun (or Baxajaun), lord of the forest, a hairy god who lived in the depths of the thickest woods. He was protector of the flocks, and when a tempest was imminent he cried out loudly to warn the shepherds so they could gather in their sheep.[3]

But if one divinity could be considered well known throughout the whole region, it was Mari—a name that in some areas meant "the lady." Mari could assume a number of forms but was usually a woman, often elegantly dressed. She was thought to live underground, and often appeared in caves, en route to or from her subterranean homes. Thus, many of her appellations referred to the caves she frequented, and differed from community to community.[4] She was sometimes known as "Andre Mari" (the lady Mari) or "Arpeko Saindua" (the saint of the cave).[5]

However, in spite of the rich tapestry of legend and myth that has been treasured, embroidered and orally handed down through the centuries, we have very little exact knowledge of the pre-Christian religion of the Basques.

We are on firmer ground when we look at the topography and geography of the future Navarra. Throughout this period and for many centuries to come, these physical characteristics were decisive in its evolution into a nation.

It covered about four thousand square miles. Most of it was mountainous. The northern third was within the Pyrenees proper. The central part was hill-encircled basins, the largest of which was to be the site of the capital, Pamplona. The southern part descended from high plateaus and steppes to the level of the River Ebro on the south. The Basque population was concentrated in the north, as it still is.

The Pyrenees were only an apparent barrier. If motivated by trade or war, the Basques could easily get through the mountains by any of a dozen passes and reach the rest of Europe— or Spain, if they were on the north side of the mountains. When pressed by enemies, the Basques could retreat far up into their valleys and either wait for the invaders to retire in disgust, or attack them from their familiar fastnesses if they ventured in.

Confined to their tight little valleys, the mountain-oriented Basques could not and would not take to the far-ranging peregrinations of their contemporaries north and south of the Pyrenees. But the fact that they did not travel widely did not mean isolation. Traders, immigrants and armies—the last usually bent on conquest not of the Basque lands but of the more appealing areas to north and south—passed through, inevitably pausing along the way and leaving some imprint on the native culture.

Two facts, then, helped shape Navarra's genesis and development as a nation: the mountain-valley habitat, and the Basques' exposure to foreigners.

Basques' devotion to their rather uninviting land was another factor. Theirs was already a strongly land-oriented society, but "ownership" of land had continued along the two paths that were laid out in late Neolithic times. Communal use of the *valle* had been an accepted concept since the early domestication of animals, when shepherds pastured their flocks in common on mountain slopes and jointly inhabited the valleys between the mountains. Later, when agriculture became important on the plains and broader river valleys, individual ownership of farmland became a mark of stability. Land was vigorously defended against invaders from outside, and sometimes against neighboring mountain dwellers who disputed rights to pasturage.[6]

For the Basques in general at this time, land meant primarily safety and survival. Later it meant economic security and enrichment and, finally, power. Strong identity with their hereditary lands and a demand that their property rights be respected have always characterized the Basques.

Such militant protectiveness of their territory was certainly not unique to the Basque people, but it is important to keep in mind as a factor that strengthened their resistance to any outsiders who were seen as a threat. For the Basques, the next few centuries were to bring many such threats. The first, coinciding with the dawn of the Christian era, came from the Romans, who in the first century B.C. arrived in the Basque Country, which they would call Vasconia.[7]

III

Four "Conquests"

UP TO THE FIRST CENTURY B.C., THE story of the Basques is seldom more than informed conjecture. But now the record becomes more precise. Thanks to surviving texts, studies in linguistics and extant cultural and ethnological traits that can be traced back to the dawn of the Christian era, we can document four decisive periods in the formation of the Kingdom of Navarra.

Each of the first three periods includes invasion, resistance and survival. These were the Roman, Visigothic, and Muslim eras. The fourth (which overlaps the third) is more complex: the time of Frankish influence, when Navarra was intermittently linked with the Duchy of Vasconia.

THE FIRST INVASION: 75 B.C.

The Roman period (75 B.C. to 468 A.D.) was a time of civilization for the wild, mountain folk. They acquired new ways, partly due to the indirect influence of the highly developed Roman culture, but equally because it was in general a time of peace, so their own institutions and customs could thrive.

The Romans reached Spain in force in 218 B.C. They did not try at once to penetrate the difficult northwest areas; they were

FOUR CONQUESTS 11

too occupied with driving out the Carthaginians in the south and east. Then they had to establish an administrative structure for the new territories. Eventually they reached Galicia and subdued the northwest. Then they turned eastward. By 19 B.C. the stubborn Cantabrians were finally defeated, with Caesar Augustus completing the conquest.

Pompey founded Pamplona (Pompaelo) in 75 B.C., on his way to subdue the rebel Sertorius, rival of the Roman dictator Silla. He intended the new town, on the banks of the River Arga in central Navarra, to be a great center of Roman culture and a powerful defense point on the route to the Pyrenees. Pamplona became a very Roman city, with temples, baths, luxurious villas, and columned public buildings. (Fragments of this culture are well represented in its Museum of Navarra today.) Latin was commonly spoken in the city. The Romans built a network of their excellent roads in Vasconia, and established a flourishing commerce with the local farmers and herdsmen, who regularly brought their goods to the city to market.

But direct Roman influence was greatest in the central and southern part of the future kingdom.[1] And even there it was not due to colonization from Rome or forced imposition of Roman customs, but to the inhabitants' adoption of what they recognized as useful new practices, some of which were brought back by mercenaries who fought in the Roman armies.

The Basques of Navarra began to farm in the Roman style (planting olive trees and grape vines), built Roman villas and incorporated Latin words into their language. Even rural towns had Roman-style mosaics, statues and inscriptions. Romanization was most intense around Sangüesa and Lumbier in the east, and along the Aragon and the Arga.[2]

In the northern mountain valleys, though, life was almost unaffected. The Basques continued to live by herding and farming, speaking their strange language, worshiping their ancient gods. For more than four centuries Rome held sway over the Iberian Peninsula, imposing its civilization on most of it to a marked degree. But toward the independent tribes in the north it maintained a live-and-let-live posture. The Basques in particular resisted or were unexposed to Roman institutions that most of the rest of the peninsula accepted: Roman law, language and religion (which, by the fourth century A.D., was Christianity).

THE SECOND INVASION

Next came the Visigoths. These partially Romanized and Christianized east Europeans had first overpowered Rome itself (410 A.D.), then moved westward, to establish a kingdom centered on Toulouse in southern France.

Their presence in Spain was preceded by waves of barbarians from northern Europe who had swept through Roman Gaul and saw Spain as their next area to exploit. The Suevi, Vandals and Alans reached the western Pyrenean passes and poured through Pamplona early in the fifth century, then collided with the aging Hispano-Roman civilization they found beyond the Pyrenees. They succeeded in occupying much of the peninsula, without pausing in Vasconia.

Rome's ability to hold its empire together had weakened. Faced with this new threat, the emperor called on the Visigoths, who had helped Rome try to keep peace in Gaul, to enter Spain and do the same service there. They occupied Tarraconensis (the territory from Catalonia to the upper Ebro Valley) in 415. By 468 they had successfully moved into the power vacuum left after the Roman decline—overcoming the barbarian invaders, but also replacing Rome as dominant presence in southern France and the Iberian Peninsula. Numbering about two hundred thousand, they were to maintain this position over a population of five million for two and a half centuries.

During the first hundred years, Toulouse remained the Visigothic capital, serving as headquarters for advances in Gaul as well as Spain. Then when the Franks pushed them out of Gaul, the Visigoths transferred their center to Toledo. But during the Toulouse period, from 409 to 507, the western Pyrenees saw an unusual amount of activity. As the bridge between Europe and the Iberian Peninsula, Vasconia was aswarm with foreign travelers, warriors and immigrants.

The Basques did not accept the Visigoths peaceably; in fact they resisted belligerently. Militarily they were not always successful. In the southern plains warfare was almost constant. Nature protected the mountain dwellers, fortunate in their isolation and the scanty attraction their homelands had for the Visigoths.

But the fifth and sixth centuries were turbulent times for the more populated areas. Pamplona was occupied more than once, but never for long.

FOUR CONQUESTS 13

Often, during the Visigothic ascendancy, the Basque tribes had to take joint defensive action. This resulted in tentative moves toward unification, if not political organization, for some small groups. During this time the old Roman distinctions of *vardulos, caristios* and *autrigones* for the different Basque peoples disappeared. These may have referred, respectively, to the peoples of Guipúzcoa, Alava and Vizcaya. But now all these, and the inhabitants of Navarra, came to be called *vascones,* which, like the name Vasconia, had survived from Roman times.

While the Basques were moving hesitantly toward nationhood, the Visigoths' hold on Hispania grew more tenuous. There had never been much intermarriage or social mixing between rulers and ruled. Visigothic law had even less impact than Roman law on the Basques. Increasingly, the Visigoths' control depended on the temporal power of their church, rather than on the rule of the aristocratic and standoffish Gothic oligarchy. And what ecclesiastical influence there was hardly reached most Basques.

In fact, Christianity of any description was by no means a universally observed religion in Vasconia even by the seventh century; some say not until the tenth.[3] During the Roman era it had reached some who lived in urban areas, but few in the countryside. The absence of inscriptions or other evidence of Christianity's presence in Vasconia during the Roman period makes it difficult to trace its beginnings. Nor is there any certain historical documentation on the widely accepted role that San Fermín played in bringing Christianity to the Basques.[4] According to the tradition that establishes him as Pamplona's patron saint, the evangelist Honesto and the bishop San Saturnino brought the Christian word from Toulouse in the first century A.D. Honesto subsequently ordained Fermín, son of a Pamplona senator. He later became the first bishop of Pamplona and its first martyr.

Whether these events really took place or not in this way, the mountain dwellers were slow to give up their old gods. And whatever advances Christianity made in Vasconia during the Visigothic period were due more to evangelization from Bayonne, just over the mountains, than to the influence of the Gothic capital at Toledo, hundreds of miles to the southwest. Even after the Visigothic King Reccared's conversion from Arianism to orthodox Catholicism in 587, and the changeover by the Visigothic church, there was little if any proselytizing of the Basques. Their active participation in the religious life of the Visigoths was occasional at best. We can pinpoint the occasions because of surviving records that show when Pamplona sent a bishop to attend the periodic Councils of Toledo. There is documentation of such ecclesiastical coexistence in 589, 681, 683 and 693, dates that coincided with Gothic occupations of Pamplona.[5]

In the early years of the eighth century the superficial and ineffective Visigothic rule in Spain, ripe for overthrow, received its death blow from an unexpected direction.

THE MUSLIMS: 714

In 711 Islam reached Spain and took over with explosive force. The Muslims, bearers of the new faith, reached the Basque Country in 714. Within five years they had overrun nearly all the peninsula.

As we have seen, the Visigothic yoke lay very lightly on the Basques, who lived virtually undisturbed and secluded in their mountains. Now the Muslims' attacks triggered the next phase in their evolution toward nationhood, setting in motion a train of events that resulted, after about two centuries, in the coalescense of the eastern Basque tribes into the Kingdom of Navarra. These events fall into a four-part sequence:

First, common defensive action (and later, offensive) against the Muslims but also against the Franks. The assaults were to come from all sides.

Second, regularization of a more or less permanent state of military preparedness, with an established command structure.

Third, gradual assumption by the war chiefs of leadership in peacetime spheres as well as on the battlefield.

Fourth, acknowledgment that the wartime organizational structure might be a workable way to govern a society that had begun to recognize and accept its common interests.

So for the Basques of Navarra, and indeed for most of northern Spain, the Muslim invasion and the immediately undertaken but long-drawn-out Reconquest turned out to be the transcendent events in their history. The conflict was primarily responsible for the birth of all the northern kingdoms.

At the time, though, the arrival of Muslim armies probably seemed to the Basques more incidental than transcendent: one more invasion of a homeland that had undergone and survived many.

The Vasconia that the Muslims ventured into in 714 had changed considerably from the land of the loosely allied bellicose tribes that the Romans had elected not to Romanize and the Visigoths had grandly ignored, after the initial battles. Agriculture was now serious business. Farmers and herders now recognized that success depended as much on human ingenuity and hard work as on the whim of the gods. Christianity was making inroads on paganism, and was enormously strengthened by the Muslim threat. Monasteries were already flourishing. According to legend, that of Leyre had been established in 435; Irache, during the Visigothic reign; Roncesvalles, in 638.

Towns were growing and being fortified. Now in time of attack, the populace no longer had to flee up the valleys.

Devoted as the Basques were to their land, it was not very attractive to the Muslims. A medieval Arab manuscript notes:

> Banbaluna [Pamplona] is in the middle of high mountains, and deep valleys; little favored by nature. The inhabitants are poor and hungry and give themselves to brigandage. They mostly speak Basque, which makes them incomprehensible.[6]

Nevertheless, when the Muslims set out to conquer the Iberian Peninsula, the eastern Basque lands were part of their target: partly because they had total victory in mind, partly because to reach France and its riches, they had to get through the Pyrenees.[7]

Musa, leader of the Muslims and the Islamized Berbers, their North African allies, penetrated Vasconia in 714 but did not conquer it. In 718 a second Muslim army came and Pamplona capitulated. In 732, the Arab governor of Spain, Abd-al-Rahman, led a force into France via Pamplona, which he made his headquarters. Proceeding with his vast army through the Pass of Roncesvalles, he reached Poitiers, but before he arrived at Tours with its tempting booty, was repulsed by Charles Martel, king of the Franks. The Muslims fell back, most of them returning to the southern part of the peninsula. During their initial ascendancy, they inhabited the Ebro Valley without much serious challenge, but never really dominated any area north of it. Raids and border battles between Muslims and Basques went on well into the eleventh century, but by and large, peaceful coexistence and even occasional alliance (against the Franks) were, from about 800, the rule, especially in the southern areas. Pamplona was frequently attacked and occasionally occupied and garrisoned, but each time managed to extricate itself from the infidel yoke.

As for the less accessible northern and mountainous areas, if any Muslim dared to come up from the plains, the maddeningly elusive Basques fought back vigorously: creeping through the woods, falling on the enemy camps, striking swiftly, then retreating in all directions before any resistance could be organized. Their way of fighting—Arturo Campión, the devoted Basque spokesman and historian, tells us—owed little to art and less to military science; it was the fruit of inspiration and a warlike spirit, goaded by patriotism.[8]

But other enemies were now worrying the Basques of Pamplona.

THE FRANKS

Since the seventh century there had been an ephemeral Duchy of Vasconia on the other side of the Pyrenees. First it was subject to the Merovingian kings, the first Frankish dynasty, and the duchy was ruled by their appointees. Later this allegiance weakened and it was governed by its own *gascon* (northern Basque) dukes. Their domain waxed and waned, sometimes reaching, at least nominally, from the Garonne to the Ebro. The common interests of the Duchy of Vasconia and that of Aquitaine to its north gave rise to the appellation "double duchy"; it lasted, at least as a military alliance, from 660 to 778. During this stage, Basques on both sides of the Pyrenees cooperated in resistance to Visigoths, Muslims and Franks. But it has not yet been established that the Basques to the south were associated politically with those who owed allegiance to the Duke of Vasconia.[9]

In the eighth century, while al-Andalus (Islamic Spain) was consolidating its emirate in central and northern Spain, and dealing with divisions and rebellions in its own ranks, the Frankish kings were expanding their borders. They took over Aquitaine in 760, then developed a renewed and lively interest in Vasconia.

Charlemagne, king of the Franks, moved south in 778, hoping to make conquests in northern Spain. His main objective was Zaragoza, where he had been promised collaboration by some rebel Muslim chiefs. But this venture failed and he started homeward, pausing on his way to demolish Pamplona's walls. Thereafter, as his army filed through the Pass of Roncesvalles, the enraged Basques swooped down from the thickly wooded mountainsides, fell on and annihilated the rearguard (where Roland memorably died), and disappeared without a trace. Charlemagne, being in the vanguard, escaped. But (the chronicler reports) the memory of the defeat eclipsed in his heart all his previous successes.

After this he paid more attention to Septimania: an area in southern France that included the northeast corner of the Iberian Peninsula (present-day Catalonia). By early in the ninth century the Franks created the "Spanish March," a buffer between al-Andalus and France.

But the Franks did not completely ignore the western Pyrenees. Though usually harassed whenever they entered the mountain passes in the west, they continued their incursions there for half a century, from about 793 to 844. For much of this time, as we shall see, Pamplona was actually under their or their *gascon* puppets' rule.

While the chieftains of Pamplona (the name was used for the whole area around the city) and the valleys of the Pyrenees felt pressures to unite and fight their foes on both sides, the other incipient nations of the northern peninsula were also organizing military drives and forming tribal alliances.

THE OTHER NORTHERN LANDS

Who were these ninth-century neighbors of Pamplona's?

First, far to the northwest, Galicia remained isolated from much of the struggle. Host to many Hispano-Gothic refugees from the initial Muslim invasions, it was not concerned with religious or territorial aggrandizement, but with absorption of immigrants and maintenance of the status quo.

Not so the kingdom of Asturias and the Cantabrian region. The legendary hero Pelayo, said to be a descendant of the last Visigothic king, led resistance by the mountain dwellers of Cantabria and routed the Muslims about 722 at Covadonga. He is generally recognized as progenitor of the Asturian dynasty that produced such brilliant anti-Muslim warrior kings in the next century and a half as the first three Alfonsos, culminating in the one who called himself "emperor" (Alfonso III, 866 to 911). Their successful forays southward from the Cantabrian mountains pushed the Christians' frontier onto the high plains of León. By the beginning of the tenth century, when Ordoño II (grandson of Alfonso III) moved the royal residence from Oviedo to León, the Kingdom of Asturias had become the Kingdom of Asturias-León.

Thence, and from the Cantabrian Mountains and the western Pyrenees, settlers (including many Basques) moved southward in the ninth and tenth centuries into the vacuum of the Duero River Valley, which had probably been largely evacuated during the Muslim-Christian wars. This frontier population was the kernel of the county, eventually the kingdom, of Castile. Under Fernán González, count of Castile (932 to 970), the Castilians were to wrest the leadership of the Reconquest from Asturias-León and prove formidable neighbors to the Basques.

East of Asturias-León, indications of the political dividing lines that would later be boundaries for the four Basque provinces were already evident. They were most sharply defined around what was to become Navarra. Pamplona with its environs served as the center for economic, military and commercial activity at the western end of the Pyrenees. It was the most accessible to France and to the Islamized lands to the southeast along the Ebro.

Of the other future Basque provinces, only Alava was a distinct entity as early as the ninth century; not a kingdom, but a seigniory, with its own lord elected by the clerics and the nobles. The other Basque lands (the future Vizcaya and Guipúzcoa) would not enter the orbit of Pamplona until the tenth century.

To Vasconia's east other states were taking shape, where the middle Pyreneans had to defend themselves against the Basques to the west, the Franks to the north and east, and the Muslims to the south. These were the future counties of Aragon, Sobrarbe, Ribagorza and Pallars. The easternmost were increasingly subject to control by the Carolingian kings and absorption into their Spanish March.

Meantime Catalonia, thanks to prosperity and good fortune, was evolving from a dependent fief of the Franks into an independent county, a husky offshoot of the empire that had created it.

This was the setting for the birth and early years of the Kingdom of Pamplona.

IV

The Young Kingdom, 824 to 1004

THE FIRST KING OF PAMPLONA ASsumed the title more than eleven and a half centuries ago. We may expect a certain amount of confusion, if not controversy, about the details of the event and the kingdom's early years.

There are two common versions. One is the legend preserved in the prologue to the *Fuero General* (the first collection of Navarra's laws). The other, much more recent, is based on research in medieval chronicles, mostly Arab.

Here is the legendary account:

> In these mountains [from the Asturias to Sobrarbe] a few people resisted [the Muslim invaders], and taking to foot they made forays and they captured horses, and they divided the goods amongst the strongest of their number until there were in these mountains of Ainsa and Sobrarbe more than 300 mounted men, none of whom had more of the booty than another. And envy developed among them, and disputes over the booty, and they came to send envoys to Rome to seek the advice of the *apostóligo* Aldebano, and also to Lombardy, whose people were notable for their justice, and to France. And they received the answer that they should have a king to rule over them; but first they should have their

laws sworn to and written. And they did as they were advised, and they wrote down their laws with the counsel of the Lombards and the Franks ... and then they elected as king Don Pelayo.[1]

Both the history and geography of this story are questionable. It is hardly likely that Don Pelayo, first king of Asturias (718 to 737), could also have been the first king of Sobrarbe—which we may assume to refer in this context to the whole Pamplona-Aragon-Sobrarbe territory of the eighth century, but which could not have stretched some three hundred miles west to Asturias.

However, flights of fantasy should not obscure the fact that the authors and cherishers of this myth displayed the same respect for law that would characterize all of Navarra's future history. They believed that the law should come before the king —and that the king must be strong, a natural leader and a just ruler.

A more realistic account of how Pamplona became the kingdom that was later called Navarra names Iñigo Arista as its first king, and includes more factors than resistance to the Muslims.

For one thing, influences from southwestern Europe, chiefly from the Franks, were equally important. The kingdom of the Franks, which under its first kings had halted the Islamic advance toward Europe and had established the Franks in the Pyrenees, had waxed under Charlemagne to become the Carolingian Empire. Its presence on Navarra's borders acted both as a spur to an assertion of independence and as an opportunity for alliance when threats from the south outweighed those from the north.

These southern threats (from the Muslim emirate), though the other major factor in Navarra's progress toward nationhood, were not constant. Navarra was not really as menaced by the Muslims as the prologue to the *Fuero General* implies. Though al-Andalus was perennially interested in conquest, Navarra was not a target it regarded with enthusiasm. And the closest representatives of Islam, almost at Pamplona's doorstep to the south, were as often allies as enemies.

These neighbors were the Banu Qasi—a powerful family of Hispano-Roman stock in the Ebro River Valley who had become Islamized when the Muslims reached their homeland

THE YOUNG KINGDOM 21

during their first sweep northward. They had exchanged their Christian religion for the right to keep property and status. Many peninsular inhabitants had thus taken the Islamic religion, and were called *muladiés*.

From the Ebro, the Banu Qasi exerted control, almost independent of al-Andalus, over the area from Tudela to Zaragoza, with occasional ventures as far as Pamplona.

Opportunists, they sometimes acted as agents for the emirate in the south, sometimes allied themselves with the Christians against it or against the Franks. Their allegiances and alliances were significant variables in the politics of the northern peninsula in the late eighth and early ninth centuries.

In 781, for example, they collaborated with the emirate in taking Pamplona and they held it for the Emir of Córdoba, Abd-al-Rahman, until 799. During such subjugations the Basques looked for help to their sometime enemies the Franks. After a successful revolt in 799, when the Banu Qasi governor was killed, Pamplona accepted as governor the *gascon* who had led the revolt, Velasco. For most of the next fifteen years Pamplona's governors were *franco-gascons*.

In 816 the pendulum swung the other way. The Pamplonese had quarreled with Louis the Pious (Charlemagne's son) over his choice of governor to replace Velasco. To counter the Franks, they sought or welcomed alliances with neighboring powers south of the Pyrenees. Aided now by the Banu Qasi, they carried on a two-year rebellion and drove out the *franco-gascon* overlords.

The alliance of the Banu Qasi and the Basques was natural, in view of their common enemies. The former needed to maintain their independence of the Cordobese emirate in the south; so did the Basques. Besides this, the Basques had to fend off the Franks, and by aiding in this, the Banu Qasi insured a buffer zone between their own principality and this potential enemy.

But the alliance was more than political and military. It was also based on blood ties due to considerable intermarriage between ruling families. For example, when the mother of Pamplona's first king, King Iñigo Arista, was widowed, she took as her second husband a Banu Qasi chief. From this marriage was born Musa ibn Musa, most famous Banu Qasi chieftain of the ninth century.

This, then, was the historical base for the formation of the Kingdom of Pamplona: a long effort to maintain independence from two powerful neighbors, the Franks and the Muslims, depending on diplomacy and nonaggression pacts as much as on warfare. Unlike many of the kingdoms taking shape in Europe, it was not the result of an imposition of force by an outsider, nor did it have a line of hereditary leaders to assume kingship. The first king of Pamplona was chosen by his fellow warlords strictly on ability.

THE IÑIGO ARISTA DYNASTY

Origins of the Iñigo family are shadowy. The family may have come originally from Bigorre, north of the Pyrenees. It produced as its first hero Jimeno el Fuerte (the Strong), leader in anti-Frank battles. The family probably settled in the Salazar Valley in northeast Navarra. Iñigo Arista was a branch of this tree.

He and his Basque warlords, with the help of the Banu Qasi, won a resounding triumph in 824 over an army Louis the Pious had sent to take over Pamplona. Once again, victory came in the Pass of Roncesvalles. This may be said to mark the birth of the Kingdom of Pamplona and the start of the reign of its first king.

Much later the archbishop Rodrigo Ximénez de Rada described the rise of Iñigo Arista:

> There appeared a man from the County of Bigorre, accustomed from childhood to warfare; he was called Iñigo, and surnamed Aritza (oak; that is, the Strong), for his ruggedness in combat; he lived at first in the high valleys of the Pyrenees; then came down to the plains of Navarra, performed great deeds of valor, and thereby earned the position of leadership of the people.

The crowning may have taken place near the present-day town of Alsasua, about thirty miles west of Pamplona. According to tradition this and future coronations required the raising of the king on a shield, while the lords of the land (in this case, the war chieftains) cried, *"Real, real, real!"* ("the royal one").

Iñigo Arista, once crowned, ruled the tiny Kingdom of Pamplona until his death in 852. He appears to have been a wise and skillful leader, as well as a rugged warrior.

During the reign of his son García Iñiguez, the emirate's power over the Banu Qasi grew stronger and the latter's old alliance with the Basques disintegrated. The neighboring kingdom of Asturias began to look to Pamplona's kings like a more dependable friend. Though Ordoño I of Asturias had waged war against Pamplona in 850, he later made peace, which was cemented by marriages between the ruling families in 858 and 868.

During the reign of García Iñiguez much of southern Europe was touched by deep Viking incursions. A persistent tale, based on Arab chronicles, recounts that in 859 they reached Pamplona from the Mediterranean, by way of the Ebro and Arga rivers, captured the king himself, and released him only after payment of a huge ransom. But lacking any evidence of their passage through Zaragoza and Tudela—which would have been necessary for such a voyage—modern historians see it as more likely that if they did reach the Basque Country, it would have been from the Atlantic, by way of the Bidasoa and Adour rivers.[2]

The dynasty founded by Iñigo Arista reigned until the end of the ninth century. Last in the line was Fortún Garcés, called "the Monk." He too was captured by enemy forces and took the crown only in 882, after returning from twenty years of captivity by the Muslims in Córdoba. Too old now to fight the Banu Qasi—who had become out-and-out enemies—Fortún Garcés yielded power to Sancho Garcés, scion of the aggressive Jimenez family. These bold warlords had moved from being generals in battle to a position almost of corulers with the Arista kings. When Fortún Garcés, perhaps involuntarily, retired to a monastery, Sancho Garcés was crowned King of Pamplona.[3]

The kingdom Sancho Garcés inherited, though only three-quarters of a century old, had already acquired shape and substance, as well as recognition from other European powers, who were girding themselves for the inevitable death struggle with Islam. They saw in the young, vigorous, strategically located Kingdom of Pamplona a vital ally in the holy war.

THE JIMENO DYNASTY

Sancho Garcés was descended from the same Jimeno el Fuerte who was a progenitor of the Iñigo Arista dynasty. Sancho was a vigorous warrior-king, something the Kingdom of Pamplona badly needed in the early tenth century. The Muslims were now a fearful menace. The powerful Abd-al-Rahman III showed no mercy, in spite of the fact that his grandmother had been a Pamplonese princess. But before Sancho Garcés died (in 925), he and his partner in the Reconquest, Ordoño II of Asturias, pushed the Muslims out of part of La Rioja and held them beyond the Ebro and Aragon rivers, thus establishing the boundaries of the future Kingdom of Navarra.

Sancho's line produced four more kings to rule Pamplona before the year 1000. But his successors were inclined more to accommodation than to attack. The most memorable exception was his widow Toda, regent from 925 to 938. She showed great political skill, astutely deploying her brood of princesses as brides for neighboring princes, counts and chieftains. León, Alava, Ribagorza, Castile and the caliphate were bound to Pamplona by marriages. Toda's energy went beyond diplomacy. According to legend, she actually fought in the battle of Simancas, when a joint Christian force defeated Abd-al-Rahman (in 939).[4]

After Toda, the dynasty was less notable. The kings joined the Leonese and Castilians in the wars of the Reconquest when it suited them, but by and large their policy was to maintain peaceful relations with Muslim and Christian neighbors alike.

THE NEIGHBORING BASQUES

Meanwhile the Alavese had also for some time been developing their own brand of nationalism. Alava never was a kingdom, but neither was it ever subjugated by the Muslims. As a seigniory and then a county, it was independent from the mid-ninth century to 1076, allied sometimes with Castile and sometimes with Navarra. Situated along the border between Muslim and Christian Spain, Alava was very important to the northern kingdoms.

Its *Cofradía de Arriaga*—a council of high churchmen and nobles—elected their lords, and also carried on the business of government. The first known lord chosen was Fernán González, Count of Castile (932 to 970), whose wife was a noble Alavese lady. During the rest of the tenth century, the *Cofradía* chose to ally Alava with Castile, but as Pamplona's star rose in the next century, the kings of Navarra were named as Alava's lords.

The Vizcayans and Guipúzcoans, farther removed from the ongoing struggles, remained more or less within Pamplona's

THE YOUNG KINGDOM 25

sphere of influence. Not until the thirteenth century did they finally cast their lot with Castile.

During this same period, the histories of Pamplona and its neighbors to the east, the counties of Aragon and Sobrarbe, were closely related. The latter were disengaging themselves from the Carolingian yoke and taking an active part in the Reconquest. In fact, from 930 on, thanks to a marriage engineered by Toda, the County of Aragon was ruled by the king of Pamplona. And the myth-shrouded origins of both nations' first fueros seem to share the same time and place.

Meantime the Muslim military threat was gradually decreasing. Warfare between the two Spains was not constant. The Muslims were often occupied with their own internal quarrels and could not give full attention to fighting the Christians. There were periods of truce and even diplomatic entente, often marked by marriages between royal or ruling families. Besides the Basque grandmother of Abd-al-Rahman III (the first caliph independent of Bagdad), his son al-Hakam II (961 to 976) also married a Basque princess. And a daughter of Sancho Garcés married Almansur, the grand vizier who was all-powerful during the nominal reign of the weak Hisham II (976 to 1013).

After their first campaigns to the north, many Muslims remained in the areas that they considered habitable. The city of Tudela, in southeastern Navarra, was populated by Muslims as early as the eighth century and remained Muslim until about 1100. The Muslim populations in Navarra's cities enjoyed their own rights and privileges, just as did other segments of the population.

Though there was not nearly as much cultural infiltration as in southern Spain, the north certainly felt the effect of the Muslim occupation and absorbed many of its customs. Much of this was due to the Banu Qasi, the semiautonomous *muladíes* of the Ebro Valley, who were in a position to function as a cultural and diplomatic bridge between the two opposing worlds.

But for the Basques of Pamplona neither the occasional conquests and occupations by the Muslims, nor the close relationships with the Arabized Banu Qasi, resulted in any permanent or deep Islamization. Culturally, economically and socially, they were affected far more by visitors and immigrants from the other side of the Pyrenees.

TRANSMONTANE INFLUENCES

Those who peacefully crossed the mountains and left their mark on the Navarrese came for two reasons: Pamplona's location on the route to Santiago, and the introduction of the Cluniac monastic reform from France.

For about two centuries, pilgrims bound for the shrine of Santiago at Compostela in Galicia were an important influence on all the lands they passed through and extremely important in Navarra.

What were believed to be the actual bones and tomb of Saint James had been found at Compostela sometime after 810. The shrine dated from about 850, when Alfonso II of Asturias ordered the first church to be built on the spot. It was added to and enriched by succeeding monarchs, and by gifts from all over Christendom during the next few centuries. Pilgrims began to flock to it soon after 850, and by the early tenth century it was the most visited shrine in Europe.

At first pilgrims faced many perils. If they took the coastal route south and west from Bayonne, they were menaced by Norman invaders. If they took a Pyrenean route, they were menaced, according to the twelfth-century guidebook of a French cleric, by the Basques.[5] One of the two main interior routes from France was through the Pyrenees at Somport, in Aragon. The other went through the Pass of Roncesvalles, then continued to Pamplona. If pilgrims came this way, the mountain dwellers were likely to fall on them for booty and, one suspects, amusement. Both routes converged at Puente la Reina in central Navarra; pilgrims *had* to pass through Navarra.

The guidebook warned travelers that the Basques of Navarra were a barbaric folk, different from all others in customs and race; debauched, perfidious, ferocious and even worse. On the complimentary side it described them as effective on the battlefield, though not very good at attacking fortresses. And it said they were consistent in their payment of tithes and in making offerings on the altar.

Aside from these possibly prejudiced judgments, the guidebook offered much practical advice on routes and stopping places. It suggested a four-day journey through Navarra. A present-day pilgrim could (and many do) follow the route and find rich architectural and artistic evidence in churches and monuments of the medieval cult of Saint James.

The pilgrim traffic swelled to a peak in the eleventh century. By then it had left its mark on Pamplona in many ways besides marble and stone.

The Pamplonese, especially the mountain dwellers, had clung to many of the practices of their pagan forebears until the ninth century. In their isolation, they were simply not exposed to Christianity. But as they saw more of other ways, they gradually adopted them. In conversations at the inns set up to cater to the pilprims, in buying and selling, they learned what the rest of the world had to offer. They liked some of it, and adopted new modes of dress, amusement, architecture and art. They acquired foreign goods and learned to deal with foreign money, even money from as far away as the tenth-century England of Ethelred II. Socially, economically and culturally, they were powerfully affected by the pilgrim traffic.[6]

Inasmuch as the carriers of the imported customs and merchandise were peaceable, not bent on military conquest or political domination, the structure of government, such as it was, was not much affected. At the ruling level the Franks and the Pamplonese were hostile. But this did not affect the everyday give-and-take between natives and visitors, nor did the fact that most of the travelers came from feudalistic societies. The habits of independence and of reliance on customary rights were strongly ingrained in the Basques of Pamplona. A feudal system such as that of Aquitaine could not take hold in the western Spanish Pyrenees as firmly as it did in the eastern, where the Spanish March owed allegiance to the Frankish kings.[7]

The second major means by which European influences were introduced was through visitors who came to found monasteries or religious colonies. The Cluniac reform had its effect on Pamplona somewhat later than did the pilgrimages, but it is part of the same historical chapter.

The great French monastery of Cluny had been founded in 910 by William the Pious, Duke of Aquitaine. Soon its emissaries were in Catalonia. Sancho the Great (whom we shall meet in the next chapter) brought the first Cluniac monks to Navarra. These monks, whose loyalty was not to kings but to the supranational church, sought to strengthen the Christian faith throughout the civilized world by placing themselves directly under Rome rather than under regional hierarchies. They had their own special liturgy; in Navarra, this in time affected the language of the whole land.

The Cluniac presence in Spain was felt in ever widening circles as more and more monks were established in more and more monasteries. As permanent residents, they were in daily contact with the natives. They encouraged and facilitated travel along the pilgrims' routes. They imported French goods. They attracted other immigrants—pilgrims, traders, craftsmen or the curious—many of whom stayed. These "francos," so called whether they actually came from France or not, became a special class in the urban centers of northern Spain. They were accepted in the cities but, like other classes, they had their own rights and privileges and restrictions—all, as we shall soon see, to be formalized in the fueros.

By the year 1000, Pamplona had changed greatly from the loosely organized kingdom that was born in the early ninth century. In 800, a veneer of leftover Hispano-Roman civilization barely adhered to the robust, rustic Basque stock. There was little social cohesiveness except what was due to propinquity and the occasional exigencies of warfare.

By 1000 Pamplona was a true kingdom in its own right, with a capital, complete with bishop; a half dozen other semiurban centers; an ongoing dynasty; dominion over a substantial portion of the Iberian Peninsula; and the respect of its partners in the Reconquest. Almansur raided Pamplona in 1000, but this was the last serious Muslim threat to the Basques.

And by 1000 the kingdom was known as Navarra. Many have postulated that the name derives from the Basque roots *nava* and *erri,* meaning flat land surrounded by mountains. But as Julio Caro Baroja points out, the little country was in fact more mountainous than flat. A later hypothesis suggests connection with an Arabic word for river, *nahar,* and that the first use of Navarra really referred to the southern part, or what is now known as the Ribera.[8]

Whatever the derivation of the kingdom's name, a king now ascended the throne who would solidify the gains of his predecessors, and give the kingdom new prominence, glory and prosperity.

V

The Pivotal Reign of Sancho the Great

SANCHO GARCES III EL MAYOR (SANcho the Great) ruled Navarra from 1004 to 1035.

When he became king, Navarra was ripe for his particular brand of kingship: an ambitious dynasticism, a relentless drive to acquire new territories to leave his sons.[1] He did, in thirty years, most of what he set out to do. But not all his projects turned out the way he expected.

What he thought would be his major achievement, the doubling of his territories (and Navarra did indeed become the most active, powerful state in the north of the Iberian Peninsula for a few decades) lasted less than thirty years after his death.

His second legacy, the new urban prosperity, was more durable. Increasingly from Sancho's time, remote mountain dwellers felt safe, because of the increased stability and decreased military activity in the kingdom. They came down to the plains and began to constitute a more urbanized, better-off class, including many artisans and tradesmen. As towns grew and life became more complex, there was more need for regulation. Customs now crystalized into laws. Thus his reign paved the way for the great period of the fueros that was to come.

But this was unforeseen by Sancho, whose central lifelong drive was extension of the power of his royal house, preferably with as little warfare as possible.

EARLY TERRITORIAL GAINS

Sancho first looked toward the County of Castile, which until 1017 was ruled by his father-in-law Count Sancho García. Sancho of Navarra married the Castilian count's daughter Munia in 1010. The king and the count seem to have been genuine friends and together waged war successfully against the Muslims. But this did not keep Sancho of Navarra from taking every opportunity for aggrandizement at Castile's expense. By 1016 he had succeeded in pushing his southwest boundary outward, acquiring La Rioja, the area beyond the Ebro River.

Somewhat later he strengthened his control over the Basque provinces, especially the seigniory of Alava, which had given its allegiance to Castile in the past. But Alava recognized Sancho as king from at least 1022. He formalized his suzerainty over Guipúzcoa and Vizcaya, naming them as seigniories within his realm in 1025 and 1030, respectively.

Having advanced on Castile territorially as far as he could, Sancho seized a chance to intercede in the county's internal affairs.

His brother-in-law García acceded to the countship in 1017 when he was only eight years old. What more natural than for Sancho to take a benign interest in the boy? Before long he was recognized as regent. In signing a document in 1023, he wrote his name first, the king of León was second, and young Count García of Castile was third. In 1024 Sancho openly claimed overlordship, as "reigning in Aragon, Pamplona, Sobrarbe, Ribagorza, Castile and Alava."

The unfortunate young Count García was assassinated at the age of twenty (in 1029). This was Sancho's opportunity. He claimed Castile through his wife, who even before García's death had been styled "La Mayor," indicating her status as direct heir in Castile. She would have been the logical successor after García, except for the fact that no woman had ever inherited a kingdom (or county) in Spain. But the Castilians recognized her primary claim, and gave their allegiance to Sancho because of her.

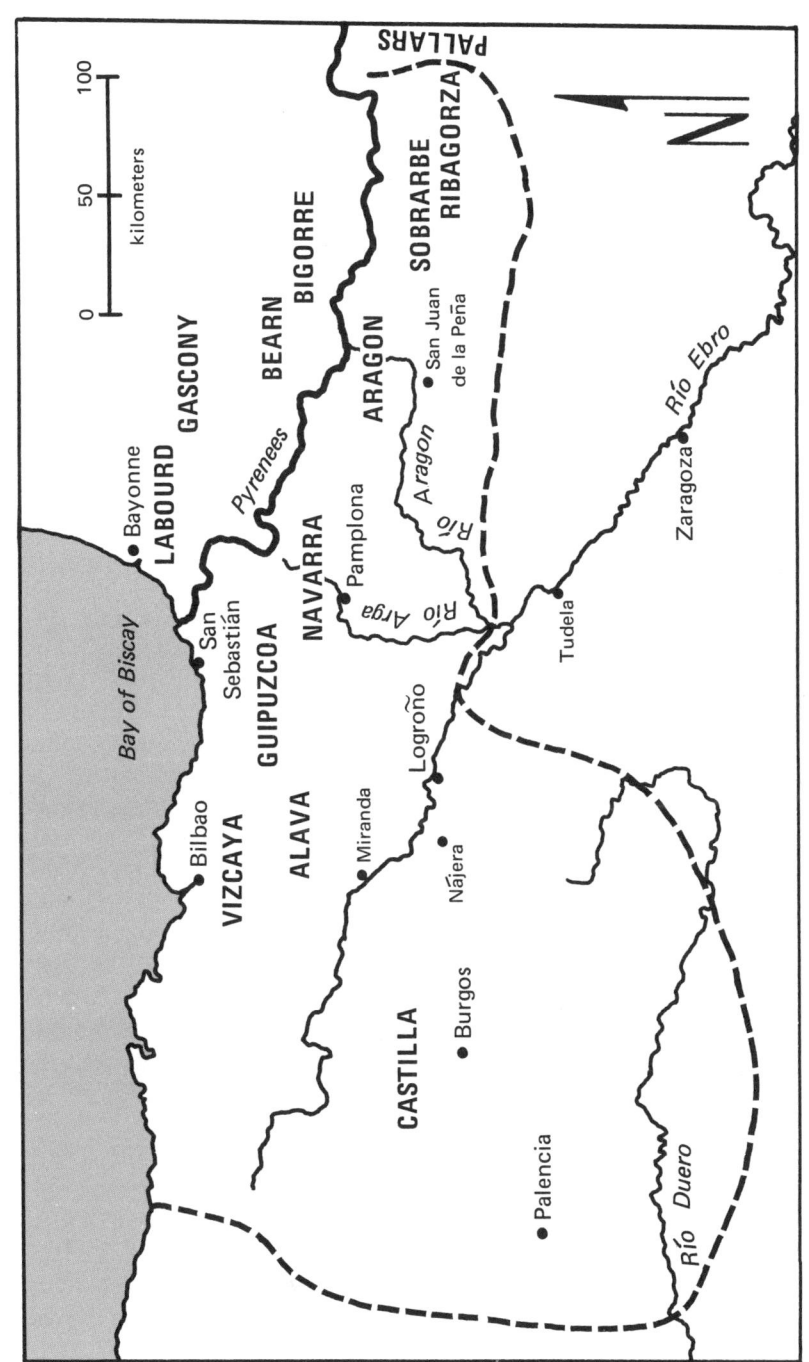

The Dominions of Sancho the Great.

Sancho had to make one concession to the Castilian nobles: to name as Munia's successor to the countship one who would not also inherit the Kingdom of Navarra. They were anxious to keep Castile for the Castilians. Thus Sancho's second legitimate son Fernando became Count of Castile when he was fifteen. But his father remained the real ruler.

This heritage and title granted to Fernando, when Sancho himself was only in his thirties, drove the first wedge in the final disintegration of the domain Sancho was to assemble so laboriously. It was politically expedient to separate Castile from the other components, but it was also an example of how Sancho, perhaps influenced by practices he had observed in France and Catalonia, saw his kindgom as a patrimony to be divided among his heirs.

To build the patrimony, Sancho also went northward and eastward.

Across the Pyrenees lay another land where he could take advantage of strong family ties: the Duchy of Gascony, also known as the Duchy of Vasconia. When the Carolingian Empire had dissolved, the *gascons,* tired of Frankish lords, went over the mountains to seek their first duke: Sancho Mitarra (in 870). His line had intermarried ever since then with ruling families in Pamplona and Aragon. By the time of Sancho the Great, Sancho Guillermo was duke of Gascony. He was technically a vassal of King Robert of France. But he chose to associate himself with Navarra because of blood ties and historical alliances. He was the son of a Navarrese princess (Sancho's great aunt) and had been brought up in Navarra. Sancho cultivated his friendship and soon established himself as protector, then feudal lord, of the French duke. In the early 1020s Sancho went to Labourd (westernmost portion of the Duchy of Gascony) to lead a successful expedition against the Viking pirates who were threatening Vizcaya and Guipúzcoa. Thereafter he acquired Labourd as his own feudal dependency.

To Sancho's east, the County of Aragon was already firmly incorporated in Navarra and had been since the preceding century, when the daughter of its last ruling count (Galindo Aznar) had been married to Sancho García of Pamplona.

To Aragon's east was Sobrarbe. This was a mountainous, poorly defined area. After the decline of the Carolingians, it had been a province under the dominion of the counts of Aragon. It became attached to the County of Ribagorza on its east, in the tenth century. During the early years of Sancho's reign the Muslims ravaged and impoverished the land. Sancho, again the opportunist, entered the fray and drove them out. The inhabitants recognized him as king and liberator in 1016. The neighboring County of Ribagorza fell to Sancho by 1018, after he had helped free it too from the Muslims.

Farther still lay the County of Pallars. Here Sancho had only fleeting recognition.

But beyond Pallars was the County of Barcelona, where he hoped to add to his power, using family ties, force and diplomacy. Sancho's wife and the wife of the young Count Berenguer of Barcelona were sisters. Sancho helped Berenguer stand up to his domineering mother, and promised to help him fight the Muslims on his southern borders.

No real additions to Sancho's domains came of this, though he considered Berenguer his vassal. And at least once (in 1033) he described himself as ruling "from Zamora to Barcelona." But Count Berenguer's wife died. Sancho grew more preoccupied with Castile and León. Barcelona ceased to be considered seriously as a possible addition to the Kingdom of Navarra.

One dream remained: the Kingdom of León, with its tattered relics of Visigothic empire. If Sancho could achieve dominance there, he could call himself not only king but emperor as well.

The Castilian story almost repeated itself. From about 1030, Sancho intervened as friend, protector and uncle of León's underage king Vermudo. He insinuated himself and his supporters into the court, the monasteries, the fortresses. When Vermudo reached sixteen the Leonese showed some sporadic opposition to Sancho. But an opportunely arranged marriage in 1033 mended matters: Sancho's son Fernando of Castile married Sancha of León, Vermudo's sister.

While Sancho's plans were progressing satisfactorily here, an event on the other side of the Pyrenees forced him to move faster. Duke Sancho Guillermo of Gascony died without an heir. If Sancho of Navarra could get there in time he might truly become lord of the dukedom. But first he had to finish what he had started in León. He hastened to occupy the capital city

(January 1034). By September he was being cited in official documents as king of León. He went so far as to have a coin minted with the inscription "Sancho Emperador."

But from this high point Sancho's dominion began to decline. He did not succeed in claiming his right as lord of Gascony, which after his death reverted to the duke of Aquitaine. But many lords of Basse Navarre (the land on the north slopes of the Pyrenees) preferred to continue recognizing the kings of Navarra.

In Catalonia, too, Sancho's tenuous claim to seigniory had been broken. Nevertheless, at the end of his reign Sancho had control (either as king or as tacitly recognized ruler) over Navarra, Castile, the three Basque provinces, Aragon, Sobrarbe and Ribagorza.

Only on his southern borders did Sancho let well enough alone. He made no effort to acquire lands held by the Muslims. While his neighboring Christian kingdoms were afflicted with raids and threats, and had to expel Muslims who occupied their lands, Navarra was relatively secure. Sancho joined his neighbors' defensive and offensive operations only when it suited his interests. He could hardly be called a warrior king. He fought no ideological wars, adding to his kingdom only in order to have a larger legacy to be apportioned among his four sons.

But he did leave permanent, nonterritorial changes in his kingdom, by encouraging the importation of European culture and customs.

SANCHO'S LEGACIES

Sancho deliberately sought out men with new ideas to introduce throughout his realms, thereby cementing the military and political ties that bound the parts loosely together. Many of the men he cultivated were of the church. For instance, the learned Bishop Oliva of Vich became his good friend and mentor. Monks and emissaries shuttled back and forth between Pamplona and the County of Barcelona. Sancho's contacts with the ecclesiastics of the Spanish March enabled him to tap the stream of communication to the rest of Europe and, especially, Rome.

Gascony was another link with the great religious and cultural changes being effected in eleventh-century Europe. Besides his vassal Sancho Guillermo, duke of Gascony, Sancho was friendly with William, duke of Aquitaine, and exchanged gifts and visits.

Through such men he learned about the Cluniac reform and saw what it could do for his kingdom—ecclesiastically and culturally—to enrich life at all levels. Sancho had always been deeply concerned with the well-being of the church—out of genuine spiritual feeling and also because he saw it as an ally in his temporal affairs. He had been careful to choose bishops who would help, or at least not hinder, him in his ambitious projects. As he extended his control over new lands, he could create new episcopates: in Ribagorza, Alava, Castile, León, Palencia, Astorga and Oviedo. Now he welcomed opportunities to associate himself with the supranational Cluniac reform.

In 1025 he installed Abbot Paterno at San Juan de la Peña in Aragon, one of his most illustrious monasteries, with instructions to put the Cluniac reforms in motion and to put an end to all religious and secular abuses of power. Paterno went on from this abbey, at Sancho's behest, to drive out wickedness and carry the reforms elsewhere.

But Sancho was careful not to go too far. He was probably far more interested in the civilizing influences of the Cluniacs on his subjects, and the upgrading of his standing among the cultured courts of Europe, than in drastic church reforms that might alienate the existing canonical order.[2]

And the Cluniac monks indeed did much more than revitalize and rediscipline a lax and worldly church. They were extremely important instruments in Sancho's efforts to Europeanize his Navarra. They introduced new interests and tastes to the curious Navarrese, including respect for art and learning, which would become even more pronounced under Sancho's sons and grandsons.

DIVISION OF THE KINGDOM

Historians still wonder what would have happened if Sancho had not followed what one has called the "detestable foreign practice" of dividing his lands among his sons in his will. He even made the apportionments public well before his death, which gave a headstart to contention among the heirs.

To Ramiro, his oldest and bastard son, went the County of Aragon, which thus was severed from Navarra after a century of union.

To García, his oldest legitimate son, went the Kingdom of Navarra, including La Rioja, Alava, Guipúzcoa and Vizcaya. Fernando, his third son, was confirmed as count of Castile. For Gonzalo, youngest and least memorable son, he created a kingdom by combining the counties of Sobrarbe and Ribagorza. Sancho thought he had created a federation of states whose rulers, united through ties of blood, would reign in harmony. He foresaw security for his major patrimony, Navarra, thanks to its protective ring of dynastically allied states.[3]

Sancho died in 1035. His story is not told in full until we see what happened to the conglomerate he had taken a lifetime to put together.

THE ARAGONESE INTERLUDE AND THE RESTORATION

Sancho had not foreseen how much stronger his sons' ambitions would be than their family feeling. They began to quarrel at once, and kept it up until they were all dead. Briefly, this is how the four heirs met their fates, and how Sancho's realm fell apart and lost its eleventh-century position as one of the most important kingdoms of western Europe.

García, king of Navarra, first was an ally of his brother Fernando of Castile, while the latter was disputing boundaries with León. But later the brothers became enemies, fighting over the southern areas of Navarra that Sancho had detached from Castile. García died in battle in 1054.

Ramiro, king of Aragon, seized Sobrarbe and Ribagorza from the youngest brother, Gonzalo, who died in 1039. Then Ramiro too died on the battlefield, while unsuccessfully contesting for Zaragoza with his brother Fernando. Ramiro's son, Sancho Ramírez, then launched Aragon on a series of conquests over the Islamic strongholds that stood between the mountain kingdom and the pasturage of the southern plains.[4]

Fernando outfought and outlasted his three brothers but succumbed in 1065, to be succeeded by his son Alfonso VI. This grandson of Sancho the Great named himself "Emperor of Spain" after wresting Toledo from the Muslims. By the beginning of the twelfth century he was guiding Castile into position as leader of the Reconquest and the peninsula's front-ranking kingdom.

Navarra, on the other hand, had been stripped of La Rioja on its southern borders by Castile, and was to be even more reduced. In 1076 King Sancho IV, grandson of Sancho the Great, died—possibly by fratricide. (He is known in Navarrese history as Sancho el de Peñalén, after the cliff from which he was said to have been pushed.) After his death both Aragon and Castile laid claim to Navarra. The Navarrese chose the former, where their late king's cousin Sancho Ramírez reigned. Thus Navarra became little more than a province of Aragon and was to remain so for fifty years.

The descendants of Sancho Ramírez ruled the combined kingdoms until 1134. This was a warlike strain, less concerned with family jealousies than alert to external threats and opportunities. And there was need for vigilance because there were new enemies.

The Muslim presence in Spain had subsided as a military threat during the reign of Sancho the Great. Al-Mansur, scourge of the Christian kingdoms, had died in 1002 and the caliphate of Córdoba came to an end. During the eleventh century, Muslim Spain dissolved into many decentralized kingdoms, preoccupied with their own differences.

But in 1086 the fanatical Almoravids invaded Spain from North Africa. They were Berbers who had been converted to Islam early in the Arab conquest and who forcibly imposed their orthodox, puritanical brand of Islam on other North African tribes. Their leader, Yusef I, was invited by the Muslim princes in Spain to help them launch a new anti-Christian crusade. King Pedro I of Aragon and Navarra (1094 to 1104) and his successor and brother Alfonso I the Warrior (1104 to 1134) joined battle against the infidel with enthusiasm. Alfonso defeated the Muslims in Tudela and Zaragoza. He recaptured La Rioja from Castile. He almost reconstructed the Navarra of Sancho the Great.

In 1134 this warrior king died without an heir, and the union of Aragon and Navarra came to an end. In his will Alfonso tried to leave the kingdom to the Templars and the Hospitalers; but neither his subjects, nor the neighboring kings, nor the military orders themselves took this seriously.[5] The nobles of Aragon elected Alfonso's brother Ramiro as their king. But Navarra's electors refused to acknowledge him and chose García Ramírez, a great-great-grandson of Sancho the Great. He was known as el Restaurador (the Restorer) because under him the Kingdom of Navarra regained its separate status, independent of Aragon. During the reign of García Ramírez (1134 to 1150) and that of his son Sancho el Sabio (the Wise) (1150 to 1194), the urbanization of Navarra made great strides, as we shall see in the next chapter.

Both Sancho the Wise and his son Sancho el Fuerte (the Strong) sought alliances to protect the integrity of their kingdom, doubly threatened, as usual, by Aragon and Castile. During the reign of Sancho the Wise an opportunity arose to strengthen ties with Navarra's third powerful neighbor, Aquitaine, and to create a counterforce to the peninsular menaces. He betrothed his daughter Berenguela to King Richard the Lion-Hearted of England, who was also duke of Aquitaine.

This important section of southwest Franch had been an English possession since 1152 when Eleanor of Aquitaine married Henry II of England, bringing the duchy—which by the twelfth century included Vasconia (Gascony) and extended to the Pyrenees—as her dowry. At the birth of their son Richard in 1157 Henry named him duke of Aquitaine, and formally bestowed the duchy on him in 1172.

After becoming king of England in 1189, and determining to join the Third Crusade, Richard saw advantages in a marriage to the Navarrese princess. It promised some security for his southernmost frontier, and gave him an ally his lieutenants could call on if need be while he was away on the crusade. And indeed, Berenguela's brother did go to the aid of Richard's seneschal in Gascony the very next year, when Raymond of Toulouse took advantage of Richard's absence to launch an attack.[6]

Though the marriage was brief and childless, it reinforced Navarra's ties with England, which were to continue for three hundred years. And more immediately, it resulted in territorial gains for Navarra. Upon his marriage Richard gave Sancho the Wise, Berenguela's father, his lands in Gascony south of the Garonne—including the predominantly Basque portion, known as Baja Navarra or Basse Navarre.

However, the English had ties with Castile too, and this resulted in a serious blow to Navarra's territorial aspirations. In 1170 King Alfonso VIII of Castile had married Eleanor, daughter of Henry II and Eleanor of Aquitaine. Alfonso felt that this gave him some rights to Vasconia. After Richard the Lion-Hearted died in 1199, Alfonso set out to establish his claims. On the way he occupied Navarra's corridor to the Bay of Biscay, near the outlet of the River Bidasoa. Navarra's king was unfortunately absent at the time, on a visit to Andalucía. Alfonso, on his way home from Vasconia, retired his forces and promised in his will to restore the lands to Navarra "because I know all these places should be part of the Kingdom of Navarra and belong to it."[7] But they remained (with all of Guipúzcoa and Alava) joined to Castile, and from then on Navarra had no outlet to the sea. This was to affect its fortunes in many ways, especially in its relations with Guipúzcoa, which controlled the nearest seaport, at Fuenterrabia.

THE LAST OF THE SANCHOS

Sancho the Strong, who succeeded in 1194, was not as fiercely anti-Muslim as his ancestors. But, with his fellow Christian monarchs, he was in at the kill in 1212, when the decisive battle of Las Navas de Tolosa dealt the coup de grace to the Muslims in Spain. Sancho led the Navarrese contingent in the combined Christian forces, which also included Castilian, Leonese and Aragonese armies.

This accomplished, Sancho subsided. He was afflicted with ill health and extraordinary obesity, and spent the rest of his life shut up in his castle atop the tallest hill in Tudela. Known during this period as El Encerrado (the Confined), he took little interest in government. His kingdom proceeded on its own momentum, with more and more control exercised by the proliferating nobility.

Sancho the Strong died in 1234. He is buried in the church he founded at Roncesvalles, where pieces of the chains he brought back from the victory at Las Navas de Tolosa are displayed. Tradition has it that the Muslim chief at that battle was protected by a ring of black slaves, chained together, and that Sancho broke through the barrier and forced the enemy general to flee. In memory of the great victory, Sancho caused the red shield of Navarra to be ornamented with golden chains. Other elements have been added to the coat of arms since, but the chains are still there.

Also displayed at Sancho's church at Roncesvalles is a seven-foot-four-inch sculptured effigy of the monarch. Many scholars believe this to have been his actual height.[8] If it was, it helps to explain his reputation for strength.

Sancho left no legitimate children, though he had four bastard sons. For a time he toyed with the idea of naming his cousin King Jaime I of Aragon as his heir, and in fact the two monarchs went through a ceremony of mutual adoption. But when Sancho died, the nobles of Navarra called upon his nephew and closest kinsman, Count Thibaut of Champagne (Teobaldo I), to assume the succession. Thus began a long series of French rulers and a period of Europeanization that even Sancho the Great might have found excessive.

We shall meet Teobaldo again in chapter 7. But first, let us look more closely at the kingdom he was to rule: thirteenth-century Navarra.

VI

The Foral Base

THE NAVARRA THAT TEOBALDO I came to rule in 1234 was far more urbanized and governed by law than the kingdom Sancho the Great had inherited two centuries earlier. Its people came together now for economic advantage, not for defense. Possessions and property had more effect on status than did military prowess.

With the changing society came new demands on the customary laws, product of centuries of expedient improvisation. Whereas in the isolated, largely autonomous valleys and towns, the law of the warrior and handed-down unwritten customs had prevailed, in the new towns the citizens had more contact with one another and less with local chieftains. More formalized legal guidelines were seen as desirable, as were guarantees that customary rights would be safeguarded. And for those who still lived in the remote valleys, similar guidelines and guarantees were also needed.

Thus, during the twelfth and thirteenth centuries the ancient customs and usages that had guided society were increasingly formalized, and by the end of Teobaldo's reign they had been assembled and codified as the law of the land.

PEACE, POPULATION GROWTH AND A CHANGING SOCIETY

The relative tranquility that prevailed in the north of the Iberian Peninsula—and indeed in Europe in general—from the beginning of the twelfth century fostered urbanization and the ordering of society. Even in the south of the peninsula, by the twelfth century the Muslims were too busy fighting among themselves to pose much of a threat to the Christian kingdoms. Living conditions improved and life expectancy increased. Immigrants, particularly in the north, added to the growing population. This influx had started with those who made the pilgrimage to Compostela and settled in towns along the route. In Navarra this accounted for considerable growth of Pamplona and Estella in particular, and was accompanied by greater commerce in goods and ideas.

Sancho the Great, receptive to European contacts, had encouraged immigration. So did Navarra's Aragonese kings from 1076 to 1134. Much of Aragon—though less of Navarra—had been depopulated during the continual seesaw warfare with the Muslims. New settlers were induced to move in and found settlements by the offer of freedom from accountability to seignorial lords, with allegiance owed only to the king.

Many of the early settlers came from north of the Pyrenees and were called, indiscriminately, *francos.* But though at first most of them were indeed from France, the term probably does not refer to the immigrants' provenance. It was applied equally to later incursions of English, Germans and other Europeans. *Franco* derives, rather, from *francus*—meaning, free from servitude.

Two other groups added to the urban population: Jews and Muslims. Their influence on society was considerable in spite of the fact that they constituted a tiny segment of the population.[1] For one thing, they possessed the rich cultural heritage of the ancient Hebraic and Arabic civilizations—based on more extensive learning and art than any of the raw kingdoms of northern Spain could claim. For another, their industriousness, both in the increasingly commercial urban areas and in agriculture, contributed enormously to the smooth functioning of the economy.

Jews had inhabited Spain ever since the Visigothic period, if not before.[2] The first Muslim invaders left them alone for the most part, but the more creedbound Almoravids and their successors of the twelfth century, the Almohads, forced them to leave their ancient dwelling places in the south, in al-Andalus. Their refuge was Christian Spain, not yet as intolerant as it was to become. The Jews settled in the cities, keeping to themselves in their *aljamas* (separate living areas), but mixing with the rest of the population in other respects. Hardworking and financially astute, many filled the role of moneylenders and other specialized occupations such as doctors. They were the only real capitalists in medieval Navarra, though they were not always free to hold onto their gains. Many a king, when he had to borrow money for wars or weddings, would not hesitate to change the terms of a contract later on, with the result that the moneylender received less than his due.

The Jews were often a persecuted minority. The Muslims were somewhat more fortunate. Muslim influence on the cities of the north had two channels: through the Mozarabs and the Mudejares. The former were Christians who had, at the time of the conquest, remained to live peaceably with their Muslim conquerors. Many of them, much later, emigrated northward to Christian Spain in the ninth and tenth centuries, bringing a certain veneer of Arabic culture and customs with them. But the impact of the Mozarabs was greater in Asturias-León than in the Basque areas.

Mudejares were their opposite number: Muslims whom the Christians found living in the cities they reconquered. They were not only permitted to remain, they were in fact granted special privileges, so serious was the Christian monarchs' need for people to settle and strengthen their towns and cities. Especially in Aragón and especially under Alfonso the Warrior the Mudejares received recognition and welcome. In medieval Navarra, however, assimilation came slowly and the Mudejares were segregated in their own precincts *(morerías)*.

Thus, Muslims, Jews and *francos* were distinct classes in the growing and newly important cities, a situation unique to Spain in the medieval world. Otherwise, Navarra's evolving society, in its broad outlines, was typical of that in many of Europe's small kingdoms with a hereditary monarch supreme over nobility, clergy, city dwellers and rural laborers.

CLASS STRUCTURE

The king of Navarra had final power over the army, justice and administration. His authority had always rested on election by his warrior-peers. This was akin to the practice of the early Franks, as well as the Visigoths who had invaded Spain in the fifth century. But in time heredity came to govern the succession, though at each king's accession there was always a ceremonial confirmation by the nobles.

Failing legitimate successors (that is, sons, daughters, brothers or sisters), a new king was elected by the nobles and *el pueblo de la tierra* (the people of the land).[3]

The nobility was the most visible class; in medieval Navarra it formed perhaps one-sixth of the population.[4] Highest in rank were the *ricos hombres*. These were the leading magnates and the king's principal advisors in his summoning of the Cortes and other important matters. Their titles were not hereditary, and each king could appoint new *ricos hombres,* to ensure their support or as reward for services. Originally there were twelve, but after the advent of the French dynasty, the number increased. The *ricos hombres* were subject only to the king, and were themselves lords of the lesser nobility—the *hidalguía.*

Members of the *hidalguía,* not necessarily rich or powerful, were certainly influential and numerous. They were not a remote, separate class, as had been the case with the Visigothic nobles. The name itself implied nothing except hereditary proprietorship: *hijos de algo* meant sons of a family with property. The right to call oneself noble was much to be desired in Navarra, as elsewhere on the peninsula. It was jealously guarded. And the *hidalguía* had to be ready at all times to back up its claims to noble lineage.

Two subgroups of this lesser nobility class were *caballeros* and *infanzones. Caballeros* were, originally, all men possessing a horse *(caballo)* and therefore in a position to take a leading role in battle. *Infanzones* were nobles of the blood. They proliferated because occasionally the king would grant nobility to an entire town or valley, and the status was hereditary.

Equal to or sometimes above the nobility in status and power was the clergy. Navarra was no exception to the pervasive influence of the Catholic Church in the medieval world, and to the power not only of the papacy but also of each country's indigenous religious institutions. Sancho the Great ruled a kingdom that embraced three papal sees: one each for Navarra, Aragon and Le Rioja. By 1200 the diminished kingdom had only one see, Pamplona.[5]

And it was in Pamplona, where the bishop was a strong force in temporal as well as spiritual affairs, that a power struggle developed between him and the nobility. The nobles preferred to be subject to their king, not to a bishop. Even the king had to be careful to keep on the bishop's good side. Teobaldo I learned this the hard way. Because of a dispute with Bishop Pedro Jiménez de Gazólaz of Pamplona over income from a *señorio,* the king was excommunicated in 1245 for two years and received absolution only by journeying to Rome and appealing to the pope.[6]

The prosperous and almost autonomous monasteries were another enclave of ecclesiastical power. Sancho the Great and his successors had been enthusiastic founders and supporters of monasteries. San Salvador de Leyre, perched on a mountainside near the Aragon border and dating from the ninth century, was Sancho's favorite. At its apogee Leyre received tribute from thirty-eight towns, including far-off San Sebastián. Until 1078 it supplied Pamplona with its bishops. Dozens of other monasteries flourished from the eleventh to the thirteenth centuries, some tracing their heritage to the Visigothic era. For example, Sta. María la Real de Irache near Estella had been an early shelter for pilgrims trudging toward Compostela and was one of the monasteries enriched by Sancho the Great, who gave it the castle of Monjardín, captured from the Muslims.[7]

As the power of these churchly institutions waxed, the support or opposition the monarch could expect from his prelates became more important to his temporal undertakings, and their counsel had greater weight. Along with the *ricos hombres,* members of the clergy had had a place in the king's council from the earliest times. He had to consult the council before he conceded important privileges, promulgated laws, levied taxes, went to war or arranged peace treaties. The council met periodically to consider, and advise the king on, matters of national concern. For example, in 1134, when the Aragonese King Alfonso the Warrior died without an heir and a Navarrese king was named, the choice was made by a body that comprised the *ricos hombres,* the prelates and deputies of the cities: a body foreshadowing the Cortes.

Next, below the lords spiritual and temporal, was the rest of the population. This included, as we have seen, three special classes: the *francos,* Jews and Muslims. The last two were less privileged and more restricted than any other class. But the *francos,* many of whom had been lured by promises of special concessions if they would settle in Navarra, were only a little below the lesser nobility in status. Their taxes were light, their privileges many. Still, they were a definite minority, with more restrictions than native-born citizens. As they became more integrated into the population, the term *francos* became synonymous with *ruanos*, which had designated the shopkeepers, craftsmen and other nonagricultural workers in the towns. (The term comes from *rua* or street, and first denoted those who lived where houses were lined along a street.)

Finally, the developing towns incorporated a growing middle class of artisans, tradesmen, merchants and innkeepers, as well as farmers who lived in the towns but worked in the fields and pastures.

Beyond the cities were the rural population and field laborers. Most of Navarra was still largely rural and unchanged, in this respect, since the early Middle Ages. Especially in the northwest toward Guipúzcoa and in the Pyrenean valleys, laborers still tilled the soil for themselves or for the landowners, and tended herds, using the same crude methods and tools that had been used for centuries. Many were practically serfs: bound to work on lands of the king *(realengos)* or of the monasteries *(abadengos)* or of secular lords *(solariegos)*.

As a class, the rural laborers were called *vilanos* (from the Latin: inhabitants of a populated place) and lived in tiny communities near their employers' lands. Their lives were not easy and they were hardly masters of their fate. But as time passed, minimal standards governing their working and living conditions were recognized. Customary law required, for instance, that they be given, with the daily meal that their lord had to provide, wine that "had the color of wine"—that is, wine that had not been grossly diluted with water.

Even so, this society was far more open than that of feudal France, for example. Here a *vilano* could at least theoretically better himself by moving from his *señorio* into a land under royal jurisidiction, though he ran the risk of retribution if he fell into his former lord's power again.

PROLIFERATION OF THE URBAN FUEROS

Navarra of the late eleventh and early twelfth centuries had built a favorable base, economically and politically, for a great leap forward into the medieval world. Relatively prosperous and secure, people were looking for guarantees of their status and rights. And in just about one century—from 1076 to 1180 —nearly every city and town in Navarra received such a royal guarantee, in writing.

This wholesale confirmation of citizens' rights and responsbilities was not unique to Navarra. The same process was taking place in Castile, Aragon and León in the eleventh and twelfth centuries.[8] The Christian kings of the peninsula, as they began to triumph over the infidel invaders, sought to attract settlers, secure their subjects' loyalty and firmly ally themselves with the increasingly puissant religious communities. Their instruments were the *fueros municipales,* the *fueros de población,* and fueros granted to religious communities or special classes—such as, for instance, all the *francos* in a city.

The *fuero municipal* was a charter confirming a "bill of rights" for the city's inhabitants. It gave no political power to the city as an entity; all such power was still vested in the king and his appointed officials.

The similar *fuero de población* probably had a much narrower purpose, though the term is often used to refer to any charter for a new city. Especially on the frontiers of Castile and Aragon freemen and laborers were encouraged to come and settle in newly founded cities on land reclaimed from the Muslims, in exchange for considerable freedom and privilege. The documents fixing the conditions under which they would live were the *fueros de población,* granted by kings and also by bishops and abbots.

So many different fueros issued during such a short period might lead one to expect the laws of the land to be in a state of wild confusion. But there was more order to the process than mere dates and statistics indicate, and there were more similarities than discrepancies among the various fueros.

One reason for the similarity was that a city desiring its own charter would often ask the king for one like the fuero of another city, usually with only a few changes or additions. There was a relatively small number of "grandfather" fueros that were subsequently adopted by many other cities.

For example, consider the wide dispersion of the first municipal fuero on record during the joint kingdomship of Navarra and Aragon—that of Jaca, promulgated by Sancho Ramírez in 1076. It is interesting not only for its broad application but also because it dealt with a specific peculiarity of the northern kingdoms and Navarra in particular: the need for and presence of foreign populations in the cities. Thus it came to be known as the fuero of the *francos*.

Jaca, in Aragon, had long been an important city. It was the southern terminus of one of the Pyrenean passes used by pilgrims and other travelers from the ninth century on. After the Muslim threat to Aragon receded, it was repopulated by Sancho Ramirez, who made it his capital. Sancho was deliberately trying to attract settlers from beyond the Pyrenees, just as were rulers in Castile and León. All across northern Spain there was not only a need for immigrants, but also a marked receptiveness to Europeans, due to the commercial activity that had grown up along the road to Compostela.[9]

Jaca's fuero was the model for many others granted to foreign repopulators of cities. Its provisions, as given in the Sancho Ramírez document, included such inducements as: the city's inhabitants need not go into battle unless they had enough bread for three days; any service in the army would be only for pitched battle, or in case the king were besieged in his own land (which would preclude foreign expeditions); and citizens could not be imprisoned for debts if they had given a guarantee that they would pay.

This fuero was the basis for the one granted by Alfonso I in 1129 to the *francos* who had just established the *burgo* (borough) of San Saturnino in Pamplona. New settlers were encouraged in Pamplona but were located in separate precincts from the old inhabitants' precinct, la Navarrería. San Saturnino was limited strictly to *francos;* no natives of Navarra were to settle there, or any cleric, or soldier, or nobleman.

Alfonso's fuero for the *francos* of San Saturnino confirmed, implicitly, the provisions of the fuero of Jaca. It also gave them an extra: a monopoly on the sale of wine and bread to pilgrims passing through the city.

Though originally fashioned for *francos,* the fuero of Jaca was in time adopted by populations of natives too. It was soon even extended to La Navarrería in Pamplona, then to another *burgo* of *francos* there (San Nicolás). But despite this similarity in their law codes, Pamplona's *burgos* remained walled off from each other and had their own separate administrations. Pamplona was, in fact, a city of separate and often inimical *burgos* until the fifteenth century.

The fuero of Jaca was model, too, for that of the *francos* of Estella (granted by Sancho Ramírez in 1090); for populators of Puente la Reina (Alfonso the Warrior, 1122), Olite (1147), Monreal (1149), Sangüesa (1122), and for the Jews of Pamplona and Huarte (1164).

But perhaps the most significant application of this famous fuero came when it was a century old, and served as the basis for the fuero of San Sebastián, to which city it was granted by Sancho the Wise of Navarra about 1180. At this time San Sebastián was still part of Navarra, and its vital seaport. There were many *francos* there, due to its active commerce, by sea and land, with Gascony. But much of the San Sebastián fuero was new, inserted to deal with regulation of the city's maritime commerce. The granting of such a special fuero may have been intended to promote the continuation of San Sebastián as Navarra's port.[10] This was during the period when Navarra and Castile, mutually distrustful, were strengthening their frontiers. Only twenty years later Alfonso of Castile succeeded in closing Navarra off from the sea.

Thus the descendants of the fuero of Jaca multiplied even further. San Sebastián's maritime version was later the model for the fueros of many other Cantabrian coastal cities.

By the end of the twelfth century most of the significant groups—geographic or class—in Navarra had received official confirmation of their status, rights and privileges, by means of their special fueros. These included most of the places important today: Pamplona, Estella, Olite, Tudela, Viana, Puente la Reina and Sangüesa.

The same thing was going on in the other Basque lands, to say nothing of the rest of Christian Spain. Inhabitants of the growingly populous cities and towns, long used to being guided by their customary unwritten laws, recognized the need for some formalization by the king's "official seal," as it were. And one city's fuero often gave birth to many others.

One such progenitor, that originated outside the Basque Country and was almost as prolific as the fuero of Jaca, was that of Logroño, a Castilian city just over the Ebro from Navarra. Alfonso VI of Castile, grandson of Sancho the Great of Navarra, granted a fuero to this city in 1095. It rapidly spread to many Basque cities, such as Vitoria, ancient capital of Alava, dating from Visigothic days, towns in Vizcaya such as Bermeo and Orduña, and others in Guipúzcoa, though the fuero of Jaca was the more accepted model there.

The Logroño fuero had some unique provisions, not to be found in the possibly more restrained and less self-conscious Basque versions. For example, a man could legally kill another man who pulled his beard—an act constituting an infringement of his personal honor.[11]

The medieval Basque fueros were even echoed overseas. The founder of the Province of Nuevo Vizcaya (in what is now Mexico) was a native of Durango in the Basque province of Vizcaya. Not only did he give Nuevo Vizcaya, of which he was governor, an old-world name, he also declared the fuero of Vizcaya to be the law of the land. This meant, among other things, that all inhabitants were automatically members of the nobility, just as they were at home.[12]

The lesson to be learned from the most cursory examination of the interrelationships of the municipal fueros from the eleventh to the fourteenth centuries is that, despite similarities and common ancestries, no two fueros were identical and few were comprehensive. A new document frequently acknowledged its basis in another fuero, such as that of Jaca or Logroño, but did not reproduce the original, simply setting down its own alterations or additions.

Therefore it is not surprising that when in 1234 a new, nonnative king became ruler of Navarra (Thibaut of Champagne, later known as Teobaldo I of Navarra), he was hampered by unfamiliarity with the customs of his new realm, so unlike feudal France. There was, undeniably, a conglomeration of overlapping, contradictory, and—worst of all—unwritten laws. Hindsight lets us recognize that the time was ripe to bring order to these accumulated fueros of the kingdom.

This is the background for the long-accepted story of the genesis of the *Fuero General* of Navarra, given currency by Padre José Moret, seventeenth-century historian. According to Moret, three years after Teobaldo's accession, he and his nobles disagreed over the meaning of the country's laws. The nobles accused the king of not abiding by the laws as they understood them. As a compromise, the king and nobles considered asking the pope for a judgment. But to acquaint the pope with the problem it would be necessary to set the laws down in writing. This was done, by Teobaldo along with ten *ricos hombres,* twenty *caballeros,* ten clerics, the king's council, and the bishop of Pamplona. The resulting document, after promulgation by the king, became the *Fuero General* of Navarra.[11]

So goes the legend. But later scholars came to believe that the document compiled by Teobaldo and his nobles was not the *Fuero General* but simply an affirmation of the nobles' rights vis-à-vis their king. If so, it was comparable to the Magna Carta, which was issued in England a few years before (1215). We know that Teobaldo, alarmed at the increase of privileged nobility and the decline in taxpaying commoners, wanted to stiffen the procedures by which a man could establish that he had noble blood. The Navarrese nobles, though they had freely chosen a foreign ruler, were naturally watchful and suspicious of any new practices he might introduce. Their special privileges may well have been the matters under dispute, not the fueros of the country in general.

It is now considered quite possible that the *Fuero General* antedated Teobaldo's reign. If it was based on the lost fuero of Sobrarbe, granted to Tudela by Alfonso the Warrior in 1117, this could place its adoption in Navarra between 1117 and 1134, when Alfonso died and Navarra lost Aragon and Sobrarbe, the small Pyrenean county east of Aragon.[14]

In any case, sometime before the end of the thirteenth century a *Fuero General* of Navarra had been set down (in Aragonese-Navarrese Romance, not Latin; and certainly not in Basque, which would not be a written language for another century).[15]

THE FUERO GENERAL, MIRROR OF MEDIEVAL NAVARRA

No matter what its exact date of origin or the circumstances, the *Fuero General* has far more substance than a mere statement of rebellion by a group of nobles vis-à-vis their king. Cutting across all classes of society, it is a compendium of rules and customs that had proven useful during several preceding centuries.

At first glance it seems to have been designed for a society where quarreling was prevalent, often leading to violence and crimes of passion.

But at the same time this was a society with few illusions, aware that human nature is frail and needs to be kept in check. The breadth, depth and practical realism of the *Fuero General* were such that it served as constitution of the kingdom for fifteen monarchs after Teobaldo I, then for three hundred years more after the kingdom was united to Castile.

The first of its six books is introduced with words that clearly hark back to the kingdom's earliest traditions and legends:

> Here begins the first book of the fueros that were made in Spain as soon as the mountain dwellers won those lands that were without a king. In the name of Jesus Christ, who is and will be our salvation, we begin in eternal remembrance of the Fueros of Sobrarbe, of exalted Christianity.[16]

It goes on to explain "by whom and by what means Spain was lost, and how the first King of Spain was elevated": Spain was lost to the Muslims through the treachery of Count Julian whose daughter the Visigothic King Rodrigo had dishonored; in revenge Julian invited the Muslims to invade and Rodrigo was killed in the battle.

As to the choosing of the first king, this prologue names him as Don Pelayo, legendary hero who fought the Muslims in the eighth century. (But Pelayo was never king of all Spain, and almost certainly never ruled any part of Navarra.)[17]

From this rather fanciful beginning, the *Fuero General* proceeds, in 508 chapters, to present a down-to-earth and comprehensive collection of remarkably precise and realistic laws.

It shows us Navarra as a limited monarchy, with a powerful and assertive nobility; a modified feudal state with a rather rigid class structure; a property-based society; a nation ruled by law with an intricate but workable judicial system.

NAVARRA AS A LIMITED MONARCHY

The kingdom did not spring full-blown from the inventive minds of the chieftains who raised the first king on a shield and cried *"Real!"* It evolved gradually from a simple, militarily-oriented power base to the precisely circumscribed monarchy defined in the *Fuero General*. Undoubtedly its evolution owed much to the examples of the past and of other European kingdoms.[18] Election of the king by his peers was similar to the practice of the early Franks, as well as the Visigoths. There may even have been a conscious effort to show a link with Visigothic tradition, in the wording describing the first king, Pelayo, as "of the lineage of the Goths."

The contractual nature of the kingship is established at the outset. The description of the procedure for the coronation includes the king's oath to uphold his subjects' fueros. A few pages later the nobles' duties to him are set down.[19]

The king had judicial but not sole power over the nobles. The *Fuero General* provides for a number of checks and balances. These were the basis for the growing importance of the nobility that became marked in the thirteenth and fourteenth centuries, during the reigns of the frequently absent French rulers.

For example, the king was not to wage war or make peace without the counsel of his native-born nobles. They were also to be consulted before he conceded important privileges, promulgated laws or levied taxes. This insistence on Navarrese advisors to the king exemplifies the *Fuero's* safeguards against foreign domination. If a foreign-born king ruled, he was not to bring with him more than seven outsiders, either as officials or personal counselors. (This provision was probably not—as most of the *Fuero* was—a statement of a customary law, but a new clause, resulting from the arrival of the foreign king in the thirteenth century, and the nobles' mistrust of his court.)

Further restraints were exercised by the fact that the king's council, from the twelfth century, also included members of the clergy and representatives of the cities, though this is not mentioned in the *Fuero General*. The only role assigned to the clergy in it is officiation at crownings. As for "the people," they are to participate in the naming of a king if there is no legitimate successor. The term probably refers to representatives of the cities and valleys. The nation's dozens of populated valleys, where geography and defense and the nature of their agrarian society had dictated the formation of effective local administration, had always participated in Navarra's government.

FEUDALISM AND CLASS DISTINCTIONS

It is generally agreed that feudal practices came to the Iberian Peninsula later than to the rest of Europe, and that they existed chiefly in those parts most subject to European influence, or that had inherited least from the Roman-Visigothic tradition. That is, it was natural for feudalism to develop in Catalonia, and to a lesser extent in the western Pyrenees.

There is evidence of feudal practices in Navarra from the time of Sancho the Great in the eleventh century. He needed loyal supporters for his expansionist endeavors, and forged reciprocal bonds of service and protection with his nobles. But the first recorded example of homage to a king of Navarra by a vassal was not until 1196, when a Gascon lord offered homage to Sancho VII, in return for which he was granted a fief. Two similar examples, also involving this Sancho and nobles from Basse Navarre (that portion of the kingdom on the French side of the Pyrenees) occurred in 1202 and 1205.[20]

With the first French king came French practices. After 1234 there were many instances when Spanish Basque lords, too, paid homage to their kings, in return for some benefit.

But the *Fuero General,* based mostly on practices of earlier years, has only one general reference to the sovereign-vassal relationship. At the opening of the third chapter, we read:

> Keep in your memory the fueros that the King of Navarra has with his Navarrese, and they with their King. The Navarrese are to serve their King as good vassals do their good lord; and the lord does well by them as his good vassals; as many men as there are in his kingdom, to all will he do well.

If feudalism was not prevalent, class distinctions were. The *Fuero* recognized—indeed reinforced—them. Especially for the lower and "minority" social orders, life was to be lived according to hard-and-fast rules.

Nearly every moment of the laborer's life was governed by some provision of the *Fuero:* from minute instructions as to types of taxes he was to pay, to exactly what he was to be given by his lord for dinner, and even extending to how many times the oil bottle was to be passed around for the soup or (as noted above) to what extent the wine could be diluted.

The laborer was also protected against more serious injuries. For example: if he were wounded so severely as to lose an arm or a leg, or to be permanently crippled, the person who had attacked him was required to pay a fine that was half that due for a murder. The amount—250 sueldos—was equal to the price of twenty lambs or seven hogs in the mid-1300s.[21]

Another protective measure required that laborers be paid every day for that day's work. If the master failed to do so by nightfall, the laborer, accompanied by two witnesses, was entitled to complain to the local judge. If the claim was admitted, the master had to pay on the following day twice the daily wage, plus five sueldos fine.

As for the minorities—Jews, Muslims, *francos*—the first were the most discriminated against. But at least their position was clearly defined in the *Fuero*. They were not completely at the mercy of unbridled prejudice. They could not be attacked without a set fine being levied on the attacker. And if the attack resulted in murder of the Jew, the fine was even more severe. In judicial disputes, if a Jew were suing or being sued by a Christian, the *Fuero* stipulated that each was entitled to a witness of his own faith.

Many of the Muslims' privileges derived from the fuero granted by Alfonso the Warrior to the Muslims of Tudela when he conquered that city in 1114. They could do business and own property, and were exempted from some religious taxes.

One final, very small but persistently present class was that of slaves. Slavery apparently existed in Navarra from the kingdom's earliest days and lasted until the fifteenth century; in 1408, King Charles the Noble accepted a Muslim slave as a gift from one of his lords.

Nearly all slaves were non-Christians. As elsewhere in Spain, Muslim captives taken in battle became slaves for their captors and could be bought and sold like animals. The *Fuero General* does not mention slaves, but some of the preceding urban fueros did. And even a slave had some protection. For example, in Tudela if a slave came into a church seeking baptism, he could not be ejected. Other evidence that religion was the main criterion of servitude was the ancient provision that if a Jew or Muslim slave became a Christian, he could not be sold by his master, but was permitted to buy his freedom.[22]

NAVARRA AS A LAND-ORIENTED SOCIETY

Ownership of property was a fundamental measure of status in medieval Navarra. Hence its disposal (through inheritance, etc.) was an important matter, and the *Fuero General* deals with it in praiseworthy detail.

Starting at the top, with the king's patrimony, the *Fuero* provides that the king's eldest legitimate son shall inherit the kingdom. Other sons, and his daughters, divide his other possessions. If the king has acquired lands from the Muslims, he may distribute them among his legitimate sons as he wishes. This was in accord with practice in the rest of the peninsula. The exception had been the division of his patrimony by Sancho the Great, who broke the pattern and broke up the kingdom in order to leave something for each of his sons. Otherwise, throughout Navarra's history, the kingdom was inherited by the king's eldest son, or the king's eldest brother, or through the king's legitimate daughter or his sister. If the king died without any such heirs, the successor was chosen by the *ricos hombres,* the *infanzones caballeros,* and the "people of the land," as we have seen.

Inheritance procedures for the nobility are also spelled out. For example, if a *rico hombre* has only one castle, the rule is the same as for the king: the castle goes to his eldest son or other legitimate heir. Younger sons receive his remaining possessions.

Property rights, as the *Fuero* demonstrates, were a source of many disputes. There must have been many arguments over who owned what. One whole title of the *Fuero* explains circumstances under which such disputes are to be settled.

These provisions dealing with property are particularly interesting because they show how central agriculture and grazing were to the kingdom's well-being—as they are today to that of the province.

Pasturage rights were of primary concern. The *Fuero* sets forth the regulations for where and when horses, oxen, cattle, pigs and even sick cattle may be pastured.

Cultivated lands—vineyards, orchards, grain fields—were not to be intruded on by flocks or cattle. Again, the *Fuero* is realistic and specific, leaving little argument as to the nature of the misdeed and its penalty. For example, if a cow strayed into a vineyard, the older the vines, the more its owner had to pay: one lambskin if vines are one year old; a lamb if two; a sheep if three. This made sense, for the purchase of vines represented a considerable investment and a wait of several years was necessary before the investment would begin to yield returns.

Reciprocal municipal property rights were also covered. For example, if one town sold water to another and the aqueduct had to pass over an intervening town, that middle town had the right to deny passage.

Not only the cultivated, inhabited lands, but also the mountains were within the purview of the *Fuero.* Woodcutting, an economically important activity, was carefully regulated. Inhabitants of one town or valley could not cut wood in the mountains belonging to another. If anyone cut wood without consent of the owners, he was fined specified amounts of barley, wheat, wine and money. Rights of the *labradores* (peasants) to cut wood were defined in relationship to those of the nobility.

As for hunting, only the king and the *hidalguía* could hunt partridge. The *vilanos* were permitted to hunt wild boar, bear, stags and roe deer, under certain conditions. Hunting seasons of a sort were enforced; no one was to prepare traps for deer in the mountains from May 1 until St. Martin's Day, in the fall. This was probably in order to protect cattle and livestock that were pastured in the mountains during the summer.

APPLICATION OF THE LAWS

The *Fuero General* did not really change much in Navarra; it simply put the customary laws in writing. It was particularly comprehensive in its spelling out of the workings of the judicial and penal system.

Medieval Navarra's judicial system was, like that of most of the medieval world, discriminatory. There were different kinds of justice for different classes.

The higher nobility was subject to the king's justice directly. The lesser nobility, and all rural laborers, were subject to their seigniorial lords' justice, or to that of the *alcaldes* (local magistrates) appointed by the king.

This left one class—the free city dwellers—nominally subject to the king and the king's appointees but enjoying considerable independence in their civil rights and choice of magistrate. Their qualification for such an autonomous condition was their claim to *vecindad*. This, according to the *Fuero,* meant being a resident of a city, town or village; owning a house of a minimum specified size, surrounded by (or with property rights to) land sufficient to plant a certain amount of grain, and a garden large enough for thirteen heads of cabbage. The benefits of *vecindad* were the rights to all the privileges the community possessed, including the right to exclude strangers.

In all judicial questions, once guilt was established by the appropriate procedure, the *Fuero* took over and decreed the penalty. It embraced the most serious and the most insignificant of crimes and misdemeanors.

The book of the *Fuero* that prescribes penalties for homicide is the second longest, and the schedule of punishments left little to a judge's discretion. Not only the nature of the crime, but also its location and consequences were factors.

For example, if a murder took place in a consecrated church, there was an extra fine of 900 sueldos. But if the church was not consecrated, this was reduced to 60 sueldos. Or if a homicide occurred in Pamplona, the fine was in money; but if it were in the mountains, where money was not so available, the fine was in oxen.

The penalty for murder by poison was death. But if the poisoner failed in his attempt and the victim recovered, the guilty party was turned over to him for disposition.

LESSONS OF THE FUERO GENERAL

The *Fuero* cannot be compared with modern constitutions or penal codes without a clear understanding of its raison d'être. Its attention to detail, its predetermination of penalties for wrongdoing and its emphasis on distinctions among classes may seem excessive to us in an age accustomed to trial by jury with verdicts affected by extenuating circumstances, and to a fluid and legally classless society.

The lesson of the *Fuero* is that it suited a deeply conservative people, who wished things to be done as they had always been done. It was a guarantee of order for a society that through centuries of dealing with disorder, had learned what worked and what did not, and wished to leave nothing to arbitration or chance.

Whether the gathering and compilation of its hundreds of laws antedated or postdated the accession of Teobaldo I, the two events marked, each in its own way, a significant moment in the kingdom's history.

The *Fuero General* was a sign of national maturity and a triumph of the distinctively conservative Navarrese character. It meant, most of all, recognition of the workability of a strong monarchy that derived its strength from the integrity of its covenant with the people.

The arrival of a non-Basque king, however, started in motion a series of dynastic developments that led eventually to the breakdown of royal power in Navarra.

VII

In the French Orbit

IN 1234 NAVARRA WAS TO BE RULED BY a monarch from beyond the Iberian Peninsula. When Sancho the Strong died, there was no native-born legitimate heir—for the first time in four hundred years. So the succession passed through the female line. Sancho's sister Blanche had married the count of Champagne and their son Thibaut became Teobaldo I of Navarra.

With the accession of a Frenchman—and not even a French Basque from nearby Basse Navarre, but a nobleman from north central France—a new element entered the kingdom's destiny. From this time on we can trace the very slow, very long decline in Navarra's fortunes that was to be climaxed by its loss of independence three centuries later.

But this cannot be ascribed only to the advent of the foreign-born line of kings. Sancho the Strong may have started the downturn when he retired from the battlefield. While he stayed shut up in his castle, the other peninsular kingdoms claimed and incorporated lands won back from the Muslims. Aragon, Castile and Portugal expanded by fifty percent during the first half of the thirteenth century. Their territorial gains were the most important in western Europe, for which this century was in general an age of expansion.[1]

Navarra, however, gained no territory and in fact lost ground. Lacking the strong leadership of an aggressive monarch, intimidated by powerful neighbors, Navarra lost its momentum among the developing Iberian kingdoms. As Navarra's kings continued to show more concern with their native France than with their obscure little Pyrenean possession, it fell prey to civil strife and the acquisitiveness of Castile and Aragon.

THE TROUBADOUR KING

Teobaldo did not come to his new realm a complete stranger. From the time of his mother Blanche's marriage to the count of Champagne there had been frequent contact between the two lands. Blanche very probably encouraged this, in order to lay the groundwork for Teobaldo's claims. She was an able and ambitious manager of her son's affairs and usually had success.[2] Sancho, aware of the need to settle the succession question, was at first disposed to recognize Teobaldo as his heir. But at the very end of his life he had a change of heart (perhaps he was affronted by the young count's unseemly eagerness) and made known his wish to be succeeded by his cousin Jaime of Aragon. But Navarra's nobles feared absorption into Aragon and the consequent likelihood of Castilian attacks. So at Sancho's death they sent two delegations: one to Jaime, asking him to renounce his claim (which he had never seemed very keen on maintaining), and another to Teobaldo, informing him that he had been chosen their ruler.

Teobaldo's qualifications for kingship were respectable. He came from one of the highest peerages in France and a family that had intermarried with English and French royalty. He was descended from Eleanor of Aquitaine. His aunt, Blanche's sister Berenguela, had married Richard the Lion-Hearted. His mother had instilled in him the conviction that he was destined to rule —certainly as one of the most powerful counts in France, possibly as king of Navarra.

But history has portrayed him not so much a leader as an adventurous, pleasure-loving romantic. Even before leaving Champagne he had earned a reputation as a notable poet and songwriter. Most prolific of all the French troubadours, he composed over four hundred melodies and wrote more than five hundred poems. Fortunately for students of this chivalric age, many of these survive.³ Whether based on experience or not, his verses speak of many an amorous adventure and attachment.

Despite some evidence of a frivolous and shallow nature, Teobaldo had his strengths: firm religious convictions and a genuine desire to rule fairly. But almost before he had a chance to pick up the reins, Pope Gregory IX summoned Europe's Christian princes to a crusade. Teobaldo was the first—in fact the only—monarch to accept the call.⁴ He recruited followers, first in Navarra and then in his native Champagne and in Brie. Always the poet, he recruited first with promises—

> Lord God, you know that whoever goes
> To that land where our Lord lived and died,
> And takes up the crusader's cross
> Will not find hardship there—
> But Paradise.
> To all who bear in their souls
> True piety and love of God,
> This is your task:
> To do battle, to avenge and liberate
> Your Lord's own land.

then with threats—

> God suffered on the Cross for us.
> And He will say, on that day when we all come together,
> "You who helped me bear my Cross,
> You will go to where the angels are.
> There you will see Me and my blessed mother Mary.
>
> But you from whom I have received no aid—
> You will all descend to the depths of hell!"⁵

Having gathered four hundred knights in Navarra and many more in France, Teobaldo set out on his adventures in 1239, reaching the Holy Land in 1240. A more or less successful crusade was marred by dissension among his followers but eventually resulted, through mediation, in restoration of much of Jerusalem's lost territory. Teobaldo returned to France late that year.⁶ There he took time out to help Louis IX win a battle with a coalition of his enemies. He returned to Navarra in 1243. It was time to settle down and be a king.

For the rest of his life, Teobaldo gave as much attention to Navarra as to Champagne—of necessity. Relations with his nobility and his clergy were difficult at best, and he had to be on the scene to keep them from nibbling away at the royal power. Early in his reign, as we saw in the last chapter, he managed to arrive at a common understanding with them of the nature and extent of the nation's laws—the endeavor that many regard as the basis for the *Fuero General.*

The chronicler Anelier, who was something of a troubadour himself and not necessarily an impartial observer, wrote of Teobaldo:

> [He] reigned fairly; he loved justice, so much so that he ordered that the kingdom's fueros should protect the poor as well as the rich; and he was such a good and wise king that while he lived, the land abounded with wheat and wine and all the fruits of the earth. He was of such a pleasant disposition that love and joy adorned his whole reign.[7]

When Teobaldo I died, in 1253, Navarra had enjoyed twenty years of peace, with the security of a strong constitutional base and expectation of continuity on the throne. (Teobaldo II had been born in 1240.) Peace, of course, is a relative term. It was even relative in regard to the Muslims, who had received a crushing blow at Las Navas de Tolosa in 1212, with Navarra's Sancho the Strong in the forefront of the Christian hosts. Still the remnants of al-Andalus remained the enemy, though doomed by anarchy. But Navarra under Teobaldo I, except for sending a contingent to take part in the siege of Sevilla, had left it to the other kingdoms to meet the Muslim threat. Sevilla fell to Fernando of Castile in 1248.[8] This was the victory that meant the successful conclusion of the Reconquest, though the small Kingdom of Granada was permitted to exist for two and a half more centuries.

Peace with the neighboring Christian kingdoms was also relative. The two rivals were flexing their muscles: Castile, which since 1230 had incorporated León; and the Crown of Aragon, now embracing Valencia, Catalonia and the small polities of the former Spanish March: Pallars, Ribagorza and Sobrarbe. The three Basque lands had moved out of Navarra's orbit and into Castile's. So Navarra was surrounded on three sides by expansionist and often bellicose neighbors. To the north lay the

IN THE FRENCH ORBIT

Duchy of Aquitaine—no enemy, but a land whose fortunes and allegiances shifted with Castilian, Plantagenet and Capetian politics.

END OF THE HOUSE OF CHAMPAGNE IN NAVARRA

Teobaldo II was only thirteen years old when he succeeded to the throne of Navarra, in 1253. Again, as had been the case with his father, a politically sagacious mother shaped his future. Marguerite of Bourbon, Teobaldo's mother, took charge expeditiously. She patched up Navarra's relations with Jaime I of Aragon and seriously considered a marriage between her young son and an Aragonese princess. This would certainly have strengthened Navarra's ties with its peninsular neighbors—ties weakened by two decades of the French ruling presence. But the pull to France proved stronger and Marguerite arranged a marriage between fourteen-year-old Teobaldo and twelve-year-old Isabelle, daughter of Louis IX (Saint Louis).

Nevertheless, Aragon remained a strong ally, supporting Navarra's resistance to the aggression, or threats of aggression, by Alfonso X of Castile. Alfonso was actually less interested in Navarra than in Gascony to the north. He claimed that land by right of its having been given as dowry by Henry II of England to his daughter Eleanor when she married Alfonso's great-grandfather, Alfonso VIII, in 1170, as we saw in chapter V. But England had never relinquished it. Now, as had happened before and would again, Navarra's geographic position threatened to make it the stepping-stone—or stumbling block—of a Castillian monarch who had European aspirations. However, Alfonso found his other concerns more pressing and had to abandon his designs on Gascony.

Under Marguerite's guidance Navarra kept on good terms with its small Pyrenean neighbors and those in the south of France. Eventually there was even a lessening of tensions with Castile. This was largely due to Teobaldo's growing friendship with his father-in-law Louis IX of France, who had entered on a period of alliance with Castile.[9] Alfonso even went so far as to make a gesture in 1256 toward returning to Navarra its outlets to the sea, San Sebastián and Fuenterrabia, which had been lost in 1200 when Navarra's sovereignty over Guipúzcoa passed to Castile. But if the repatriation was ever formalized, it did not last.[10]

Teobaldo's short reign was a time of détente not only externally but within the kingdom as well, where ruler, clergy and nobility had so frequently been at odds. Teobaldo came to an agreement with the bishop of Pamplona whereby the city's revenues, formerly property of the church, would be shared equally by church and king.

Teobaldo also continued his predecessors' encouragement of the kingdom's municipalities, granting charters to dozens of towns, including many in Basse Navarre: St. Jean Pied de Port, St. Michel de Cize, Ostabat, for example.[11]

By 1267, his fourteenth year as king, Teobaldo had spent less than one-quarter of his time in Navarra. He was more often in Champagne, where he was count, or in Paris, where his father-in-law the king held court. Still, either personally or through his seneschals, he had governed well.

Now, like his father, he was attracted by the notion of a crusade. But for this Teobaldo it was not a triumph; it was a disaster.

Meeting cermoniously at Notre Dame in Paris in June 1267, he and King Louis agreed on their plans, which imposed severe conditions on Navarra: it was to devote ten percent of its revenues for three years to this Eighth Crusade.

The flower of the kingdom's nobility signed up, and Teobaldo embarked in July 1270 to meet King Louis and proceed to Palestine. But for reasons unknown, they sailed first to Tunisia. The heat was intense and plague broke out. Before the armies were much affected by this, Teobaldo, perhaps wishing to win military renown quickly, impulsively launched an attach on the king of Tunisia, winning a resounding victory. According to the chronicler Anelier, the Saracens were stunned by the fierceness and fearlessness of the Basque warriors, declaring them to be not men but living devils. "Against such creatures it is not well to fight!"[12]

But the plague soon became so devastating that the crusaders gave up the plan to go on to the Holy Land. King Louis himself died in Tunisia and the disheartened, depleted army finally set sail for home. On the way, in December 1270, Teobaldo too succumbed, aged only thirty-two. He left no heirs; Enrique I, his brother, succeeded him.

Little is remembered of Enrique's short reign except that he was exceptionally fat, he quarreled with the bishop, and he very

IN THE FRENCH ORBIT

nearly fomented a civil war in Pamplona. The last was due to his granting (perhaps for a price) permission to the borough of La Navarrería to strengthen its fortifications, which enraged its neighbor San Cernín. But actual hostilities did not break out until after Enrique's death (of obesity, the prince of Viana surmised in his history), in 1274.

THE HOUSE OF FRANCE

Enrique's only son Teobaldo III had died when he fell from his nurse's arms out a window of the castle in Estella. Thus, his sister, two-year-old Juana, inherited the throne, becoming the first queen of Navarra in her own right.

Before her father died, the infant queen had already been betrothed twice: first to Henry, son of Edward I of England, and after his death to Philip the Bold—Philip III of France—considerably her senior.

Immediately after Enrique's death, interest in the kingless kingdom led princes of Aragon and Castile to present themselves as prospective husbands for the young heiress. But Juana's mother, a neice of King Louis, preferred to work toward alignment with France, as had been the custom of the House of Champagne.

She also sought French support when Pamplona's civil war began in earnest, in 1276. An army sent by King Philip marched into the city and settled matters by razing La Navarrería. But the enmities among the boroughs were to linger for another hundred years.

Juana was married to Philip the Fair, son of Philip the Bold, in 1284. She was twelve and he was sixteen. When his father died in 1285, Philip became Philip IV of France. He and Juana called themselves the king and queen of France and Navarre—a dual title that the kings of France were to cling to until the French Revolution.

Juana and Philip, like her forefathers, spent much of their time in France and ruled Navarra through governors. France was more than enough to keep them busy: there was a quarrel with the pope and a war with England. Throughout the 1290s Edward I made several attempts to regain Gascony (which he had pledged temporarily to Philip but which Philip decided to keep). Navarra suffered, despite being a noncombatant, when the English armies carried their marauding southward. But an energetic governor, Hugo de Conflans, drove the English out of the kingdom.

Juana bore seven children during her twenty-one years of marriage to Philip. When she died, in 1305, the Navarrese sent a request to Philip that he dispatch his eldest son Louis to Pamplona to take the oath as king of Navarra. They had never considered Philip their king, only the consort of their queen. Hence he could not succeed, lacking the required antecedents; but his and Juana's son could, in complete conformance with the *Fuero General*. He was the first of three of her sons who were to reign briefly and with little distinction over France and Navarra.

But Louis was slow to respond. He kept delaying his acknowledgment of the repeated invitations from the nobility, representatives of the cities, and the clergy. (The assemblies that met to send him reminders of his duties were evolving into the kingdom's Cortes—i.e., parliament.) Even after they threatened disobedience to his governors until he came to swear to uphold the fueros, Louis procrastinated. Finally, in 1307, two years after his mother's death, he found the time. For two months he visited Estella, Olite, Tudela, Sangüesa and Pamplona, then went back to France for the rest of his life. He ruled through governors, who were not well received.

The most enduring result of his short reign was his order to build a fortified castle next to La Navarrería, which was still a potential site of civic strife. Though the castle has disappeared, its memory is preserved by the name of Pamplona's colorful Plaza del Castillo, heart of the city's social life, and transition zone between the old city and the new.

Louis died in 1316, after two years as King Louis X of France and eleven years as Luis I of Navarra. In both kingdoms he was given the sobriquet "the Quarrelsome."

His six-year-old daughter Jeanne (Juana II to her would-be subjects in Navarra) should by rights have succeeded as queen of Navarra.[13] But French policy outweighed the fueros. The traditional fiat against female succession in France (later to be called the Salic Law) was extended to Navarra, and there was nothing the people or Cortes could do about it. In fact, the Cortes never even went through the motions of sending a formal call to her, simply accepting the *fait accompli*. Louis X's younger brother Philip the Tall was recognized as king. His reign was most noted for its brevity and the fact that he never visited Navarra. He took the oath in Paris before a delegation from Pamplona.

Despite his unpopularity and that of his governors, his reign saw a good start toward a resolution of the age-old quarrels between king and bishop over jurisdiction of Pamplona. Again, as had happened in 1291 when Philip and Juana I made a pact with the clergy, the church yielded more than did the monarch.

After Philip's death, in 1322, the third son of Juana I and Philip the Fair came to the throne, again usurping the place of his niece, the lady the Navarrese still considered their rightful queen: Juana II.

Charles IV of France (Carlos I of Navarra) was called "the Fair" in France but "the Bald" by the blunt Navarrese, who never acknowledged him to be their king. They had finally run out of patience. When summoned, they refused to send a delegation to Toulouse to witness the swearing in.

With Charles's death, in 1328, the line of Capetian kings in France came to an end, as did the House of France in Navarra. Though he was a rather insignificant king, Charles's demise had far-reaching significance for all Europe. A dispute broke out between Edward III of England and Philip of Valois for the French throne: Edward was a grandson, and Philip of Valois a nephew, of Philip III of France. Their rival claims ignited the Hundred Years' War. Philip won the first skirmish—the right to recognition as King Philip VI of France—but other issues kept the battle flames burning.

The disappearance of the House of France in Navarra did not mean the end of French rulers. First Philip of Valois claimed the throne, but the Cortes indignantly rejected him, holding out— this time successfully—for Juana II, their legitimate queen. Her naming as monarch in 1328 must have seemed to the Navarrese an auspicious turning point. For one thing, they had won the argument that had begun in 1316 when she first became eligible to rule them—but when her uncles began their series of usurpations.

For another, the swearing to uphold the fueros took place in Navarra, not in France. Juana and her consort, Philip of Evreux, were enthusiastically welcomed in Pamplona in 1329.

But though Juana was descended from the ancient line of the "Pyrenean" kings of Navarra, she was far more French than Navarrese. Both she and her husband were direct descendants of Saint Louis (Louis IX). The Cortes, mindful of this strong

French orientation, permitted Philip to be crowned with Juana, but insisted that both agree publicly in advance to step down from the throne as soon as an heir reached age twenty-one.

Shortly after the coronation Philip promulgated the *Amejoramiento* ("Improvement") of the *Fuero General,* a collection of thirty-four amendments. The *Fuero* had been unchanged for a century, and the monarch and Cortes agreed it was time to bring it up to date. (For purposes of comparison, the first amendment to the U.S. Constitution—after the ten in the Bill of Rights, adopted in 1789—was added only ten years after ratification.)

One of Philip's aims was to completely revise the fueros so there would be a separate fuero for each of the three classes: the nobility, city dwellers and rural laborers. But this interesting idea went no further than publication as Article 25 of the *Amejoramiento.*[14]

However, other more modest amendments were enacted and as far as we know enforced. For example:

The legal coming-of-age of a young *hidalgo* was raised from seven to thirteen years; he was then considered able to bear witness and enter into contracts.

Christians were prohibited from lending for profit.

Fines were established for misrepresenting goods sold (e.g., claiming cloth was from Bruges when it was really from Carcassonne).

Blasphemy was prohibited, and fines for it were laid down.

Even the partridges were protected: penalties were to be exacted of those who took the birds before their young had left the nest, or who took eggs from the nest.

Most of the amendments were what we would call "housekeeping" provisions, bringing the *Fuero* from the thirteenth into the fourteenth century. But the fact that a half dozen of them dealt with activities and lending practices of Jews (and to a lesser extent, Muslims) indicates some deterioration in relations between Jews and Christians. And indeed this is borne out by events.

Early in the new reign there was a violent outbreak of anti-Semitism in the southern part of the kingdom. This was uncharacteristic of Navarra, where Jews had nearly always been accepted and easily absorbed in the population. (In fact, during the thirteenth century a pope wrote twice to scold Navarra for too much benevolence to the Jews.)[15] The outbreak of the 1330s was probably due more to resentment of the practices of Jewish moneylenders than to religious or racial prejudice. In any event, the monarchs and their governors took prompt action to punish the ringleaders and normalcy presently returned.

Aside from this, most of Juana's and Philip's brief stay in Navarra was productive and harmonious. But France was their home, to which they returned in 1334, ruling Navarra through a series of generally able governors.

The kingdom continued to provide them a good income. The tax-collection machinery ran smoothly, in accord with a well-established foral tradition of who paid which taxes. *Pecheros*, the bulk of the taxpayers, included nearly everyone who was not at least an *hidalgo*. Exempt from the *pecha*, or principal tax, were the *hidalguía, caballeros, ricos hombres* and the clergy. However, these classes contributed to the *ayudas* or *servicios*—periodic donations to finance the monarch's wars, ceremonials, weddings and special events. And the nobility had the additional duty of fighting for the king. This involved all kinds of outlays—from outfitting their contingents (as the *ricos hombres* had to do) to paying some one to fight for them (as many *hidalgos* did).[16]

Hence Juana and Philip could live well in France, bringing up their family of seven—of which three were sons. There were no uncertainties now about the succession. Philip busied himself in aiding his cousin King Philip of France in his wars with Edward III of England and Edward's Flemish allies. Juana took charge of administering their French domains: Evreux, Angoulême and Longueville.[17]

Philip of Evreux, like his predecessor Teobaldo II, died during a crusade, albeit a less ambitious one. When Alfonso XI of Castile sought support from other princes in his battles with the Muslims, who still clung to their corner of Andalucia, and when the pope added his authority, calling the warriors of Europe to join the Crusade, Philip was one of the first to respond. He collected funds and followers, some from his French lands but most from Navarra, and proceeded to Algeciras. There, the Navarrese troops performed with customary distinction, but Philip fell ill and died, in 1343, at Jerez de la Frontera.

Juana continued to reign with benevolence and firmness until her own death in 1349. The heir, Carlos, was seventeen years old.

VIII

Dynastic Decline, 1349 to 1517

WHEN CARLOS II CAME TO THE throne, in 1349, Navarra was already beginning its nearly two-century drift toward obscurity, weakness and eventual loss of independence. It would be hard not to ascribe the course of the nation's history to the character of its kings during this period.

For much of the first hundred years Navarra appeared to be a vigorous, active kingdom. Two memorable monarchs of the Evreux dynasty assured it of potency and a prominent, if often belligerent, place on the European stage.

But then came the disastrous, strife-torn reign of Juan II of Aragon. Not all the wisdom of the *Fuero General* could protect Navarra against this ultimate affront: rule by a "foreign" king, who was not recognized by the Cortes, who repudiated his son and heir, and who consistently exploited the kingdom for his own ends. He created and perpetuated enmities so deep that the kingdom lost its national will, ceased to be an actor and became a pawn. The weak Foix kings of the late fifteenth century who came after Juan II were unable to turn the country around—even if they had cared to.

THE TROUBLED REIGN OF CARLOS II

The last two Evreux kings were not so indifferent to their kingdom as their predecessors of the late medieval period had been.

They were Carlos II (the Bad), son of Juana and Philip, and his son Carlos III (the Noble).

Carlos II, a king at the age of seventeen, reigned from 1349 to 1387, during which time he was almost continuously involved in foreign adventures, often requiring considerable military and monetary support by his subjects. If the French kings had largely ignored Navarra, neither had they called on its people for subsidies. Now, a resident king demanded men, money and arms of a kingdom that was in poor shape to provide them. Navarra had barely survived a sixty percent population loss due to the Black Death that devastated Europe from 1348 to 1349.[1] Also, the country still felt the loss of thousands of its most industrious and cultivated citizens, killed during the wave of attacks on Jews at the outset of Juana's reign.

Barbara Tuchman has called Carlos one of the most complex characters of the fourteenth century.[2] He was, besides being ruler of a small but long-established Pyrenean kingdom, a man of his age and his continent. He interacted with contemporaries such as Pedro the Cruel and Pedro's half-brother Henry of Trastámara, locked in combat for the throne of Castile; ruthless Pedro the Ceremonious of Aragon; Edward III of England and his war-nurtured sons, the Black Prince and the Duke of Lancaster; and the Valois kings, who defended the French throne by fair means or foul against Edward and Carlos and their own kinsmen and countrymen. To say nothing of the dread French Captain du Guesclin and his Grand Companies, who ravaged whatever land they went through in pursuit of their careers as mercenaries. These were all contentious men, playing for high stakes. Carlos too had great ambitions.

His desire was to reestablish his dynasty as a top-ranking European or at least peninsular force.[3] Though it does not excuse, his consuming wish explains most of his foreign adventures and his pacts and broken alliances.

During his troubled reign he repeatedly dragged his followers into France, though the *Fuero General* denied his right to take a Navarrese army on the offensive to foreign soil. His persistent intrusions into French affairs, which necessitated off-and-on war with Castile and alliance with France's enemies, were due to his conviction that somehow he could and should regain his family's hereditary lands and honors, and that he had a better claim to the French throne than did the reigning monarchs. This was despite the fact that his mother, Juana II, had renounced her rights to the French succession when she married Philip of Evreux. (She may have had reason; her uncles had expressed doubt about her legitimacy, citing the promiscuity of her mother, Marguerite of Bourbon, queen of Louis X.)[4]

For a time after his accession, Carlos—allied with anti-royalist factions in Paris—seemed to be close to his goal and was named Captain of Paris in 1358. But the future Charles V of France bested him, and Carlos went back to Navarra to see if he could patch up his relations with England, which had deteriorated during his assault on Paris.

As we have seen, the English had long been a continental power. England's fourteenth-century involvement in events on the Iberian Peninsula explains why Carlos felt it to his advantage to ally himself with them occasionally.

During the twelfth and thirteenth centuries the descendants of Henry II and Eleanor of Aquitaine had clung to their European base, defending it not only against the French kings, but also against other neighboring princes: Teobaldo II of Navarra, Fernando III of Castile and James I of Aragon. Its possession, and their Norman lineage, supported the English kings' occasional claims to the throne of France. Their differences with the French had broken out in open warfare in 1338, with Edward III disputing Philip VI of France not only for the traditional English possessions, including Aquitaine, but also for France itself. This opening skirmish of the Hundred Years' War was to attract Carlos as a means of furthering his own French ambitions.

In 1367 Carlos decided that his and England's interests were close enough to merit an alliance. Edward, the Black Prince, had been named duke of Aquitaine by Edward III of England, his father. He was charged with holding Aquitaine and Gascony against the French. In a side maneuver he allied himself with his father's cousin Pedro the Cruel of Castile. The objective was to help Pedro wrest the Castilian throne from his half-brother Henry of Trastámara. The Black Prince, who was always ready for a good fight, saw this fraternal dispute as a chance to break the Castilian-French alliance, which threatened Aquitaine. With Henry supported by the French and Pedro by the English, the struggle for the throne of Castile became the excuse for a resumption of the Hundred Years' War, and a reason for an English army to be on the Iberian Peninsula.

Carlos was lured to the Black Prince's side by the promise of restitution to Navarra of Alava, Guipúzcoa and La Rioja, all held by Castile. He agreed to let the English armies march through Roncesvalles and Pamplona, on their way to Burgos in Castile. After their great victory over Henry of Trastámara at Nájera, the English armies marched back again. They pillaged the countryside and the people suffered greatly, but Carlos was on the side of the victor, and did manage to recover three important cities: Vitoria, Salvatierra and Logroño.

He was not always so fortunate, as he shifted his support from one faction to another. He finally had to give up his aspirations to the French throne, when (in 1378) he lost all the Evreux holdings in Normandy, as well as his last French possession in the south, Montpellier.

For the last ten years of his reign Carlos had to content himself with action on the narrower stage of Navarra, with peninsular powers as his adversaries. He fared badly. In 1379 the kingdom suffered the indignity of Castilian occupation of twenty of its fortifications, including the important castles of Tudela and Estella. Finally in 1387 Carlos, old before his time and miserably ill, died.

NAVARRA IN GREECE

Beginning during Carlos's reign, and continuing almost to the end of his successor's, a curious and protracted overseas adventure took place: the Navarrese expedition to the eastern Mediterranean and Greece. Though quite unrelated to Carlos's involvement in European affairs and in a way only a footnote to the main events of the period, it is interesting as evidence of the proclivity of the Basques for far-ranging explorations and voyages.

The pretext for the expedition, led by Carlos's younger brother Luis, was the recovery of Albania, which was to have been the dowry of Luis's wife Juana of Sicily and Durazzo. Carlos encouraged Luis to go fight for it (possibly to give him something to do), and pried 50,000 ducats out of the royal treasury to finance the effort.

This was, to that date, the largest and most organized Navarrese venture into the Mediterranean, but it was by no means unprecedented. The Basques had long had a world reputation as incomparable seafarers—whether for whaling, commerce or piracy. Though Navarra lacked the Cantabrian seacoast that Vizcaya and Guipúzcoa enjoyed, its seamen could go overland to Pasajes or Bayonne to embark. They also had the Ebro River, which had been their pathway to the Mediterranean from remote times.[5] This was Luis's route. In 1376 his four hundred men took ship from Tudela and sailed down the Ebro to Tortosa, south of Barcelona, and set out on their 1,500-mile voyage. They arrived safely in Albania, did battle, and recovered the kingdom. But Luis died shortly thereafter.

Lacking resources to go home, the Navarrese constituted themselves an "autonomous military republic."[6] Under a succession of leaders, they stayed on, fighting Catalan mercenary forces and French and all comers for possession of much of Greece. They took Athens in 1380. They were still in Greece in 1390, with Venetians as allies. They were still there in 1404, with the widow of their last general, San Superano, regent over themselves and the feudal lands they had acquired. Their last recorded battle was in 1419. For fifty years the Navarrese had virtually dominated the Peloponnesian Peninsula, and toward the end played a role in the terminal struggles of the Byzantine Empire and its allies against the encroaching Ottoman Turks.

ACCESSION OF CARLOS THE NOBLE

Meantime, back in Navarra, Carlos II had been succeeded in 1387 by his son Carlos III. Arturo Campión says of this reign that it was "like a peaceful, smiling morning that succeeds a tempestuous night." Carlos III was a good and perhaps great king, who showed considerably more prudence and moderation than his father. He brought peace, order and unity back to the kingdom, fostered culture and learning, and shored up Navarra's standing among the kingdoms of Europe.

One of his chief aims was to rebuild good ties with France. He successfully negotiated with Charles VII, trading his rights to Cherbourg, Champagne and Brie for an annual subsidy, and trading his title of Count of Evreux for the dukedom of Nemours.

Carlos, a genuine enthusiast of the arts, imported painters and architects from France and distributed their works throughout the kindgom. His most splendid monument, the royal palace at Olite, about thirty miles south of Pamplona, began to rise a few years after his coronation; work went on until 1418.

Olite had a long, distinguished history and was well qualified to serve as a royal seat. It was a fortified native town when the Romans arrived, and kept its importance through the Visigothic era. It had been, for a brief period, part of a tiny kingdom belonging to Castile but surrounded by Navarra in the twelfth century: the Kingdom of Artajona.

During the early years of the Kingdom of Navarra, Olite was one of the five cities with fortified royal palaces—designed more for defense than for luxury. Nevertheless, the city was attractive to the kings, with a more healthful and pleasant climate than Pamplona and free of that city's strife and contention. Both Teobaldos spent time there. Juana, queen of Carlos II, was fond of Olite. It was natural for her son to look on it as an appropriate site for his splendid court.

Here he built his luxurious palace with fifteen towers, inspired by the Gothic castles in France. It was said to have as many chambers as there are days in the year. There were gardens, bowers, galleries, and exotic birds and beasts. He built well: after more than five centuries the palace is largely intact, is being restored, and is a major tourist attraction.

Carlos also improved the old cathedral of Pamplona, which had suffered earthquake damage in 1390. But not all his monuments were in stone. He succeeded, where others had failed (or had not cared to try), in reconciling the differences of the three inimical boroughs of Pamplona: San Nicolás, the Navarrería and San Cernín. Ever since the *francos* of San Cernín had been granted special foral privileges, there had been jealousy and dissension among the boroughs.

In 1423 Carlos promulgated and the Cortes approved the *Privilegio de la Unión,* requiring that the walls separating the three boroughs be torn down and that henceforth they were to be governed by one mayor and administration. Pamplona at last became a unified city.

Also on the governmental front, Carlos tried to bring some order into the by now quite confusing set of conflicting and overlapping laws of the kingdom. He ordered that a book be kept at court with all the commonly understood rules, laws and customs of the court, interpretations of the fueros, and records of how difficult cases had been settled, thus providing a precedent and avoiding future disputes. And he gave his attention to the *Fuero General* itself, issuing in 1418 a set of fourteen amendments, most of them referring to rights or obligations of the nobility. This was a class that had proliferated greatly during his reign.

Carlos III, unlike his father, cared about ceremony and appearances. He ingratiated himself with his nobles and showered them with privileges and titles, in order to add luster to his royal court. But in the long run the kingdom suffered from this added importance given to an already top-heavy class.

Toward the end of his reign Carlos unwittingly laid the groundwork for more troubles. He agreed to the marriage of Blanca, his daughter and declared heir, to Juan, younger brother of Alfonso, newly crowned king of Aragon.

There was another contender for Blanca's hand, Jean I, count of Foix. Alliance with the House of Foix would have strengthened Navarra's ties with France, and created a state that would have been undisputed master of the western Pyrenees. But Carlos III, whose orientation was more peninsular than his father's, knew his people and their repugnance for French kings. Furthermore, the Aragonese prince had inherited a fabulous collection of counties, dukedoms and cities in Castile from his father Ferdinand of Trastámara (Ferdinand I of Aragon). To his death, in 1416, Ferdinand, an insatiably ambitious king, had sedulously advanced the Navarrese cause for his son Juan.

All these factors led Carlos to choose Juan of Aragon for Blanca's consort.

As for the bridegroom, he was eager for the match, though the bride was thirteen years his senior. Earlier, when Blanca was only second in line for the throne, Juan had been betrothed to her younger sister Isabel. But as soon as the oldest sister Juana died, and Blanca became the heiress, Juan threw Isabel over, in order to make himself eligible to wed a princess with greater prospects. He and Blanca were married in 1420.

Throughout his lifetime Juan's motivations were deeply complex, but one persistent objective was the diminution of French influence on the Iberian Peninsula. Marriage to Blanca put him in a favorable position to move on this front, and reduce Navarra's cultural subjection to France. It also gave him his first real status. He was only a second son of a king, with no prospect of rising higher except by marriage.[7] His older brother Alfonso had succeeded to the Aragonese throne in 1416. Though childless to date, Alfonso could still have heirs. Juan had little reason to expect that he would ever succeed his brother.

Nevertheless, while arranging his daughter's marriage, Carlos III recognized the off chance that Juan might some day become King of Aragon and subject Navarra to that crown. He saw to it that safeguards for his kingdom's independence were written into Blanca's and Juan's marriage agreement. All officers of the kingdom and court, and commanders of forts and castles, were to be Navarrese. Juan was not to permit Blanca to give, sell, hand over or dispose of any part of the kingdom. Children of the marriage were to be brought up in Navarra. If there were no children and Blanca died first, Juan would have no claim to the kingdom.

But the document was vague as to what would happen if Blanca died first *with* heirs—as came to pass. This ambiguity of the provisions for the inheritance was the root of most of Navarra's fifteenth-century troubles.

In 1423 Blanca brought Carlos, their firstborn, to Navarra where his grandfather created for him the principate of Viana. Henceforth an heir to the throne of Navarra was automatically given the title Prince of Viana, comparable to the title Prince of Wales in England or Prince of Asturias in Spain. Carlos, prince of Viana, aged two, received the oath of loyalty from the Cortes, and was declared heir to the kingdom.

His grandfather, Carlos the Noble, died in 1425 at Olite, his favorite palace. He had reigned thirty-eight years. His goodwill and good sense had not only promoted peace for Navarra, but had often helped prevent all-out war between his quarrelsome neighbors on the Iberian Peninsula.

But the rest of the fifteenth century was the most confused, discordant period in Navarra's history.

FATHER AGAINST SON

The kingdom was increasingly caught up in the struggles of Castile and France. These protracted disputes had been, and would be, fired by the ambitions of three generations of Aragonese kings: Ferdinand of Trastámara, Juan II and Ferdinand II. After his marriage Juan continued to connive with his brother the king of Aragon and their younger brother Enrique to turn the turbulences in Castile to the family's advantage. He was so intent on his enmity for Juan II of Castile and Juan's majordomo Alvaro de Luna that he drew Navarrese troops and money into his campaigns. This did not sit well with the kingdom, or with Blanca. A peace-loving queen, she tried without much success to curb her husband's belligerence. And for a few years there was relative tranquility within the kingdom, if not without.

One important task for a monarch as ambitious as Juan was arrangement of advantageous marriages for his young prince and princesses. In 1434 he and Blanca set about the delicate negotiations. That same year Leonor, their youngest, was wed to Gaston de Foix. In 1439 the prince of Viana, aged eighteen, married Princess Ines of Cleves. Until her death in 1448, she did her best to enliven with festivities the prince's serious, studious court at Olite.

In 1440 Juan carried out another move in his complicated games with Castile when he arranged the marriage of his daughter Blanca, heiress after Carlos to the throne of Navarra, to the heir of Castile, Enrique IV.

Shortly after this marriage Queen Blanca, still grieving over her husband's preoccupation with war, went on pilgrimage to Santa María de Nieve to pray for peace. There, in 1441, this gentle queen died. Even in her will she tried to bring her aggressive husband and her unassertive son to a compromise. She affirmed that Carlos was heir to the Kingdom of Navarra and the Duchy of Nemours, but prayed him to obtain his father's consent before taking the titles. Juan never consented.

Blanca's will also stated that if Carlos should die without heirs, his sisters (first Blanca, then Leonor) were to succeed.

Carlos was twenty-one when his mother died. He governed Navarra for nine years as "lieutenant" for his father, who by now had assumed not only the role but also the title of King of Navarra. The cleavage between the two grew, and gave the nobles an issue to focus on. There had been considerable rivalry among the nobility ever since Carlos III granted so many new titles and honors to his courtiers. Now one great house, the Beaumontés, took the son's side. Juan de Beaumontés was his chief advisor. The Agramontés faction, much of whose strength derived from a bastard son of Carlos III and his descendants, supported the father.

Three years after Queen Blanca's death her widower Juan married Juana, daughter of the admiral of Castile. Juan insisted that she should govern Navarra jointly with Carlos—a further humiliation for the prince who should have been king. All this came to a head at mid-century. Navarra became caught up in one of the bloodiest civil wars in Spanish history. Everyone, from nobles to humble laborers, took sides. Juan's supporters, including many of the Agramontés faction, were generally pastoral traditionalists from the mountains and valleys; those of Carlos were lords and peasants from the south.

Between 1451 and 1461, Carlos's life was like that of a hero of a tragic opera. First his father conquered him in battle and imprisoned him. Then he released him, whereupon Carlos fled to Naples to seek help from his uncle King Alfonso of Aragon.

Meantime, Navarra's parliament—the Cortes—entered the fray. In 1457 Juan convened his Cortes at Estella to disinherit Carlos and his sister Blanca, and to declare their younger sister Leonor and her husband Gaston de Foix heirs to Navarra. Almost at once a rival Beaumontés Cortes assembled in Pamplona and swore its loyalty to Carlos, who was still in Naples.

In 1458 the plot thickened when Alfonso of Aragon died without an heir, and Juan, as younger brother, succeeded him. Now legal king of Aragon, he nevertheless continued his Machiavellian tactics in Navarra. He again arrested his son, while the latter was on his way back from Naples. The conflict broadened, with the Catalans revolting and clamoring for Carlos to be recognized as Juan's heir to the Crown of Aragon—that is, as their own king, because Catalonia was joined to Aragon. They succeeded in getting Carlos freed from prison, but he died suddenly, in September 1461, possibly poisoned by his stepmother Juana. So closed a tragic story.[8]

After the death of the prince of Viana, perhaps a very strong king could have rallied his subjects, picked up the pieces, and restored Navarra's dignity and integrity. Juan was indeed strong, if strength be ambition and perseverance. But though he was undeniably king of Aragon, he was not viewed with enthusiasm by his rightful subjects there or in Catalonia. And he was still not accepted as king by most Navarrese.

For eighteen more years Juan intrigued with Castile and France, losing and then regaining Catalonia and securing for his son Ferdinand a brilliant future by marrying him to Isabella, heiress to Castile. Through it all he never loosened his hold on Navarra. His daughter Leonor had been governing there for him for fifteen years, wishing she were queen. Her consort Gaston IV de Foix was equally hungry for a crown. Leonor's position as legitimate heiress had been secure ever since the death of her elder sister Blanca in 1464. (Again, poison was suspected.) But Juan would not let go. When the octogenarian king finally died, in 1479, Leonor was duly proclaimed queen by the Cortes, meeting in Tudela. But hers was an ephemeral reign. She died only fifteen days later. "Of all the kings and queens of Navarra," wrote Moret, "she was the one who had the briefest reign, after wishing for it the longest."[9]

DECLINE UNDER THE FOIX-ALBRETS

So in 1479 began the wavering, ineffective rule of the Foix-Albret dynasty, with the succession of Leonor's twelve-year-old grandson Francisco Febo (François Phebus, so called by the French because of his blond beauty). Anarchy was rampant in the kingdom, with Agramontés and Beaumontés at swords' points and no one to keep them in check. Though Francisco was recognized as king immediately after Leonor's death, his mother, the regent Madeleine de Foix, did not bring him from Béarn to Pamplona for the crowning until 1481, and then stayed less than three months. They returned to Pau, where in two years Francisco died. It may have been tuberculosis, or it may have been poison. Meantime, Navarra's civil strife and lack of leadership grew ever more acute.

Francisco was succeeded by his fifteen-year-old sister Catherine de Foix. With her husband Jean d'Albret she presided over the gradual weakening and eventual demise of the independent kingdom. But it was not due to deliberate negligence. The monarchs of Navarra had many other responsibilities. Navarra was only one of a half dozen possessions of Catherine and Jean. Small wonder that they were distracted, and usually absent from Pamplona, when they were also rulers of Andorra, Assua and other east Pyrenean polities and, to the north, of Béarn, Bigorre, Foix and much of Gascony, Perigord and Limousin. As for the continuing disruption caused by the warring Beaumontés and Agramontés factions, they had inherited, not encouraged, it. There was a lull in the strife during the coronation ceremonies in Pamplona in 1484. But the enemies of tranquility soon came alive again: the Beaumontés nobles who had never wanted the Foix-Albret alliance, and the minions of Ferdinand, who like his father had a lifelong obsession with Navarra. During these difficult times for the Foix-Albret kings, help came from an unexpected source: the valiant warrior son of Pope Alexander VI, Cesar Borgia, brother-in-law of Jean d'Albret. Of Spanish lineage, he had been named bishop of Pamplona in 1492 at the age of fifteen. It was largely an honorific appointment; no record remains in the archives of any official action he took as bishop. And he was seldom (if ever) at his post. But fourteen years later he happened to be in Pamplona (a consummate international adventurer and *condottiere*, he was deep in the intrigues between Castile and France) and service to Jean d'Albret seemed worth a try. Jean named him captain-general of the royal troops. This was good for everybody's morale, but before Cesar Borgia could win any victories over the Beaumontés enemies, he was killed in battle at Viana.[10] And the civil war went on.

END OF INDEPENDENCE

The unsettled state of Navarra made it vulnerable to interference by its more powerful neighbors, in particular by the Catholic Monarchs, Ferdinand II (of Aragon) and Isabella I (of Castile). When they had joined their two kingdoms in 1479, they united nearly all of Spain. Navarra was the only missing piece, except for the small Muslim remnant in Granada. When the latter was finally taken in 1492, Ferdinand could give the north his full attention.

The Catholic Monarchs had already involved themselves in Navarra's domestic affairs where they could. For example, with the excuse of preserving the Christian faith, they called the city of Tudela to account in 1486 for giving asylum to heretics who had fled from Aragon. The officials of Tudela dared to threaten the representatives of the Inquisition, and stood up for their rights in defiance of the foreign princes to whom the city did not owe allegiance. But such firmness was not supported from Pamplona. In 1488 Tudela submitted under threat of excommunication.

Nevertheless, Navarra never agreed formally to accept the Inquisition. Yanguas y Miranda tells us that "it was sanctioned first through terror, then through silence—then through custom it became venerated as a bulwark of religion."[11]

Now in 1512, at the age of sixty, with much accomplished but one goal still ahead of him, Ferdinand set out to subjugate Navarra for once and all. He found a valued ally in Henry VIII of England, who saw a good chance to join in an attack on their common enemy Louis XII of France. The plan was for Ferdinand, supported by a strong contingent of English troops under the marquis of Dorset, to invade Guyenne (lost by England at the end of the Hundred Years War), which would then be reincorporated into England. Meantime Henry would take Normandy.

In March 1512 the allies declared war on France. In June Dorset and his army disembarked at Pasajes on the Guipúzcoan coast, whence they were to march into France. Still ostensibly intent on this invasion, Ferdinand pressured Navarra's monarchs (Jean and Catherine d'Albret) and the Cortes to permit his and Dorset's troops to enter the kingdom to forestall a supposedly imminent French counterattack. The kings and the Cortes resisted, but in July the Castilian army crossed the frontier into Navarra anyway. The worst fears of Jean and Catherine were realized: Ferdinand was interested only in their kingdom, not in a march to France, or their protection against a French invasion. The Albrets fled across the frontier, with their noble supporters and most of the army.

Ferdinand's general, the duke of Alba, took possession of Pamplona on July 24, 1512, leading his army into the city to the sounds of trumpets and kettledrums—a conquering hero who had made his conquest without resistance.

In the short term, Ferdinand and his lieutenants were scrupulously careful to assure the Navarrese that nothing would be changed except the name of their king. In Ferdinand's name the duke of Alba received the submission of the Pamplonese and swore to uphold their privileges. He urged them to be loyal vassals to the new king—who would guard their fueros if they did him good service.

But the Pamplonese demurred and asked for three days to think about the duke's remarks. They then announced that, first, they would take Ferdinand as their lord but could not accept him as their "natural" king, because Jean d'Albret was still living and they had already sworn him allegiance. Secondly, because their ancient fueros prevented them from swearing allegiance to more than one king, and because Ferdinand had confirmed their fueros, he of all persons could not subvert this, the principal one.

King Ferdinand's lawyers then presented his case. It was based largely on the assertion that Ferdinand's father Juan II had ruled "seventy years, peacefully" *(sic)* as king of Navarra, which established his line's right to the kingship. The Pamplonese at last gave in, after exacting one last promise that they would not lose their rights or liberties.

By the end of 1512 Pamplona was entirely Ferdinand's. When the other cities of Navarra saw what good terms Pamplona had achieved, they soon joined in the capitulation, each by its own separate document. Though Jean and Catherine tried to recover their kingdom for another half dozen years, their cause was hopeless, and they could only console themselves with quasi sovereignty over Basse Navarre, which they anxiously watched from their royal seat in Béarn.

IX

Ten-Year Transition

NAVARRA NOW HAD TO ADJUST TO an unprecedented situation: to be merely one among many in the newly assembled Hispania.

The kingdom's immediate reaction, when Ferdinand's conquest was seen as irrevocable and further resistance useless, was to try to salvage as much traditional foral liberty as possible, while recuperating from the ravages of seven decades of civil war. To some extent the Castilian presence must have seemed almost welcome, inasmuch as it promised, at least, more peace than the Navarrese had enjoyed since the reign of Carlos III.

For a time a few in Navarra and more in Basse Navarre worked for restoration of the Albrets and reunification of the two Navarres. Whether this step could or should be taken became the much-wrangled-over Navarre Question. It absorbed the Albret dynasty, relocated on the other side of the Pyrenees. For ten years Jean and Catherine tried to put the pieces back together by force, but then had to admit that force was not the answer.

The people of Navarra, however, soon accepted their new status philosophically, with its respectable vestiges of autonomy.

FERDINAND'S THIRTY-NINE MONTHS

Ferdinand of Aragon was past middle age when he took Navarra. He had seen many of his and his late queen Isabella's dreams dissipate or take strange forms. But Navarra was real and it was his. He knew how important it had been to his father, and he too gave it a great deal of attention. From the evidence, he was firm and fair, a vigilant if jealous guardian of his new acquisition.

He soon had reason for vigilance. During the next decade the Albrets were to make four open efforts to retake Navarra.[1] The first and most nearly successful came when the ink was scarcely dry on Pamplona's capitulation.

Ferdinand had assumed the title of King of Navarra on August 28, 1512, though some cities (including Estella and Tudela) and valleys (including Roncal) were still holding out. In September several factors looked favorable for the Albrets: the possibility that Ferdinand's English allies would desert him, the confusions naturally attendant on the change in rulers, reports that Pamplona was calling for Jean d'Albret, and the poor condition of the duke of Alba's army of occupation. Though Alba had reached St. Jean Pied de Port on the other side of the Pyrenees, his forces were isolated, shelterless, hungry, wet, sick and outnumbered. Nevertheless the Spanish succeeded in subjugating much of Basse Navarre, thanks to the brutal tactics of General Villalva.

The marquis of Dorset and his English troops were upset because Ferdinand had taken Navarra instead of keeping his previous promise of a joint Spanish-English invasion of Guyenne. After some weeks of haggling between Alba and Dorset, Ferdinand—to gain time and keep the protection of the English presence on his French frontier as long as possible—proposed a number of ambitious joint endeavors to Henry VIII: occupation of Béarn, Bigorre and Gascony; a blockade of Bayonne; a siege of Bordeaux—none of which he had any intention of even beginning.

The English troops had been thoroughly miserable during their hot summer of inactivity in Guipúzcoa. A great number had deserted and gone home at the end of August, an un-English act that infuriated Henry VIII. By October Dorset was completely disillusioned by Ferdinand's duplicity, and on October 15 the entire force left for home.

Ferdinand had also been conducting halfhearted negotiations with Louis XII of France, in another effort to gain time. But Louis refused to sign anything until the Albrets got all their kingdoms back. These parleys stopped by the end of September. Louis, still willing to help the Albrets, assigned General de La Palice to lead Jean's army, which prepared to launch an attack on Navarra through the Valley of Roncal.

By acting quickly, the army probably could have eluded the duke of Alba, reached Pamplona and taken it. But La Palice was dilatory and Jean was inexperienced. They were no match for the skill and decisiveness of the duke, who got to Pamplona first (October 26) and tightened Castilian control over the capital and the kingdom. The French forces' efforts had consisted in little more than a great deal of marching about the countryside.

But Jean and La Palice immediately tried again. This time it was to be a siege of Pamplona, which Jean was still convinced was full of loyal subjects, waiting for the chance to rise in his support.

Alba was again too much for them. He kept the Pamplonese firmly under his thumb: he exiled two hundred of the Agramontés faction of doubtful loyalty, ordered lights kept on all night to help his watchmen, and issued frequent false alarms to test the citizens' alertness and obedience.

The besieging army was an undisciplined and uncooperative mélange of Gascon and Béarnais volunteers, German and Albanian mercenaries, and French men-at-arms. The mercenaries were interested only in pay and pillage. Jean protested at the devastation the army left in its wake. Mills, vineyards and orchards were burnt. Churches were sacked. Citizens were infuriated at what this "liberating" army had done to their land. But La Palice paid no attention and gave the army its head.

The eventual attack on the ramparts of Pamplona, November 27, 1512, was an anticlimactic failure. After accepting defeat and taking a final look at the towers of the city that he would never see again, Jean crossed the frontier into France. He and his miserable army were not even able to get through the mountains without more disasters. They were attacked by mountain dwellers of Guipúzcoa and the Valley of Baztán. When they straggled into Bayonne where young Francis, duke of Angoulême and heir to the throne of France, was awaiting them, he greeted them with what Correa, the contemporary chronicler, called "the discretion appropriate to the circumstances."² Francis should indeed have been apologetic as well as discreet in his greetings: he had done very little to help in the campaign. His assignment had been to create a diversion by an assault on San Sebastián, but the Basques of Guipúzcoa and Vizcaya, no friends of the French, came to the aid of the besieged city and Francis had to retire ignominiously.

POSTCONQUEST STABILIZATION

These annoying incursions into Navarra having ceased, Ferdinand could concentrate on solidifying his position. Though he ruled a united Spain with a considerable degree of absolute power, he was nervous about possible cracks in the new structure. In his most vulnerable realm, Navarra, he strengthened some fortifications, especially in the Valley of Baztán, route to Bayonne, and in the Valley of Roncal, route to Béarn. He also tore down fortifications that could enfeeble the kingdom's defense by spreading it too thin, and could encourage internal insurrection.

Whether there was as much internal dissatisfaction with the new regime as Ferdinand feared is not clear, but he and his deputy Cisneros were taking no chances. Cisneros is credited with ordering destruction of twenty-one small castles in all.³

Ferdinand obtained the complete submission of St. Jean Pied de Port and its environs, and manned it with good troops, as a bulwark against France. Some of his counselors advised abandoning Ultrapuertos (Basse Navarre), but Ferdinand refused: "It would be inhuman to amputate from such a splendid body a member which is not even its weakest."⁴ This attitude pleased his subjects in Navarra, as jealous as he of the integrity of their realm.

As an administrator, Ferdinand made few changes. He respected the people's rights and waited for the passage of time and the fairness of his rule to bring about a healing of the kingdom's deep wounds.

During these years, as a counterpoint to the preparations for defense (by Ferdinand) or offensive action (by the Albrets), there was an intermittent diplomatic interchange about the status and possible reunification of Navarra and Basse Navarre.

Jean and Catherine tried to interest any and all in their cause: Emperor Maximilian, Archduke Charles (Ferdinand's grandson, and heir to the Spanish throne), the French, the pope. They sent emissary after emissary to Rome to ask for a revocation of the papal bull that had excommunicated them.[5] This bull of excommunication was Ferdinand's main legal claim to Navarra. It had been based on the Albrets' alliance with a king of France (Louis XII) who had harbored an anti-pope. Its continued existence was a serious deterrent to the Albret fortunes, because many potential supporters in Navarra held back, fearing the excommunication would be applied to them if they openly helped the exiled rulers.

The Albret kings had no success in their protestations. The papacy had nothing to gain by revoking the bull, and so did not.

As for their efforts to enlist Louis of France, he talked generosity but gave very little. For example, in March 1513, he wrote Jean d'Albret that he would do everything he could for his cause in the truce terms he was then negotiating with Ferdinand (the Truce of Iturbie). The very next day the papers were signed, and there was not a word about the Albrets and their rights.

A few weeks later, Louis went further and openly recognized the pretensions to Navarra of Ferdinand's second wife Germaine de Foix. She was connected with the House of Foix that had preceded the Albrets on the throne of Navarra. But this avenue was too serpentine for even Ferdinand's devious diplomacy to pursue seriously.

The next year Ferdinand and Louis renewed their truce. Louis was asked to affirm that he would not help the Albrets, but balked at such a promise. However, again they were not mentioned in the documents, and Ferdinand was referred to as king of Navarra.

Ferdinand's aim in all this negotiating was, still, to gain time to firm up his defenses, both military and political. In the summer and fall of 1514 he succeeded in obtaining the support of most of the Basque nobles of Basse Navarre, through either bribes or threats or military action. He proceeded to take charge of the administration of the province: tribunals, the Cortes, tax collections. Jean and Catherine, from their court at Pau, had no choice but to accept these takeovers in their hereditary territories. That fall, the Estates (Cortes) of Basse Navarre swore fidelity to Ferdinand.

The year 1515 saw more correspondence and negotiation than saber rattling on the Navarre Question. Francis I had succeeded Louis on the French throne in late 1514. He at once became the target for a barrage of pleas and demands from Jean and Catherine. Like his father, Francis dealt in promises. He and Jean solemnly swore to friendship, but he gave no concrete help. And with the other hand he signed a treaty of alliance with Archduke Charles, in anticipation of Charles's accession to the Spanish throne. Most of all, Francis wanted to avoid trouble in the Pyrenees while he was preoccupied with his position via-à-vis the Spanish in Italy.

THE NEXT KING

Ferdinand had the royal succession to worry about, as well as his international adventures. Almost as soon as he and Isabella had been married they had begun to try to insure that there would be a suitable inheritor of the thrones of Castile and Aragon. Yet in spite of a series of carefully arranged royal marriages for their children, they saw one scheme after another come to nothing, through untimely deaths or, as in the case of the last heir, through mental incompetence. Their daughter Juana, married in 1495 to Archduke Philip of Austria, son of the Holy Roman Emperor, became quite mad after his death.

Ferdinand continued to maneuver frantically after Isabella's death, in 1504. He broke his promise to her and immediately remarried. Wed to Germaine de Foix, he hoped vainly to produce at least an heir to his own patrimony of Aragon. But in his last few years, he had to face the fact that the inheritor of the entire peninsula (except Portugal, still independent) would be an absolute stranger to Spain: Charles, son of Juana and Philip, who had been born and brought up in the Low Countries.

Ferdinand, understandably, doubted that Charles, lacking his own personal involvement, would show proper zeal in holding onto his last and most precious acquisition. Should he permit Navarra to remain in Aragon's sphere, where it had fallen naturally as the personal prize of a king of Aragon? If he did, it might after his death drift back into independence, or worse, be snapped up by France, through the inattention of the Aragonese Cortes, less devoted to peninsular unity than were the Castilians. To guard against this, Ferdinand determined to cement this little jewel firmly into the Spanish crown by uniting it to Castile.

On May 8, 1515, the Castilian Cortes had voted him a sizeable subsidy for his war expenses. As a reward, on June 11 Ferdinand donated the Kingdom of Navarra to Castile, providing that after his death it would go to his daughter Juana and after her death to his grandson Charles. (Inclusion of poor, mad, widowed Juana was largely a formality, a gesture to the legalities and to avoid alienation of her Castilian supporters.) He charged Juana and Charles to respect the customary fueros. Three deputies from Pamplona succeeded in obtaining from the Castilian Cortes promises of administrative autonomy. But command of the kingdom's fortresses, and the presidency of the *Consejo Real*—the royal council—remained Castilian.

There only remained for Ferdinand to impress on his grandson the significance of the kingdom. Five months before his death, he wrote to Charles (then fifteen years old):

> You know the justice of my rights; you know I have acted for the good and security of my Spanish realms in assuring myself of its [Navarra's] possession. You will inherit this state some day along with the others, and I do not think you will consent to do anything contrary to your own interests. No good counselor would advise you other than I do, and you have too much prudence and discretion not to understand me.[6]

Ferdinand died in January 1516. Neither sixteen-year-old Charles nor his Flemish counselors were in any hurry to leave their familiar surroundings for what they rightly suspected would be a stern and inhospitable country. The counselors knew that in Spain their power would be less. Chièvres, Charles's chief minister, saw himself being displaced by Cardinal Cisneros, designated regent by Ferdinand. Cisneros had been Isabella's chief advisor, was a stalwart of the Inquisition, and had little sympathy for the light-minded northerners.

ANOTHER ALBRET ATTACK

There was, therefore, an eighteen-month interregnum, during which Jean d'Albret made his third and most solitary strike into his lost kingdom. King Francis seemed to encourage him. There were again reports of strong sympathy for Jean in Navarra. And the change in monarchies promised an atmosphere of restlessness that should work in his favor. He could hope for support from members of the Agramontés party, who had never liked Ferdinand and were outraged when he ordered razing of the kingdom's fortresses. He could even expect support from the Beaumontés, who also had grievances: the occupying Castilian army's abuses, the command of fortresses by non-Navarrese. And many in Navarra, Jean was told, were still smarting from the ignominy of being attached to their old enemy Castile.

So he tried again. His tiny volunteer army set forth bravely, with more enthusiasm then cohesion, in February 1516. Francis had not yet sent a single man. But the army was heartened when it captured one fort at St. Jean Pied de Port. There was a pause while Jean sent fierce pleas to Francis for his promised help. None came.

The forces then began an advance southward through the Pass of Roncesvalles and the Valley of Roncal, in Navarra's northeast corner. But many deserted, and the expected reinforcements from the mountain valleys failed to join up. Many mountain men, when they heard that the dread Castilian General Villalva was at Roncesvalles, joined him instead. A brilliant forced march by Villalva from Roncesvalles to Roncal, and his quick defeat of Jean's remnants, ended the endeavor. Jean retreated to Béarn.

Meantime the regent Cisneros had done his part by suppressing any signs of support in Navarra. Normality prevailed: the Cortes met on February 22, and the viceroy, in the name of Juana of Castile and her son Charles, exchanged the customary foral oaths with the deputies.

In May of 1516 the pendulum swung back to negotiation. Representatives of France, Spain and Basse Navarre held a conference at Noyon, in Basse Navarre. Charles's Flemish counselors, led by Chièvres, temporized, and would only agree that Charles would study the Navarre Question when he got to Spain and made a "satisfactory arrangement." This oblique and vague statement was soon transformed in the minds of the Albret faction into a promise of restitution. But Charles and his counselors viewed it merely as the prelude to the inevitable formal denial of the pretenders' claims.

Jean d'Albret died in June 1516, some say of chagrin, certainly a disillusioned and discouraged man. Catherine carried on.

The Albrets' emissary, Pierre de Biaix, was given a virtual replay of the Noyon statement when he confronted Charles himself later that summer in Brussels. Charles pointed out that he had only inherited Navarra, had not taken it by force. He promised to look into the matter thoroughly when he got to Spain, and if he found Catherine had a just claim, he would not wish to keep a kingdom that did not belong to him. He advised Catherine to be patient.

Catherine continued as queen-in-exile until her death in February 1517, still hopeful if not patient. Her heir, Henri d'Albret (Enrique II of Navarra, were he to regain the throne), was only fourteen years old. His grandfather, the Sire d'Albret, acted as regent.

CHARLES V AND THE NAVARRE QUESTION

Meantime, Charles was by now able to extricate himself from his other concerns and come to assume his position as king of Spain. He arrived in September 1517. One of his first acts was the dismissal, even before a meeting, of the aged, faithful regent Cisneros. This demonstration that the Flemish counselors were to be dominant, the fact that Charles spoke no Spanish, the general air of frivolity that surrounded his court—none of this was conducive to a warm welcome on the part of the Castilians. However, Charles began the obligatory royal progression around the peninsula to convoke the various Cortes. In spite of considerable prickliness on the part of his new subjects, he succeeded in getting through the ceremonies and formalities in Castile and Aragon by July 1518.

The Castilian Cortes, assembled at Valladolid early in 1518, was informed of Charles's Noyon and Brussels commitments to study the Navarre Question. But its members were also privately assured that he firmly intended to keep the kingdom. The Cortes, in fervent agreement, put itself on record as opposing restitution of the kingdom "acquired by Castile because of the schism," and offering, if necessary, to sacrifice life and property to defend it, "the principal key to Spain."

It would have taken a more secure and less astute monarch than Charles to go against these sentiments.

But the emissaries of the Albrets, who were following Charles around Spain, still hoped for a definite indication that he might be persuaded to return the kingdom. They trailed him from Valladolid to Aranda del Duero to Zaragoza (where the Cortes of Aragon was to meet), then finally gave up and returned to Béarn to report no progress to Henri.

Finally, in May 1519, Charles did make a definite statement: he would not give up Navarra. But out of affection for the king of France, he would give the Albrets a monetary settlement. This they naturally rejected, because acceptance would have implied an abandonment of their claims.

Thus ended seven years of the Albrets' efforts to make a king of Spain see reason. The only two avenues left were intrigue and war.

Charles's royal progress, bogged down in Catalonia, had not yet gotten to Valencia, much less Navarra, when news arrived of the death of his grandfather the Emperor Maximilian. Charles left Spain to look after his candidacy and subsequent election as Holy Roman Emperor. This was not entirely a formality; his two major European rivals, Francis I of France and Henry VIII of England, were also candidates.

These events kept Charles out of Spain from May 1520 to July 1522. During his absence, revolts against what the Castilians saw as a high-handed new regime of foreign despots broke out in cities throughout Castile: the *comuneros* uprisings. Navarra, far from the disturbances and the irritating presence of the Flemish, was not involved in these peninsular conflicts, but soon became deeply involved in an external attack.

Francis I, the aggressive young king of France, had been maintaining an outward show of civil relations with Charles since the latter's accession to the Spanish throne. Now his hostility began to be manifest when his rival was elected emperor. In the *comuneros* uprisings, Francis saw his first chance for action. His ally and tool was Henri d'Albret.

Henri had spent the first nine years of his life in Navarra, his parents' kingdom, and was totally committed to reunification. And Francis, now, was serious about bringing the southern territory back into the French orbit, at a time when he saw the conflicts in Castile and Charles's absence favoring his chances. But for him it was only one step toward his broader goal: victory in the Hapsburg-Valois struggle, which had Italy for its main theater.

THE LAST CAMPAIGN

Francis first warned Charles that all clauses of the Treaty of Noyon would be void if Navarra was not returned to Henri. No response. It was then arranged that Henri would send an army to Pamplona. Meantime, Francis would distract Charles by harassing his forces in the north, at Luxembourg.

In the winter of 1520-21, conditions looked as favorable as could be expected for the attempt. Troops from Pamplona had been sent to Castile to help against the *comunero* rebels there. Pamplona, hence, was lightly defended. There were also, again, reports that it was ready to rise for its legitimate ruler. St. Jean Pied de Port, too, was not likely to offer much resistance. Finally, there was a good chance that Francis would find allies in Castile for his pet project: an invasion of Charles's Spanish heartland. Emissaries from the *comuneros* were in touch with Henri and Francis early in 1521, hinting at cooperation if they entered Navarra.

Unfortunately for Henri, by the time his army was ready to march (May 1521), the tide had turned for the Castilian dissidents and they ceased to be a significant factor. However, the army at first had good success. It was commanded by André de Foix, Seigneur de Lesparre (Asparros), who had apparently been given the post because of his high connections (with Henri d'Albret, and with Francis's mistress), not because of his military qualifications. But at least he had youth and enthusiasm, both qualities that had been sadly lacking in the last French general assigned to the Albret cause, cynical La Palice, in 1512. The French force also outnumbered the Castilian army of occupation in Navarra.

Lesparre advanced through the Pass of Roncesvalles, after meeting no resistance at St. Jean. Basse Navarre rose for Henri. All else was successful and by May 19 Navarra was Lesparre's. Pamplona's submission was remarkably rapid. In the viceroy's absence (he was trying to get reinforcements from Castile), the citizens broke into the armory and opened the gates to the French army. The city's council drew up a list of conditions under which it would submit, presented it to Lesparre, and he agreed to comply with nearly all. The council swore fealty to Henri and he to it, through Lesparre, acting as his viceroy.

Lesparre did find it necessary to attack the Castillo, that grand new fortress begun by Ferdinand in 1514, but not yet completed. The Spanish commander, Francisco de Herrera, defended it but, short of men, soon had to yield. This action was chiefly memorable for the following event, without mention of which no history of Navarra would be complete: During the attack on the Castillo, a soldier in the defending forces, Iñigo de Loyola, was wounded in the leg and fell on the battlefield. While recovering, he read the lives of the saints and determined to emulate them. Later he left the army for the church, founded the *Compañía de Jesús* (Society of Jesus —the Jesuits), and still later was venerated as San Ignacio. A statue showing him being carried from the field by two companions may be seen on the Calle de San Ignacio in Pamplona. A plaque in the sidewalk nearby marks the spot where he fell.

Lesparre, after his victory in Pamplona, left two thousand men there and proceeded to Estella, which also yielded, as did Sangüesa, Tudela and Olite. Thus all of Navarra's main cities and fortresses (except Maya) were in French hands. This was the high-water mark for the Albrets' struggle to regain their kingdom.

But conquest and retention were two different things. Lesparre—young, inexperienced, impetuous—proved a foolish and harsh administrator, and an ineffectual, shortsighted general. He exerted absolute power as viceroy, revoked amnesties, alienated the Beaumontés who would have come over to him, and all in all convinced the Navarrese that this was no liberation, but a war on behalf of the king of France.

Probably at Francis's orders, Lesparre moved toward Logroño, just over the Ebro in Castile. En route, he stopped a few days to pillage Los Arcos, a Navarrese town not far from the northern banks of the Ebro.

By now the Castilians charged by Charles with defense of Spain in his absence had been able to scrape together an army to meet the French threat. It included nobles who had compromised themselves in the *comunero* revolt—and were offered pardon if they were willing to fight the French—and volunteers from the Basque provinces. The Castilian army moved toward the invader. Meantime, Lesparre's pause at Los Arcos had given the Castilians time to fortify Logroño, where they quickly repulsed his attempt at a siege. The leader of the imperial forces, the duke of Nájera, forced Lesparre to turn tail and pursued him to Noain on the Plains of Quiros, just southeast of Pamplona. There, on June 30, 1521, the Spanish enjoyed a spectacular victory. They claimed losses of only three hundred men, in contrast with six thousand for the French. Lesparre was taken prisoner (and later ransomed in France by his captor, Francis de Beaumont, for 10,000 ducats). His army retreated north, past Pamplona and beyond Ultrapuertos.

The last fortress to capitulate, Maya, did so after heroic resistance, on July 19, 1522. The Castilian commander during the siege of Maya, Viceroy Conde de Miranda, was filled with astonishment and admiration at the bravery of the defenders. "Why not?" said Luis de Beaumont. "After all, they are Navarrese." The implied comparison with the French troops defeated at Noain was obvious.[8]

All Navarra was reconquered in less time than it had taken Lesparre to win it.

Aleson calls the Battle of Noain the "definitive sentence that struck Navarra from the ranks of the nations." It tolled the knell for Henri's dreams of reconquest. The defeat, however, was due as much to Francis's involved motivations as to military ineptness. With his main purpose a quick march on Castile while turmoil there made it an easy target, he deliberately did not encourage Henri to go to Navarra in person and rally his subjects to his cause. Francis feared that any such popular rising would only delay Lesparre's advance to the south. Yet he fostered the notion that the whole venture was an Albret enterprise, not supported by the Crown of France. This was in order to avoid undue offense to either Charles or Henry VIII of England. Lesparre, thus left on his own, proud and vainglorious, did not ask Francis for more troops during the critical final days of the campaign—when they might have made all the difference.

There was one last faint attempt to revive the Navarre Question. During negotiations between Francis and Charles to sort things out (with Henry VIII as mediator), a French army took Fuenterrabia in Guipúzcoa, in Henri's name. With this important seaport, Francis now had a new card in his hand, and offered to return Fuenterrabia to Spain if Charles would restore

Navarra to Henri. The proposal was not accepted. And in due course, Charles's armies retook Fuenterrabia (1524).

After the dust of the French retreat had settled, the Castilian governors of Pamplona imposed strict order. Many of Henri's supporters fled to France rather than stay for disgrace and retribution. The rest of the country settled down to business as usual, relatively unaffected by the change in dynasties that had taken ten years to become a firm fact.

Henri d'Albret, observing events from France, never did accept the change, as we will see.

In 1527 he married Francis's sister Marguerite de Valois. During the first few years of the marriage, Henri, his queen and his brother-in-law the king of France were agreed, for their various reasons, on the need to regain Navarra: Henri, because of the inborn and unshakeable sense of his rights; Marguerite—who was a Valois first and an Albret second—because she was in favor of anything her brother was in favor of; Francis, because he was in favor of wresting European hegemony from the House of Austria, and still saw Navarra among the desirable firstfruits of that process.

For thirty-five more years the Albrets, using whatever means and allies they could, kept at the Spanish monarch to restore their realm; but, as we will see in the next chapter, they never succeeded.

X

Navarra Under the Hapsburgs

UNDER CHARLES V AND HIS SON PHILIP II, Navarra settled comfortably into its role as a minor cog in a very large wheel. To the Hapsburg rulers of sixteenth-century imperial Spain, with its global concerns, Navarra was chiefly interesting as a bargaining unit in their European power politics.

Neither monarch had Ferdinand's deep sense of possessiveness about the kingdom, and though they never really intended to give it up, they did not hesitate to pretend that they might, especially in their dealings with France. Fortunately for the peace of mind of the average citizen of Navarra, this kind of diplomacy was very secret indeed. And meantime the new rulers showed a commendable respect for the kingdom's traditional independence.

CHARLES V IN SPAIN

When Charles returned to Spain in 1522, he was ready to take up his kingly duties in earnest. He was not yet, strictly speaking, Holy Roman Emperor, and would not be crowned by the pope until 1530. But he was already deeply involved in continental politics, and needed money to keep his European and American empires going. So he started another round of convocations of Cortes throughout the peninsula, to obtain grants of funds or *servicios*. And his subjects had accumulated a number of petitions to present to him in return.

From the moment of Charles's accession, the Navarrese had been awaiting and requesting his coming to swear to uphold their fueros and be properly sworn to as their king. (This custom had been essential to every coronation since the creation of the kingdom and, as described in chapter VI, the ceremony was prescribed in the *Fuero General* to legalize the contract between the king and his subjects.) Charles finally crossed the Castilian border into Navarra in October 1523, and remained in the kingdom for nearly three months. He first visited Los Arcos, Estella and Puente la Reina; then he spent the rest of his time in Pamplona.

He performed the customary swearing to uphold the fueros, and received the pledge of loyalty of the Cortes. He further cemented good relations by pardoning many of the nobles who had supported Henri d'Albret.

Like Ferdinand his grandfather (and in obedience to his last wishes), Charles paid close attention to the defenses of this vulnerable land, concentrating them still more. He strengthened those of Pamplona, Lumbier, Puente la Reina and Estella. But he ordered the destruction of many other fortifications, lest they serve as centers for dissension or rebellion.

The Navarrese appreciated the attention from their monarch. They saw hope at last for stability and peace, sadly lacking for a century. They had reason to sorrow over the loss of their independence and the violence that had been done to their land by foreign armies during its loss. But other than that, they had little to regret, with the end of a dynasty that had been more French than Basque, more absent than present. And with the passage of time this realistic people concentrated on holding fast to what independence it still had, and educating its Hapsburg kings in their foral duties.

But Charles was preoccupied with questions much more crucial than the self-esteem of a tiny kingdom in the Pyrenees: the shifting positions of Spain and his other European dominions vis-à-vis France and England (he fought four major wars with France in thirty years); the need to come to some kind of accommodation with Lutheranism; what to do about the Turks and their piracies and encroachments all around the Mediterranean;

and protection and exploitation of the Spanish possessions in the New World.

He made Spain his headquarters, but it was twenty years before he paid another visit to Navarra, on his way to Aragon in 1542. He again entered the kingdom at Los Arcos, and stopped in Estella and Puente la Reina before Pamplona. On June 15, accompanied by his son, fifteen-year-old Prince Philip, he inspected the Castillo and other city fortifications, ordering what was necessary to strengthen them. Although a ten-year truce with France had been in effect since 1538, Charles knew better than to trust in truces.

After three days in Pamplona, he proceeded to Tafalla, stopping en route near Noain, scene of the definitive defeat of the French, and inspecting 3,000 troops from Pamplona's garrison. Before leaving the kingdom, he visited Olite's royal palace, that magnificent masterpiece of Carlos III the Noble, sadly neglected by all royalty after the prince of Viana.

For the rest of his reign, Charles kept a steady stream of directives flowing toward Navarra, but entrusted on-the-spot government of the kingdom to his appointed viceroys. By and large, the kingdom's foral customs and tradition of self-government were observed. The Cortes continued to meet regularly. The citizens, with their lively consciousness of their rights, did not hesitate to point out to the viceroy or to the king any lapses from correct procedure. One tradition that they continued to insist on until well into the seventeenth century was that each heir to the throne must come in person, swear to uphold their fueros, and be formally recognized by them as a legitimate potential ruler. Therefore, Charles's heir Philip II came for this purpose in 1551 and performed the ceremony at Tudela.

Shortly afterward Charles, tired and grievously ill but still bearing heavy responsibilities, decided he had had enough of empire and determined to step down in Philip's favor.

He declared his intention to abdicate in 1555, did so in 1556, retired to a monastery, and transferred his imperial crown to his brother Ferdinand and the rest of his dominions, including Spain, to Philip. He died in 1558.[1]

AGAIN THE NAVARRE QUESTION

Charles's will revealed that throughout his reign he had had qualms about his legal rights to Navarra. These doubts persisted for two more generations.

In his will, Charles counseled Philip to study the matter of whether Navarra should be restored to its legitimate rulers, or whether some other compensation should be made. And that whatever was "found, determined and declared to be the just course, should be put into effect, so that my spirit and my conscience may be clear." His spirit had cause to be troubled for another half century, through the reign of his grandson.

THE ZEALOUS PHILIP II

When Philip II of Spain succeeded his father, in 1558, he received an inheritance that was not as uncoordinated and unmanageable as his father's had been. It consisted basically of Spain, the Netherlands, Italy and the New World possessions. But it was still extraordinarily complex, and it took all his vigilance, all his life, to try to keep one jump ahead of all that menaced it.

As self-appointed champion of Catholicism he tried, largely in vain, to stave off the encroaching Protestant tide in Europe. His mighty armada failed to take England for God and Spain in 1588. His efforts to hold onto the Netherlands ranged from savage warfare to uneasy periods of pacification. He finally gave that battle up, the year before his death. And as defender of the faith (and Spain's coasts) against Islam, he fought the Turkish menace until the 1571 victory at Lepanto reduced it considerably. Within Spain itself, he had to put down the specter of Islam that had come to life in the Morisco revolt in Granada, in 1568. Though he gained an empire when he appropriated Portugal in 1580, he almost lost a kingdom when Aragon tried to break away in 1591—the first sign that Spain, seemingly all-powerful, was subject to internal rebellion.

Philip's reign had opened with another French war. The peace, or rather armed truce (Treaty of Cateau-Cambrésis), that he signed with Henri II of France, in 1559, was to endure more or less for the rest of the century, but Philip took nothing for granted. His zealous defense of the Catholicism of his subjects made him extremely sensitive to real or imagined Protestant inroads. He felt most vulnerable on his French borders, from Catalonia to the Atlantic. Even before the French Wars of Religion broke out, in 1562, he was alarmed by the fact that the reigning Albret queen in Béarn had fervently espoused Calvinism, and by the danger that Navarra might be infected or abducted. So its defense, through diplomacy and physical fortifications, was dear to his heart, and was in fact the only reason he ever came back to Navarra, after his visit in 1542 to be sworn to as rightful heir.

Like Ferdinand and Charles, Philip was chronically concerned about Pamplona's fortifications, and continued the periodic wall-strengthening program. By 1571, he decided that Ferdinand's Castillo, dating from 1514, was no longer adequate, and ordered the building of the Fortaleza. Later it was called the Ciudadela (Citadel). This was a huge pentagonal fortress just southwest of the city. He commissioned the leading military architect of the day Jacobo Pelear, who modeled it on the fortress of Ambéres in Flanders. Philip kept in touch with its progress through the rest of his reign, inspecting it for the last time during a state visit in 1592. The Ciudadela was to serve as a vital intimidating stronghold for centuries. It experienced its finest hour in 1823, when it withstood five months of bombardment by the French. It was not besieged during the first Carlist War, but was during the second. Thereafter it saw no action, but was not considered expendable until, during World War II, the Germans easily subdued its prototype at Ambéres. Only then did the city fathers feel safe in authorizing its dismantling, to give the expanding city more room.[2]

However, back in the sixteenth century, Philip was not so worried about his own Navarra with its loyal, unrebellious subjects, as he was about Basse Navarre on the other side of the Pyrenees, which from the tenth century had been an integral part of the Kingdom of Navarra.

In 1530 Charles V had decided that Basse Navarre was too remote and inconsequential to bother with, and turned it loose. To the dismay of many French Basques, he told them they were no longer his subjects, though they could keep their Spanish citizenship rights.

This meant that the Albrets, who had claimed both Navarres all along, were at least kings *de jure* of the northern segment, and had a broader base for their machinations. Henri d'Albret and his son-in-law and successor Antoine de Bourbon tried by schemes and threats and proposed bargains with the Hapsburgs to reunify the two Navarres, but the project died with Antoine in 1562.[3]

The last Albret queen, Jeanne, who became a militant Protestant, was a different kind of antagonist. She succeeded in converting much of Béarn and tried hard in Basse Navarre, while Philip watched with trepidation. But most Basques north of the Pyrenees, except in Bayonne, violently rejected all attempts to introduce the "new thinking." Bayonne, on the sea, was a pocket of tolerance, where a populace accustomed to commercial intercourse with all the world saw nothing to condemn in varying creeds and customs. Philip, aware of the need to seal off this weak spot near his borders, obtained a bull in 1566 from Pope Pius V to permit separation of part of Guipúzcoa and all of Basse Navarre from the diocese of Bayonne "while the Protestant heresy lasts in France."[4]

By and large, though, Philip had little cause to worry about defections from orthodox Catholicism on either side of the Pyrenees. His hold on Navarra remained secure. As to the matter of whether he really had a right to it, he never did get around to reopening the question, though his father's will had counseled him to do so. Finally, he passed it on to *his* son in his will. He excused his failure to comply with his father's request by citing the many serious projects, wars and expeditions he had been busy with all his life. He charged Philip III to submit the problem to "men of science and conscience, who will be able to get to the bottom of the matter of whether the Catholic Kings, my great-grandparents, proceeded with justice in regard to the Kingdom of Navarra." So the Navarre Question remained alive—barely.

XI

Less War, More Government

BY PHILIP'S REIGN, WHICH COVERED the second half of the sixteenth century, the process of adjustment that had begun, willy-nilly, as soon as Ferdinand's conquest was a fact, had gone a long way. Navarra was a kingdom within a kingdom, and getting used to it. Government had settled into a fairly smooth-running machine, with predictable rattles when local authorities thought the king or his representatives had strayed too far from the foral path.

As far as the structure of government was concerned, the pattern was established for the next three hundred years. This was a longer period of stability than any other Spanish territory was to enjoy, and merits a pause in the narrative for examination.

The main components of the governmental machine were the viceroy (executive), the *Consejo Real* (judiciary) and the Cortes (parliamentary). Later, the *Diputación* played a regular supporting role. And the *Cámara de Comptos,* dating back to the fourteenth century as the royal Department of the Treasury, continued as fiscal management body under the Castilian regime.[1]

All these outlived their counterparts in the rest of Spain: the Cortes of Castile, Aragon and Valencia were combined in Madrid in 1709. During the eighteenth century, only Navarra had its own judiciary (*Consejo Real*); the courts of the other kingdoms were subordinate either to the chancellery of Valladolid or that at Granada, and had been since the sixteenth century. And by the end of the eighteenth century, only Navarra still had a viceroy, a *Diputación* and a *Cámara de Comptos*.

The effectiveness of these institutions depended on their checks and restraints on each other, on their mutual respect, and on a considerable degree of doughty rectitude, displayed most consistently by the Cortes. This body set the tone for the others and held firmly to its major objective: to keep things as they had been and always should be.

THE VICEROY

Viceregal government with variations obtained throughout the Hispanic empire in the sixteenth century. Viceroys represented the monarch: he could not be everywhere at once. There were nine of them: for Aragon, Catalonia, Valencia, Navarra, Sardinia, Sicily, Naples, New Spain (Mexico) and Peru.

In most of these areas the system worked slowly. The viceroy would send from his regional headquarters a dispatch to the appropriate Royal Council at court, which council was composed of natives of the land it represented. The council took the matter under advisement, made recommendations, and sent it on to the king. He either forwarded it to other experts for opinions and advice, or returned it with his decision to the council, which then sent orders back to the viceroy.

But in Navarra action could be taken much more quickly and efficiently. The kingdom really did enjoy a high degree of autonomy, higher even than the other areas that had been incorporated in Hispania with many of their fueros intact: Aragon, Catalonia and the Basque territories. Navarra's *Consejo Real,* unlike the others, had its seat at home. The three main governing elements—viceroy, *Consejo Real* and Cortes—though often opposed to each other, maintained a workable balance and were able to administer affairs without constant "checking with Madrid."

There had been government by viceroy in Navarra as early as the thirteenth century, during the reign of the second Teobaldo. Then the later French kings, often absent, named French viceroys to rule in their stead. Next, during much of the fourteenth century, when the House of Evreux came to the throne, records of viceroys cease. They appear again under the Houses of Foix and Albret, whose kings preferred or were constrained to tend to their interests in France at the expense of close surveillance over Navarra.

Though Navarra's viceroys under the Hapsburgs had extensive power, some of those appointed by the French monarchs had had even more. They could make foreign alliances and arrange truces and peace treaties. But otherwise, Charles's and Philip's viceroys were instructed to govern and administer just as the king would. Their average tour of duty during the sixteenth century was about five years: long enough for the viceroy to establish good working relationships with his fellow administrators.

He was usually a Castilian. Only in Aragon was a native viceroy permitted—in fact, insisted on by the Aragonese. Ferdinand had felt more respect for his own hereditary kingdom's customs and wishes than for Navarra's; and perhaps more faith in its loyalty.

Navarra's viceroys were automatically commanders-in-chief of the armed forces and governors of Pamplona's major fortress, the *Ciudadela*. The Cortes was careful to keep it this way, wanting no separate military commander in the kingdom. In peace or war, the viceroy had sole say over the military. Even the *Consejo Real* was excluded from advising him in such matters.

Both Charles and Philip kept in close touch with their viceroys. Philip especially, wherever he was, kept a two-way torrent of paper flowing between him and Pamplona. Each new viceroy received a royal order as to what was expected of him. For instance, in June 1552 the duke of Alburquerque received his orders from Philip (acting for Charles, who had not yet abdicated), outlining specific duties and prerogatives, such as appointing mayors and other officials; cautioning against too freely pardoning misdeeds and too liberal a distribution of the royal patrimony.

Philip's careful hand seems evident in this passage:

> Call the Cortes to meet only from the palaces or houses from which they traditionally have been called—and from these, the fewest you can, as much to avoid cost to the kingdom,

as to avoid disturbances and confusion that come about if there are too many in the Cortes—as has been the case in the past.²

And later:

Try to free yourself from other business and meet with the *Consejo Real* as much as you can.³

The viceroys attended the opening and closing of the Cortes, but were not permittted at the working sessions.

THE CONSEJO REAL

Every Saturday afternoon this body met at the viceroy's palace to take up matters on which it was empowered to advise him.

But the consultative role was subordinate to its function as the highest tribunal of the land. Before Navarra's conquest, the *Corte Mayor,* presided over by the king, had been responsible for administration of justice. But by the end of the fifteenth century it had been effectively replaced by the *Consejo Real.*

In other Spanish realms, Castile controlled the judiciary. But Ferdinand had permitted an exception in Navarra because of his policy of placating the Navarrese as much as possible without endangering security. And there was the undeniable provision in their fueros, which he had sworn to uphold, that no judicial matters involving Navarrese were to be taken out of the kingdom.

The sixteenth-century *Consejo* consisted of six councilors and their president, or, as he was also called, the regent. This officer was appointed by the Crown for a life term, or until promotion to one of the other Royal Councils: perhaps of Castile, or the Indies or the Military Orders. He was not usually a native of Navarra.

Two of the councilors were ordinarily nonnative as well. The Cortes, throughout the century, complained about this inclusion of foreigners, recalling the provisions of the *Fuero General,* but to no avail. Councilors were usually men with legal experience (though they could not function as lawyers while on the *Consejo*), were never "new Christians" (converted Jews), and were distinguished from the ordinary populace by their prescribed costume: the *traje talar* (a suit with a long coat reaching the ground). For a time, they changed to capes, but when other men also began wearing capes, they went back to the *traje talar*.

They had a number of duties besides presiding at trials and passing sentence. Two councilors had to visit the jail every week. Two were supposed to be present when the Cortes met, and sometimes the whole *Consejo* accompanied the viceroy to the opening of Cortes, though they were not made welcome.

The *Consejo Real* of Navarra was smaller than any of the other Royal Councils of Spain and had a wider range of responsibilities, which included gubernatorial and legislative, besides judicial. The legislative acts were usually worked out in collaboration with the viceroy, and usually were more like administrative ordinances than broad laws, which remained the exclusive domain of the Cortes. However, the *Consejo Real* had the final say over all royal ordinances: those sent directly by the monarch to the kingdom, and not originating in the Cortes. This approval was the *sobrecarta*.

THE VISITS

Though we have emphasized the degree of autonomy left to Navarra after incorporation into Castile, the kindom was by no means left totally to its own devices. Besides his viceroy, and the controls he exercised on the *Consejo Real,* the king had another powerful check (this too was common to other territories of Spain, including the Americas): the Visit.

The Visitor was sent to see if justice was being done as it should and if anything was lacking for good government and efficient administration. The Visit was not a regularly scheduled event and was seldom in response to a specific situation that needed remedy. There were other means for that. It was, rather, an occasional quality-check on the *Consejo Real's* performance, and lasted a year or more. During his stay the Visitor gathered quantities of information. He took it back to Castile to digest and to make recommendations from it to the king. The result, in Navarra, was always a batch of new ordinances, usually greeted unenthusiastically by the Cortes, which legally was solely responsible for issuing laws.

One of the many formal protests was that of the Cortes of 1556:

Neither the Viceroy nor the King can make general laws, because before the incorporation, the kings of Navarra would seek counsel from the Cortes, and the laws were not made in any other fashion; the Visitor is here only for reform of judges and the courts, but with that pretext the Visit may not lead to promulgation of general laws.[4]

The Visits, nonetheless, continued to lead to laws.

Publication of the new ordinances was always an impressive ceremony in the *Consejo Real* audience chamber. The highest officials of justice were in attendance and the viceroy was usually in charge. The king's authority was implicit. After the reading of the new laws by the secretary, the viceroy and other officials then took the documents in their hands, kissed them and held them aloft over their heads, promising to uphold them and obey them as instruments of his majesty.

Two other checks on the kingdom's government were the *Residencia* and the *Pesquisa*. *Residencias* were routine inspections and investigations of city and town governments, carried out by judges named by the regent in the king's name. The *Pesquisa* was a commission sent from court to investigate a single specific matter.

THE CORTES

If the fueros were the life source for medieval Navarra, the Cortes was the life preserver in the modern era. Viceroys came and went, the *Consejo Real* buzzed about, the king hovered remotely in the background, but the Cortes marched purposefully on, determined to do its duty by the status quo.

Navarra's representative, three-armed legislative body was not unique. Cortes or *Estados* had existed in Spain since the later Middle Ages. Though many valid claims to be the "first" Cortes may be supported, twelfth-century Castile has a strong case, if the presence of representatives from the towns is a criterion. At Castile's Cortes of León in 1135, Alfonso VII was crowned emperor, and representatives of the cities were present. However, the early forerunners of the Cortes did not yet serve the purpose of permitting the towns to negotiate *servicios*—subsidies to the Crown. Rather, they were primarily forums for the king's oath to respect the laws, and for his noble and ecclesiastical subjects (and, increasingly, representatives of the town dwellers) to swear their fealty.

In any case, Navarra, though the oldest kindom in Spain, was the last to adopt the custom of a Cortes called by the king and including representatives of the towns. This is understandable in view of the late urban development of Navarra, where until well into the fourteenth century the kings were still granting conciliatory municipal charters to new or developing towns, in an effort to create a counterforce to a powerful nobility.

During the thirteenth century there were several assemblies in Navarra with most of the characteristics of the later Cortes: one in 1253, to decide the procedure for the minor Teobaldo II to swear his foral oath, for example. The three classes were represented. In 1274, an assembly included prelates, nobles and town representatives to name a regent during the minority of Juana I, daughter of Enrique I and Blanca. Campión believes this could be called Navarra's first Cortes.[5]

In 1297, the league called *Infanzones de Obanos* met, with representatives present from the noble class (*infanzones*) and from twelve cities plus two *burgos* of Pamplona. But it was not convoked by the king; in fact it was born out of anti-royal and anti-French sentiment. (It was during the reign of Philip I, first king to simultaneously occupy the thrones of Navarra and France.)

By 1319, the Cortes was a fact. Representatives of the three estates met then to agree on sending emissaries to France to receive the oath of the new king, Philip II (Philip V of France). In the oath Philip swore in Paris (he was never in Pamplona), reference is made to the three estates of the kingdom.

Of the three, the *Brazo Ecclesiástico*—ecclesiastical branch—was first in prestige. In the sixteenth century it included ten prelates, increased to twelve in the seventeenth century. The bishop of Pamplona was always the presiding officer of this *Brazo* and of the Cortes as a whole.

The *Brazo Militar*—that of the nobles—was a descendant of the twelve *sabios* whom the *Fuero General* designated as advisors to the king and without whose counsel he could not take major action. *Sabio* meant "powerful and wealthy" rather than "wise" in those days. The *sabios* were later called *ricos hombres,* and were the leading nobles of the land. During medieval times they had all been distinguished from the lower nobility in the

Cortes, but in the sixteenth century all members of the second *Brazo* were referred to interchangeably as nobles or *caballeros*. Their number varied greatly, as did the conditions under which they were eligible. The king appointed them. Some appointments were a reward for service, or even for donations, if the king's coffers were seriously depleted. Some were hereditary (and these seats could be inherited through women, though women could not sit in the Cortes). Some were only for life, but became hereditary because of short official memories and inadequate records.

Accordingly, the number of nobles in the Cortes varied considerably. There were at least forty-one in 1494, and some seventy-five by 1576. During the seventeenth century the number grew, as did the applications to the king for seats. Eventually, a complicated eight-step procedure was established:

1) The candidate petitions the king.

2) The king asks the viceroy and the *Consejo Real* to verify the petitioner's qualifications.

3) The candidate provides proofs, including that of *limpieza de sangre* (purity of blood).

4) The application is sent to the *Real Cámara de Castilla*, and from that body to the king.

5) The king gives it his official sanction (or not).

6) If approved by the king, the file is reviewed by the viceroy and sent to the Cortes.

7) The Cortes votes in secret ballot whether to grant a "License for Seating."

8) In addition, candidates from outside Navarra must submit proof that they have obtained citizenship.[6]

Besides meeting the criteria of noble blood (manifested by possession of a palace bearing an escutcheon) and Navarrese citizenship, members of the *Brazo Militar* had to be at least fourteen years old to vote. (For a time, younger nobles were permitted in the chamber, but could not vote.)

CITIZENSHIP AS A CRITERION FOR OFFICEHOLDERS

Citizenship had always been an unquestioned, fuero-based requirement for any one appointed to a legislative or judicial position. Even the French kings had been made to toe that line. But after 1512, there was a continual battle between Navarra and Castile on the point. Naturally, the "outsider" kings wanted their own loyal, experienced men on the spot to protect their interests. So they appointed Castilians to posts in the church (no bishop of Pamplona from 1523 to 1735 was a Navarrese), the *Consejo Real* and the Cortes. Time after time the Cortes complained of this as a *contrafuero* (an act contrary to the fueros). Sometimes the legislators even suspended the session of Cortes in protest and went home. Time after time the kings ignored the complaints, or equivocated.

Charles set the example. During his reign, a royal order permitted the vicar general of Pamplona to sit in the Cortes, though he was a foreigner (1523). That same year, when Charles recieved a petition concerning foreign judges, he promised to right the wrong in half a year, but apparently did not. A few years later, he declined to promise that he would always appoint native judges, saying the best interests of the kingdom might sometimes be served best by foreigners. He did add, though, that if any judge failed to do justice, he wanted to be told.

Unable to make the king change his ways, the Cortes finally found a face-saving formula: granting of honorary citizenship —*naturaleza.* Increasingly during the sixteenth century this was the way out when the king's foreign appointees insisted on attending the Cortes.

The solution was not a novelty. Naturalization of foreigners to make them eligible to hold office in Navarra had been started by the Albret kings when they wanted to bring their trusted magistrates from Béarn. Catherine d'Albret, for example, after much persuasion, got the Cortes to naturalize Raymond, a judge from Bigorre, in 1501.

Another problem was the poor attendance record of the ecclesiastical branch. Sometimes there was only one prelate present, sometimes there were none, in which case the Cortes could not function. Inasmuch as many of them had been granted *naturaleza* as a concomitant of their service in the Cortes, that body, having failed with persuasion, tried threats: to withdraw citizenship if the prelates did not attend. But to no effect. The representatives of the church never did take their legislative duties as seriously as did the other two arms.

The third branch of the Cortes was the *Universidades,* representing the *estado llano* (the middle class).

Of the three segments of the population represented in the Cortes, this was the last to arrive. As prescribed in the *Fuero General*, the king had been taking counsel from the leading prelates and nobles ever since the birth of the monarchy. But not until the fifteenth century was the third estate a regular participant.

The name derives from the medieval *universitas:* a city or fortified place whose inhabitants exchange oaths with their king or lord, and who are thereby bound by certain laws. In Navarra, according to Yanguas y Miranda, the *Universidades* were the cities and *buenas villas* (most important towns; the monarchs designating as few as possible, to limit representation in the Cortes) in which lived free persons, recognizing no other lord than the king, and the governed by an official (the *alcalde*) named by the king.

The number of cities and *buenas villas* was twenty-seven or twenty-eight before Ferdinand's conquest, and about ten more by the end of the seventeenth century. Pamplona's representatives always had the seat of honor in the Cortes, with Tudela and Estella chronically disputing over second place, setting in motion a whole series of quarrels over seats by the rest of the cities. (Theoretically, seating order was determined by the order in which the cities had been granted charters or *fueros municipales*, but records and interpretations varied.)

Similar disagreements were frequent in the ecclesiastical branch. In fact, the Cortes agenda eventually had a regular heading for "Protests over Seating."

The cities' representatives, called *procuradores*, were elected either by the town councils or by *insaculación* (see below).

LOCAL ELECTION PROCEDURES

Town council elections varied according to local taste and habit, and with the passage of time. The electorate usually consisted of all male heads of families. In smaller towns their meetings were known as *batzarres* (a Basque word, still extant in Navarra and the rest of Vasconia). The *batzarre* was concerned with all kinds of community and family matters, besides the election of *procuradores*.

In larger towns the town council represented, and was elected by, all heads of families; the electorate at large, therefore, did not vote for *procuradores* but left this to the council.

The second electoral method, *insaculación* ("ensackment"), was introduced by the Castilian rulers in territories where the citizens' volubility and contentious rivalry made the council method too unruly. It became widespread but not universal in Navarra during the sixteenth century. It was a curious combination of popular representation, a self-perpetuating oligarchy, and pure chance. In typical circumstances, it worked as follows:

Names of all men in the community deemed fit to hold public office (in the judgment of the existing town officials: mayor and councilors) were written on separate pieces of paper, encased in lumps of wax, and placed in a sack. Each name had to be approved unanimously. To be *insaculado* a man had to be a resident; independent—that is, not serving a noble or lord; twenty-five years old; able to read and write; of good habits; and worth 200 ducados if from a city or *buena villa*, 100 if from a smaller town.

Once in the sack the names were guarded with utmost secrecy, under lock and key.

On "election day," in the presence of all citizens who wanted to see the ceremony, the secretary opened the sacks, drew out the wax-wrapped names, and tossed them in a jug of water. A child picked them out one by one; they were opened; the first to be drawn out were named, in corresponding order, to the highest offices of the new town council and down the line until all offices (some half dozen) were filled. Because the mayor was nearly always the *procurador* in the Cortes, the *insaculación* automatically elected that representative too. The other names went back in the sack until the next election. Every four years the current town government reviewed all the names to bring the lists up to date.

In some cities, *insaculación* was the method used for naming only the town council, which then nominated and voted on *procuradores*.

There were many variations and refinements to the system, as well as objections. At the Cortes of Sangüesa in 1561, most of the cities were reported as discontented with the method, for various reasons. Tudela, for one, even after *insaculación* had been in common use for a century, petitioned the right to return to the open-council system, which, in truth, gave a more direct vote to more electors.

However elected, the *procurador* was sent to the Cortes with broad powers to act for his constituency. Nothing annoyed the Cortes more than to have to postpone action because some member had to send or go home for instructions. Though there were no precise limits on the number of representatives per town, each *Universidad* had only one vote. Most towns sent one or possibly two men: it was expensive to maintain them, especially when the Cortes sessions ran on for months or even years, as they occasionally did. Pamplona usually sent three representatives.

FUNCTIONS OF THE CORTES

The Cortes considered itself the guardian of the ancient rights of the Kingdom of Navarra and bulwark against Castilian absolutism. In fact, the members saw themselves as personification of the kingdom, and frequently so referred to themselves: "*Los pidimentos que el Reyno envía . . .*"; "*Queda satisfecho el Reyno . . .*"; "*El Reyno lo dijo al Virrey . . .*" ("The requests that the Kingdom sends . . ."; "The Kindgom is satisfied . . ."; "The Kingdom so informed the Viceroy . . .").

Navarra's Cortes met much more frequently than those in the rest of Spain. It had petitioned Charles to let it meet annually, to which he agreed, and it did so with few exceptions through most of the sixteenth century. (Meantime, Castile's Cortes was meeting every two or three years, Aragon's about every five years.) Eventually, the intervals in Navarra became two or three years, in the seventeenth century. In 1617 the Cortes ruled that it must meet at least every three years. By the eighteenth century, there were much longer gaps, as long as seventeen years. But the *Diputación* (see below) was alert and active between sessions and acted on behalf of the Cortes. In the nineteenth century, Navarra's Cortes met only three times before its dissolution (in 1841).

In the kingdom's days of independence, the Cortes had been accustomed to participation in top-level decisions. Up to the time of the Albrets, it was consulted about (or intervened in) such questions as royal marriages, alliances, the succession and defense of the realm. Though such "international" matters could not be in its purview after 1512, Ferdinand tried hard to keep the Cortes feeling important. He wished it involved in the creation of a peaceful postwar kingdom, and he sent it flattering messages. When he convoked the Cortes of 1513, he said, through his viceroy, "You, who are best informed on matters having to do with this kingdom, are to set forth all that you think needs remedy, so that after informed discussion it may be resolved for the universal good of the kingdom."[7]

Charles and Philip, too, made special efforts to maintain good relations and mutual respect. In 1595, Philip received a complaint from the Cortes that, contrary to the fueros, foreign (Castilian) troops were lodged in Olite. He replied with an order to remove them to the frontier of Castile and to see that the citizens were paid for what the soldiers had consumed or appropriated. He said: "My royal intention and wish is that in no way shall the laws to which I have sworn be contravened, but they shall be kept inviolate."

But the main and often desperate concern of all the monarchs was that the Cortes should grant *servicios* (subsidies to the king) and, in wartime, men for the army—and as expeditiously as possible. The Cortes, on the other hand, saw its main function as getting all its *agravios* (complaints) remedied and all *contrafueros* righted, before a penny or a man were committed. As early as 1510, it had put itself on record as being implacably opposed to granting of *servicios* before settlement of its complaints:

> Not in these Cortes here assembled, nor in any which henceforth shall be held, shall at any time any concession or granting of funds be undertaken or any matter connected with same, until all *agravios* shall be effectively and unconditionally remedied, with all necessary auxiliary matters dealt with.

Because the contributions were always voluntary, and not a regular set amount, the Cortes was able to continue to hold to this firm line.

But the seesaw never stopped. The kings always pled for and ordered short, efficient sessions. The Cortes always proceeded deliberately through all its business, only then turning its attention to Castile's requirements. Not until 1801 had the power of the Cortes eroded enough for the king to actually set a time limit on the session, and prohibit any business except the *servicio*.

Nevertheless, the *servicios* were always granted—eventually. There was no question of the kingdom's basic loyalty and sense of duty to the king.

Nor was there any question of what Navarra saw as its king's duty to his kingdom, in regard to legalities and properties. As late as 1828, when what was to be the last Cortes was convoked, the *Diputación* requested a revised document from the king because the first one had two mistakes. First mistake: Ferdinand VII was described as "King of Castile, León and Navarra," whereas he should have been styled "King of Castile, Navarra and León." Second mistake: the king named Pamplona as the meeting site, whereas it was not his but the viceroy's prerogative to name the site. The corrections were made and the Cortes permitted itself to be convoked (in Pamplona).

Relations with the viceroys were marked by respect and sometimes even partisanship in opposition to the *Consejo Real*. The viceroys, though never natives of Navarra, were seldom the unsympathetic autocrats they could have been. Their interests and views often coincided with those of the Cortes, and their terms of several years gave them time to develop local loyalty and pride.

The Cortes always maintained enormous respect for itself. Assemblies were conducted with impressive ceremony and a deliberate, formal order. Take, for example, the manner of address in the formal letters inviting *procuradores* to come to the Cortes. There were four forms to choose from in addressing representatives from the *Universidades*. For those from Pamplona, *"Magníficos y mui nobles señores"* ("Magnificent and very noble sirs"). For Tudela and Estella, *"Mui nobles señores"* ("Very noble sirs"). For lesser towns, *"Nobles señores"* ("Noble sirs") or *"Honrados y especiales amigos"* ("Honored and special friends"). Members of the other two arms, the clergy and the nobility, were to be addressed by the appropriate honorific from this list of eleven: *"Ilustre señor, mui ilustre señor, magnífico y mui reberendo señor, mui reberendo señor, reberendo señor, mui magnífico señor, magnífico señor, mui noble señor, noble señor, magnífico y mui noble señor, señor"* ("Illustrious sir, very illustrious sir, magnificent and very reverend sir, very reverend sir, reverend sir, very magnificent sir, magnificent sir, very noble sir, noble sir, magnificent and very noble sir, sir").

The meeting chamber was the *Librería Vieja* of the cathedral, off the cloister, entered by way of an elegantly sculptured stone arch called *La Preciosa* (which is still there). Within, a precise seating arrangement was held to: ecclesiastics to the viceroy's right, nobles to his left, *Universidades* below and in front.

The business that preceded granting of the *servicios* included means of raising money through property and sales taxes. Other items for the agenda came from several sources: messages from the king, lists of *agravios* drawn up by the *Diputación* (especially after the sixteenth century), the mails, petitions or memorials from the towns brought by their representatives, members' motions made orally in the chamber, or finally, via the *ratonera* or suggestion box, which Huici Goñi calls the "authentic voice of the people."

THE MOUSETRAP, VOICE OF THE PEOPLE

The Cortes had been receiving anonymous memorials throughout the seventeenth century, and possibly much earlier. Presently it decided to regularize the communication method by causing a small door to be cut in the large door to the assembly room. Citizens could put their written suggestions for official action through the small door. It was called the box for secret memorials or, more familiarly, the *ratonera*—the mousetrap.[8] Traces of the aperture in the great wood door of *La Preciosa* are still visible in Pamplona's cathedral.

The mousetrap proved a rich source of material for the agenda of the Cortes. So rich, in fact, that a commission had to be appointed to review all suggestions to see if they were suitable for reading aloud in the Cortes. If found to be indecent, frivolous or otherwise improper, they went no further. But the sensible memorials received full consideration, and there was hardly a day when the mousetrap did not yield several. For example, in 1795 a citizen sent a plan for defense of the kingdom against the French. In 1817 there were suggestions for civil and criminal codes. (This must have been a long-term problem: in 1829, the Cortes offered a prize of 50,000 reales for the best criminal code for the kingdom.) In 1828, a defense of the formation of a royalist volunteer force came from an anonymous correspondent who must have had some premonition of the Carlist wars that were to break out in 1833.

Passing laws was not the main function of the Cortes, as it is in most modern representative bodies, because it had to be constantly on the defensive. Hence the emphasis on righting wrongs and dealing with grievances. But the legislative function was important, and went back to the very early modern period, though no written laws passed by a Cortes before 1512 are known. No law could be passed except by the Cortes, after which it was sanctioned by the king. And even after this sanction, the Cortes could decide not to publish the law, thus holding a final veto power.

The legislative power also worked in reverse. If the Cortes considered a royal disposition to be contrary to the fueros, it could reject it with the courtesy formula, *"Se obedece pero no se cumple"* (loosely, "We hear you but we will not comply"). Such decrees could become law only if then given the *sobrecarta* (approval) of the *Consejo Real;* but the opposition of the Cortes would be on public record.

THE DIPUTACIÓN

As demands on its time grew, and concern about the integrity of the kingdom's foral liberties continued, the Cortes saw it would need help, especially during the periods between its sessions.

For a time, it named deputies or *síndicos* to function while the Cortes was not sitting. They were to gather *agravios* and present them to the Cortes when next it met.

By the 1570s it seemed expedient to turn the body of deputies into an institution. The Cortes created a permanent *Diputación* of five members, to begin serving as soon as the Cortes adjourned and continue until its next session. The number of deputies was soon increased to seven: one representing the clergy, two the nobles, and four the towns. Two of the last were from Pamplona; the other two represented, in rotation, Estella, Tudela, Sangüesa and Olite.

The *Diputación* soon acquired more duties than merely to serve as a foral watchdog. It gave each new Cortes a report on what had taken place since the last session, as well as a memorandum outlining what matters the new Cortes should take up. It conceded certificates of naturalization. It administered issuance of franchises for dealing in wool and tobacco, for example.

It administed *fondos de vínculo* (funds for Cortes and *Diputación* expenses). It was charged with maintenance of roads and passes, and with public education. It received all royal orders before they went to the *Consejo Real* for the *sobrecarta*. It became the body charged with proper observance of such ceremonies as raising the standard for a new king, mourning a deceased monarch, proclaiming a new heir to the throne, and welcoming a visiting monarch to the kingdom.

As the Cortes met less frequently during the eighteenth and nineteenth centuries, the *Diputación* became more important administratively. It also became more self-important. Like the Cortes, it was legalistic, protocol-conscious, and a stickler for conventions, all the way down to proper dress.

In 1708, a deputy appeared wearing a necktie: an innovation. The conventional neckwear was the high ruffed collar. The novelty provoked a discussion. The Prior said he did not particularly mind, because he knew the king was wearing neckties in Castile. Another member said he supposed it was all right this once, but not in future, pending some ruling by the Cortes. A third agreed with the Prior, and told how he had seen council presidents wearing neckties at court. He had even seen the viceroy in a necktie, though he was not permitted to wear it in a council meeting until he got authorization from the king. A fourth was completely opposed: it was all very well for the viceroy to wear a necktie becasue he was captain general; but just because it was accepted in Castile, it was not necessarily acceptable in Navarra. He favored nullification of the entire session of the *Diputación*. Finally, the body voted to tolerate the necktie for the present but could not agree on a policy for the future.[9] (Actually, the ruff had been officially discouraged since the reforms of Olivares, Philip IV's minister, in 1623. Navarra was about seventy-five years behind the rest of Spain in accepting new fashions.)

The *Diputación* outlasted not only its counterparts in the rest of Spain, and the absolutist monarchy it had been created to guard against, but also the Cortes it had been designed to assist. The present *Diputación Foral* is the direct descendant of this *Diputación*.

The Cortes, too, enjoyed a remarkably long life. Its final adjournment in 1841 came well over a century later than the end of Spain's other regional parliamentary bodies.

LONGEVITY OF NAVARRA'S CORTES

There were to be many stormy periods before the end, but at first, under the first two Hapsburgs, a considerable degree of mutual respect between monarch and kingdom obtained, with a shared desire to keep the system working. Later relations were not so smooth. How did Navarra's Cortes keep its vitality in the face of the encroaching power of Castile during succeeding centuries, in the face of the ministerial absolutism of the Bourbons, and the liberal absolutism of the nineteenth century?

For one thing, remoteness from king and court meant less factionalism and intrigue among the nobles vis-à-vis the king and the royal councils. In Castile, where the king would play one faction against another, and where he gave his councils much of the power formerly exercised by the Castilian Cortes, the latter lost prestige and effectiveness.

For another, the equilibrium maintained by the three branches kept them all afloat. If not numerically equal, they were equal in aspiration, with an unwavering allegiance to the constitutional tradition and the status quo. The rule that all major laws had to be passed unanimously fortified this purpose.

The third life-preserving factor was loyalty to the monarch. The kings of Spain knew they could always count on Navarra's support and fidelity. Other territories might rebel, seek independence, refuse *servicios*. Not Navarra. After the doomed attempts by the Albrets to get their kingdom back, there was little sentiment for a return to independence. In 1598, when there were rumors that Philip might recognize the French king's rights to Navarra, the kingdom expressed consternation. Calm was restored only when the *Diputación* was assured that the king had no intentions of giving Navarra away, and was well pleased with the evidence of the kingdom's loyalty. Out of respect for such fidelity, it was certainly in the Castilian government's interest to avoid undue hacking away at the power of the Navarrese Cortes.

Finally, the Cortes was open-minded about the changing world. No one could accuse the Navarrese of flexibility, if that implies constant shifting with every wind. But they were a people with a realistic appreciation of the need to adapt somewhat (usually as little as possible) to new situations. As Huici Goñi points out, the willingness to entertain all kinds of suggestions (recall the *ratonera*) was an indication of this. Another was the continual revising, discussing and perfecting of the rules under which Navarra governed itself and dealt with its monarch.

All these characteristics were evident in the sixteenth-century institutions of Navarra and remained so as the kingdom continued to adapt to the exigencies of coexistence with other states in a growingly complex Spain.

XII

The Kingdom Within a Kingdom

IN THE SEVENTEENTH CENTURY SPAIN was almost continuously at war with one or more European countries. The most famous conflict was the Thirty Years' War, which turned out to be a forty-year war for Spain. The nation also experienced two major and four minor internal revolts, three terrible plagues, three unremarkable kings, the expulsion of the Moors, the slowing to a trickle of the silver supply from America, and a population decline of seventeen percent. Perhaps the wonder is not that Spain managed to get into such an "exceptional concurrence of adversities,"[1] but that she did indeed survive them.

Surrounded by such events, it was impossible for even a kingdom so small and so skillful at minding its own business as was Navarra to keep out of the mainstream of history. From now on, Navarra's development would be linked more closely than before with that of her near neighbors and of Europe. Spain was still a global power, if a fading one. And Navarra was part of Spain.

Still, the Navarrese in general preferred noninvolvement both in the monarchy's international adventures and in peninsular affairs. And the record shows the kingdom was quite successful at staying in the shallows, while maintaining a scrupulously correct and respectful posture toward Castile and the Hapsburg monarchs.

Within its borders, life went on. The institutions that had undergone changes in the previous century to adjust to the Castilian rule perfected and solidified themselves. Times were hard; but there was considerably more stability and prosperity than in most of Spain.

THE RESTIVE PENINSULA

This was the Spain within which Navarra cautiously threaded its way during the seventeenth century:

Philip II's lackluster son Philip III inherited four kingdoms in 1598. They were Castile, Portugal, Navarra and the Crown of Aragon, which last included the kingdoms of Aragon and Valencia and the principality of Catalonia. Castile accounted for about sixty-six percent of the peninsula's area; Aragon, seventeen percent; Portugal, fifteen percent; Navarra, two percent.

In spite of nearly a century of nominal association as one kingdom, there was practically no sense of national unity or even alliance. Each realm continued to go its own independent way, and Aragon went three ways. Thus the king actually had six loosely federated states to deal with, and the only one where he had much leverage was Castile.

Most of Philip II's enterprises had been of an international nature, depending on his and Castile's reactions to events outside Spain, not involving the other peninsular kingdoms. But during the disaster-strewn seventeenth century, the battles came closer to home and internal affairs became more turbulent.

Philip III, though well intentioned, paid little attention to any of his kingdoms, finding it simpler and far pleasanter to amuse himself at court and leave the hard work of government to others. While heir to the throne he had performed the customary swearing to uphold Navarra's fueros *in absentia,* in 1586, and came in person with his father to swear again in 1592. He did not come back.

His *valido*—favorite—for most of his reign was the duke of Lerma. Not only did Lerma assume the bulk of the monarch's responsibilities, but the ponderous system of councils and courtiers became even more difficult to deal with because of the growing presence of the *juntas.* These were special committees

THE KINGDOM WITHIN A KINGDOM

to handle special problems, appointed by the Crown. They took over much of the royal councils' work during this reign. They were effectively bypassing the more position-conscious royal councils, which were usually bogged down in detail. Later, under the weaker rule of Charles II, the nobles and the councils regained much of their power.

Philip III's reign opened with a period of comparative calm on the international front. Spain had made peace with England in 1604; had signed a truce with the Netherlands in 1609, which lasted until 1621; and Philip II's 1598 treaty with France kept the lid on that bubbling pot for twenty-nine years.

Nevertheless, signs of internal discontent and decline were all too obvious. In a move to please the populace and set the seal on the holy war of reconquest, begun six centuries before, the government expelled the *moriscos* (Christianized Moors) from Spain, starting in 1609. The effects were most noticeable in the southern and eastern parts of the peninsula, where the *moriscos* had been an important element in agricultural and commercial life. But few *moriscos* had ever settled in Navarra or the northwest, or emigrated there after their forced dispersal from Andalucia in 1570. Most of the two hundred seventy-five thousand who left Spain went to Africa, but some ten thousand passed through Navarra and its Pyrenean passes, en route to France and beyond.

Even during periods of comparative peace in Spain, the Hapsburgs had to maintain armies elsewhere. Having practically exhausted Castile's resources, they turned to their other kingdoms for money and men. In most cases response was minimal. In Aragon, which had a foral tradition fully as long and strong as Navarra's, the Cortes consistently resisted attempts to impose taxation instead of the voluntary *servicios*. The Catalans, too, were uncooperative and, in the end, rebellious.

In contrast, Navarra's Cortes continued to meet and regularly vote *servicios* to the king, averaging a meeting every four years during the reigns of Philip III and Philip IV. Troops were also forthcoming, but with reluctance, especially if the war was outside Spain. However, Navarra sent a token three hundred men to join the army of the two General Spinolas (brothers) in the Palatinate, in 1618. This action was an attempt to shore up Spanish strength vis-à-vis the United Provinces, which were rapidly slipping away toward complete independence.

Philip III was apparently the last monarch to take up the Navarre Question. And in contrast to his father and grandfather he did take action, of a sort. To be sure, by his accession in 1598, the question had become somewhat academic. The legitimate Albret dynasty that ruled Basse Navarre and Béarn had merged with the direct line of the Bourbon kings of France. It was hardly likely that a king of Spain would voluntarily "return" such a strategic property to his chief European rival. However, Philip III asked a royal commission to study the case. Though the commission admitted it had not been able to find the pertinent documents that told of Ferdinand's assumption of the kingship, it presently produced an opinion: that there was not, and never had been, any reason to have any scruples about the way Navarra had been disposed of, nearly a century before.

Philip III died in 1621, and was succeeded by sixteen-year-old Philip IV, brighter than his father but also inclined to depend on others for decisive action. His *valido* for twenty-two years was the Conde Duque de Olivares, who gave at least an appearance of taking hold and initiating constructive action to wrench Spain out of its economic and spiritual decline.

And the wars began again, and the calls for support. Navarra's enthusiasm for Castile's wars was still lukewarm, but slightly greater if they were close to home.

In 1635 France declared war on Spain, attacking in Flanders and Italy. In 1636 Spain responded with two moderately effective incursions into Labourd and Narbonne. With considerable reluctance, Navarra participated in the former. When asked to provide troops, the kingdom protested, and cited ill omens. Padre José Moret's contemporary account describes ominous portents before the outbreak of hostilities. Two eagles fought daily in the skies over Lumbier, some twenty-five miles southeast of Pamplona, then each nightfall one flew northward over the Pyrenees, the other south into Spain's heartland. This went on for three days, when both fell to earth dead: a warning, the Navarrese thought.

But eventually, after an order from the king, the Cortes sent an army under the viceroy, Marqués de Valparaiso, to march through the mountains and into Labourd for a campaign that lasted seven months. This was considerably longer than the three days specified by the fuero.

THE KINGDOM WITHIN A KINGDOM 127

These expeditions inspired Richelieu to open the Spanish-French chapter of the Thirty Years' War by invasions at both ends of the Pyrenees. In 1638, he besieged Fuenterrabia in Guipúzcoa with an army of twenty-two thousand. This, the first presence of foreign troops on Spanish soil since the days of Charles V, astonished and roused all Spain.

For once, the monarchy's calls for help were heeded. Contingents to lift the siege came from Castile, Valencia and Aragon. The new viceroy of Navarra, the fifth Marqués de los Vélez, even sent for cannon from his ancestral castle in Murcia, far to the south. Navarra, after making sure its own kingdom was safe from French attacks at St. Jean Pied de Port and Vera, sent four thousand troops off to the neighboring province, where they saved the day.

This action was outside Navarra's frontiers, hence it was against the fueros to send troops there. Here is how the Cortes got around the dilemma: a deputy from their number was sent to the border to the viceroy, where he publicly put Navarra's protest on record. Having complied with the laws by this demonstration, the deputy then took up a spear and announced that up to that point he had been acting as a deputy; from now on he would act as a Navarrese and a warrior.

The scene of battle next shifted to Catalonia. Olivares, energetic but high-handed, outraged the principality by insisting on billeting a "foreign" (i.e., Castilian) army there, in 1639, to meet the threat from France. This and other assaults on their liberties goaded the Catalans into rebellion and war with Castile in 1640. They asked help from Navarra, Aragon, Valencia, Portugal and France. The king of France responded at once, by recognizing Catalonia's independence, appointing a French viceroy and sending an army.

The peninsular kingdoms, however, declined to get involved on either side. Not only were they indifferent to Catalonia's requests: they resisted their own king's demands for troops to put down the rebellion.

Speaking for Philip IV, the viceroy in Navarra—the count of La Coruña—argued to the Cortes that Navarra's own borders would be endangered if a Catalan Republic were allowed to emerge and if the French protectors went on to occupy Aragon. The Navarrese, unmoved by such a hypothetical threat, replied that it was still against their fueros to send an army to fight outside Navarra, and that men were needed at home for the harvest, and to protect their own French frontier.

Finally, in a compromise, they sent a contingent of thirteen hundred men to serve four months at the king's expense. (Normally, the kingdom paid its own military costs.) There were many desertions.

The principality's experiment in independence, at the end without much French protection, lasted until 1652, when, in exchange for a grudging recognition of its liberties, a weakened Catalonia rejoined the Spanish fold.

The Portuguese seized the opportunity to revolt immediately after the start of the Catalan disturbance, and their efforts were eventually successful. But their rebellion had even less impact on the rest of the peninsular monarchy than had the Catalan. Portugal had been acquired only in 1580 and was not regarded by anyone except Castile as a possession worth fighting for. In spite of valiant efforts to regain it, Castile gave up by 1668.

The Catalan and Portuguese rebellions were the major internal conflicts during this century. But the spirit of unrest they typified had its precursors and repercussions in a number of smaller outbreaks, from Andalucia to Navarra.

One of the first was almost next door to Navarra, in the Basque province of Vizcaya. Olivares, looking everywhere for revenue, imposed a salt tax which, together with forced military service, provoked open revolt. The protests were bloodily quelled in 1632, the price of salt was lowered, and peace was restored. (Another protest arose in Vizcaya in 1637 when an attempt was made to impose a stamp tax: a fee for the official seals required on documents. As a result of such indignities, many Vizcayans emigrated to France, saying their land no longer enjoyed its ancient privileges.)

In 1641 a conspiracy to establish Andalucia as an independent kingdom, with the duke of Medina-Sidonia as king, was nipped in the bud by Olivares. Two years later Olivares had to step down from his high post in disgrace. No one of stature took his place, and Philip IV tried to assume the reins of government himself. But the rebellions continued.

In Aragon in 1648, as in Andalucia in 1641, the nobles conspired against Castile. Their grandiose scheme was to involve France and Portugal, handing over Galicia to the latter and Navarra to the former, as rewards for help. The plot was impractical and poorly planned, and failed abysmally.

The same year saw a secessionist attempt in Navarra itself, possibly involving the descendants of the Albret family, and certainly aimed at restoring Navarra's independence. It too got practically nowhere and the leader, Miguel de Iturbide, was executed. Though there does not seem to have been much popular support, the event was symptomatic of the general discontent throughout Spain.[2]

It also illustrates the longevity of Navarra's memory of independence, and served to remind the Castilian rulers that they still could not press the little kingdom too far. In spite of their desperate need of support for their wars, they could not risk demanding too much from Navarra or they might still lose it altogether.

As if his domestic troubles were not enough, Philip IV had to deal with uprisings in Italy, and with Spain's final renunciation of authority in the United Provinces. He kept a semblance of claim to the southern Netherlands. His treaty with the Dutch, in 1648, and the Peace of Westphalia the same year, marked the official end of the Thirty Years' War, but did not deter the powers from renewing hostilities as soon as they had licked their wounds. In 1658 came the resounding defeat of the Spanish army at Les Dunes at the hands of the French and English. Now Philip had to treat for peace with Louis XIV. The negotiations were held on the Isle of Pheasants in the mouth of the River Bidasoa, only a few miles from Navarra's border with Guipúzcoa. The site was chosen so that the treaty table could be half in Spain, half in France. The treaty, known as the Peace of the Pyrenees, was signed in 1659.

One major purpose was to set a lasting French-Spanish boundary. France held out for a geographic line, along the summits of the Pyrenees. Spain preferred a division according to historical frontiers, which would have been considerably to Spain's advantage in Catalonia. France won. Spain gave up Roussillon, but did get some concessions: the Cape of Creus, which juts out into the Mediterranean at the northern end of the Costa Brava, and some parts of Cerdagne and Puigcerdá. The western border remained a line along the peaks. By recognizing this, Louis XIV definitively renounced any French claims to Navarra. The Navarre Question would not be raised again.

The negotiations for the Peace of the Pyrenees also included settlement of the marriage terms for Louis XIV and María

Teresa, Philip IV's daughter. One clause was to be a vital discussion point some forty years later: the agreement that María Teresa would renounce all claims to the Spanish throne for herself and her descendants.

The main negotiators were Luis de Haro (who had somewhat replaced the fallen Olivares as chief minister) and, for the French, Cardinal Mazarin. But Philip put in an appearance, after a royal progression that skirted Navarra, and during which the bishop of Pamplona and several nobles representing the *Diputación* came to pay their respects to him and his queen in San Sebastián.

Philip IV died in 1665. His four-year-old son Charles II succeeded. The queen mother, Mariana of Austria, was regent until Charles's fourteenth birthday.

Under this last and least Hapsburg, things went from bad to worse. Charles lacked physical and mental strength, and no other capable leader arose during his long, sad reign. He traveled little, and never to Navarra: the oath to uphold the fueros there was taken in his name by his viceroy, the count of Fuensalida, in 1677.

The Peace of the Pyrenees last only fifteen years. In the 1670s Louis XIV resumed hostilities in the Low Countries, Italy and Germany. In 1684, in a burst of aggressiveness, he took Luxembourg, attacked in Italy, and invaded not only Catalonia but also Navarra.

A Navarrese regiment was scraped together in 1677 to join in the defense of Catalonia. But they and their fellows in the Spanish army were not notably successful in the Catalonia campaign. The Peace of Nimega (1678) closed that chapter in French-Spanish hostilities.

The French attack on Navarra, though abortive and probably intended largely as a diversionary action to test the kingdom's defenses, was well mounted: the Cortes estimated fifteen thousand enemy troops. The French, under Marshall de Bellefont, marched through the Pass of Roncesvalles and on toward Pamplona. The Cortes, at the instigation of the viceroy, Iñigo de Velandia, sent orders to the valleys nearest the French line of march—Erro and Estenbar—to defend the frontier. Eight hundred men were hastily deployed. There were no important battles and the French retreated through the Valley of the Aldudes to St. Jean Pied de Port. Pamplona was safe.

THE KINGDOM WITHIN A KINGDOM 131

NAVARRA AND ITS NEIGHBORS

Except for the fright of 1638 and that of 1684, Pamplona and Navarra were in no real peril throughout the century, and enjoyed the longest peaceful period in the kingdom's history. How did Navarra use this unprecedented respite? To keep Castile at arm's length, and to march along its own road at its own pace. If the kingdom did not make any major advances, neither were there setbacks.

As we have seen, Navarra remained loyal to the Hapsburg kings, but resisted getting caught up in their foreign adventures. Nor did it, seemingly, feel any need for much cooperation with its sister kingdoms, the conglomerate that would later be known as Spain. Up to and during the seventeenth century, the name *España* was seldom used and, when it was, it usually had a geographic rather than a political meaning. *La monarquía* was the convenient and usual term.

In the deliberations of the Cortes of Navarra, when reference was made to the overall political body, it was usually to "Castile," "the States of Castile," or "the Kingdom of Castile." But other than that there is little indication in Navarra's records of any sense of political community or even interdependence with the other kingdoms. Navarra's refusal to help and reluctance to hinder Catalonia's rebellion in 1640 illustrates this. With Aragon, on Navarra's eastern borders, there was more contact but most of it was quarrelsome, each accusing the other of restraining its trade in wine and wheat. Navarra was always jealous when Aragon was permitted to trade with France and Navarra was not.[3]

With Guipúzcoa, the sore points were wheat and iron. Guipúzcoa complained, probably with reason, that Navarra's iron was inferior to its own and should not be exported on the same basis. But, on the whole, Navarra and Guipúzcoa, with common geographic and defensive interests, cooperated. In 1638 they jointly petitioned Madrid for a revision of the customs duties on fish and paper entering *La Provincia*, as Navarra called the neighboring province.

And from the fourteenth century, the two had been trying, sporadically and never successfully, to get action on a project that would make the River Bidasoa navigable from Santesteban (in north central Navarra) to the sea. This would have given Navarra a direct water route to a port, and would have facilitated Fuenterrabia's commerce with the Valley of the Bidasoa.[4]

Another involved project in which inhabitants of both territories were interested was the improvement of the Guipúzcoan port of Pasajes, near Rentería. This would threaten the monopoly that nearby San Sebastián, Guipúzcoa's capital city, enjoyed in sea commerce, but would give Navarra a good and more accessible port for its iron and wood products from the Valley of the Bidasoa. Partisans in this dispute were not only the two contending Guipúzcoan cities, but also the *montaña* and *ribera* of Navarra. The former favored Rentería: it was closer to the mountain valleys; the latter favored San Sebastián: it was nearer to such Ebro Valley towns as Viana. The cities of the *ribera* also felt reluctance to antagonize San Sebastián, whose defensive capabilities could be very helpful to them in war.

Unlike the canalization of the Bidasoa, this project actually succeeded, in 1620, after only four years of controversy.

INSIDE SEVENTEENTH-CENTURY NAVARRA

By and large, the kingdom's institutions and preoccupations during this century were more like those of the pre-Castilian era than what they would become when Madrid's pull would draw Navarra closer into its orbit. Not much had changed in two hundred years. And while the rest of the peninsula was suffering from three great plagues, Navarra was relatively immune.

Spain's population overall declined from 8,485,000 to 7,000,000 during the century, but that of Navarra and the Basque provinces remained almost constant at 350,000.[5] (In spite of fewer deaths from the plague than in the rest of Spain, population did not increase: living was not easy, and emigration accounted for the loss of many young men.) Although Spain was officially at war with France for about one-third of the century, commerce between French and Spanish Basques went on, by their accustomed Pyrenean and maritime routes, even with official approval occasionally.

While other parliamentary institutions were atrophying, Navarra's Cortes grew ever more vigorous, aided by a zealous *Diputación*. (During the reign of Charles II, the Cortes of Castile disappeared, that of Aragon met only twice, and Catalonia's and Valencia's not at all.) Much of the energies of Navarra's

Cortes were directed to the losing battle to keep Castilians out of the local government, especially on the viceroy's staff. Nevertheless, Navarra loyally and regularly granted *servicios* to the king. Navarra's citizens paid no taxes directly to Castile, but the kingdom taxed them to raise the money for these periodic "voluntary" payments to the king. The taxes were known as the *alcabala* (a five percent sales tax) and the *cuarteles* (a property tax based on the number of hearths or families in each town, and calculated in terms of quarterly collections: hence the name). These were the main revenue-raising sources from the Middle Ages until 1817.[6]

The *alcabala* (a tax common to much of Spain) had been initiated in Navarra in the fourteenth century during the reign of Carlos II to satisfy his demands for money to pay for his chronic French wars. It was imposed on everything bought or sold in the kingdom except horses and arms. Though originally specified as a temporary expedient, the royal requests continued and the Cortes continued to accede.

The *cuarteles,* too, went far back, to the fifteenth century. At first the reason for the contribution was specified—for example, the marriage of a princess, war expenses, a prince's trip abroad. The payments were usually spread over several years, to make the taxpayers's burden easier. For example, the Cortes might grant a *servicio* of two and a half *cuarteles,* to be paid over three years.

There were a remarkable number of exempt persons: clerics, of course; members of the *Consejo Real;* the high nobility, as well as all who could call themselves *caballeros.*

From these sources, the Cortes unfailingly granted *servicios* to the king—on the average, every two or three years during the seventeenth century—in marked contrast to Aragon, Catalonia and Valencia. In fact, the Cortes was so faithful and regular that its generosity came to be accepted as a matter of course. The Cortes, sensitive, objected, pointing out that it should not be referred to as "the ordinary *servicio.*"

Other than the *servicio,* the king got very little out of Navarra. Though the Royal Patrimony there yielded something, it was barely enough for the hereditary benefits he was obligated to pay to certain nobles, and for the salaries of his own officials. The Royal Patrimony was also charged with maintenance of roads, passes and the palaces at Olite and Tafalla.

And the *servicio* itself was usually earmarked down to the last penny for internal expenses: chiefly, for salaries for the *Consejo Real,* military governors, and other officials, war expenses, and maintenance of the army.

Far from being a bargain for Castile, Navarra at this time usually cost more than it gave. Because of the kingdom's special status as guardian of a vital frontier, the Castilian government was committed to very large defense expenditures there. During construction of Philip II's *Ciudadela,* annual costs of the fortress frequently came to more than annual receipts from the kingdom's *servicio* of *cuarteles.*[7]

Nevertheless, Navarra certainly had a better record than some. As evidence of how its contributions compared with those of other states during this period: in 1610, Navarra contributed one-sixth as much as the much larger Kingdom of Aragon; in 1616, half as much as Aragon. True, most of Castile's income came from Castile itself, and from outside the peninsula (from the New World and Italy).

Navarra's comparative stability in the midst of the continuing crises that afflicted the peninsula does not mean it was free of hardship or friction. For one thing, Pamplona overpowered the other cities, and they resented it. Pamplona was superior in population (about ten thousand inhabitants in 1637, as compared with about five thousand in Tudela, next largest); in influence, being the seat of government; and in wealth. Its commercial leadership was insured by the right, dating from the fourteenth century, to hold an annual twenty-two-day fair. It monopolized the wine supply in the city, limiting it to producers in the immediate vicinity. This caused complaints not only from the wine producers in the rest of Navarra, but also from consumers in Pamplona, who disliked paying high prices for an inferior product. One complaint claimed the wine was so bad that even doctors advised against drinking it.

But the citizens' pleasure in a good controversy between capital and provinces was not limited to such worldly matters. A question that absorbed both the Cortes and the people from 1622 to 1656 was: Who is Navarra's patron saint? It became a battle between Pamplona and the rest of the kingdom.

There had been no official patron saint until the *Diputación* named Francisco Javier (Francis Xavier) in 1622, and confirmed the action in 1623. But Pamplona, where San Fermín had been revered since the seventh century, objected. Both candidates had excellent credentials. San Fermín had seniority. He had been a native of Pamplona, son of a pagan senator and a Christian mother, and a priest at the age of eighteen. He dedicated himself to preaching and was martyred for his faith at Amiens (France) in 614.

Francisco Javier, on the other hand, was not Pamplonese and was thus more appealing to inhabitants of the rest of the kingdom. And he had the Society of Jesus on his side. He was born in 1506 in Javier, near the Aragonese border. He had illustrious ancestry, being in the direct line of the lords of the Castillo de Javier. While studying in Paris he met and was influenced by Ignacio de Loyola, the Guipúzcoan founder of the Society of Jesus who had fought in Pamplona in 1521, as detailed earlier. Francisco devoted his life to spreading the faith in the East Indies, India, the Moluccas, the Philippines and Japan, and is credited with the conversion of more than a million unbelievers. He died in 1522 and was canonized a century later, whereupon Navarra's *Diputación* named him patron.

The rival claims were disputed until 1650. Then someone suggested a compromise: revere both saints equally. But partisans on both sides preferred to continue the argument. The Jesuits, naturally, supported San Francisco Javier, and carried on the battle at the Roman level.

Various efforts were made to mediate between the Cortes (holding to the original nomination of San Francisco) and the city of Pamplona (still holding out for San Fermín). But not until 1656 was the 1650 compromise accepted, with the proviso that if both saints were honored in the same procession, San Fermín would take precedence in Pamplona. The pope confirmed the accord in 1657.

Such preoccupations took citizens' minds off the high cost of living and the scarcities of basic goods. Navarra was still a developing country. It had not yet recovered from its depopulation caused by the devastating plague of the fourteenth century, and the civil wars of the fifteenth. With the rest of Spain, it suffered inflation. Its economy was almost exclusively agricultural: grainfields, vineyards, livestock. It could export a few commodities—some wheat, wool and wine—but there were hardly enough of most basic products to meet the kingdom's own needs. Forestry was not yet developed enough for much export of wood products, though some wood from Navarra's mountains went into the ships of the sixteenth-century Spanish Armada.

There were no exportable manufactured products to speak of. One exception was munitions (cannonballs at first; later on, high-quality armor), made at the Royal Arms Works at Eugui.[8] But these brought the kingdom no income, except from their transport, because the whole operation was subsidized by the king. Navarra did have deposits of iron, and exported some to Guipúzcoa.

Wheat prices and restrictions on its export provided the most sensitive barometer of the economy. Price controls came and went. When the price was high, the poor suffered the most, and, judging by records from the time, the price was often high. Others profited: smuggling to get a high price abroad during periods of scarcity, stockpiling in time of plenty in order to sell later at a higher price. The church was among those who engaged in such profiteering.

Because of the hard life, as well as the uncertainty of prices and the many restrictions on where and how they could sell wheat, many growers and laborers gave the whole endeavor up as a bad job. Wheat farmers turned to viniculture, where there were fewer controls. This of course led to even more severe wheat shortages.

On the whole, it was an importing rather than an exporting kingdom. And because of the many customs barriers, the high duties, and the difficulty of manning all the checkpoints, it was also a kingdom where contraband flourished. There were forty-nine customs posts in 1607, seventy-two by 1621, in all five of Navarra's divisions or *merindades* (Pamplona, Estella, Sangüesa, Tudela and Olite), covering all internal and external frontiers.

During war Castile's need to seal the border against illegal commerce was acute. At the outbreak of the Thirty Years' War, the French were expelled from the kingdom, and commerce with the enemy was forbidden. This was a sore hardship for Navarra, which received some revenue from wool shipped to France and depended on French imports of some basic necessities. At the same time, troops were being called up for the unpopular 1637 expedition to Labourd, the harvests were bad, and the king's armies billeted in Navarra took what they pleased without paying. (Idoate tells how the much-abused Valley of Guesalaz complained in 1637 about the soldiers' depredations, saying they descended on the community like "so many lightning strokes.")

During such periods, traffic in contraband increased.

The most rigid laws were against the export of horses, which could be used in warfare against Spain. A sixteenth-century law stipulated the death penalty for the third offense, if the horses were destined for France. Export of iron was also closely controlled, with one curious exception: Yanguas tells us that the *Cinco Villas* (five towns in the Valley of the Bidasoa, near the French border) could send iron to France even in time of war in exchange for food products, if they obtained a license from the viceroy. This indicates how much Navarra still depended on imports for the very essentials of life.

But this dependence was to change. Hard work on the part of the industrious Basques at home, and their growing commercial contacts outside the kingdom, laid the groundwork for the prosperity that was to accompany the new century.

XIII

Cautious Progress

AT FIRST GLANCE, THE COINCIDENCE of the dawn of the eighteenth century with the arrival of the first Bourbon on Spain's throne seems to make history fall into neat and manageable blocks. But if this is a hasty conclusion for Spanish history as a whole, it is still less valid for Navarra.

For Spain, the Hapsburg dynasty's extinction was accompanied by a violent war over the succession, involving most of the countries of Europe before it was settled in favor of Philip V, the French contender. But once the Bourbon was securely on the throne, the same lethargy and stagnation, or at best only halting progress, that had characterized Spain under the later Hapsburgs continued. Castile, synonymous with Spain to a growingly materialistic, rationalist world, became an international laughingstock for its outmoded devotion to "noble" blood and its scorn of "crass" commerce. The monarchy was not revitalized. The Bourbon kings, like their predecessors, lacked the strength of character to rule alone and depended on ministers of varying ability.

What of Navarra? The two major wars in which Spain was involved during the 1700s touched it, but not as scathingly as they did the rest of the Iberian Peninsula.

The War of the Succession came very close. Navarra officially supported the Bourbon Philip in battles on Navarra's own soil, but the population as a whole remained indifferent or obstructionist. The War against the Convention at the end of the century was fought in Navarra but again failed to arouse a strong crusading zeal, in contrast with the subsequent War of Independence, 1808 to 1814.

The more penetrating effects of social and economic forces at work in Navarra had very little to do with Castile or the rest of Spain, and stemmed from the kingdom's own private past. As Caro Baroja has pointed out, regional history does not necessarily adjust to the pace and rhythms of national history.[1]

Navarra in the eighteenth century continued to work toward the solid commercial prosperity that had begun to take shape in the previous century. Its middle classes began to venture farther away from home base, as they saw opportunities for enrichment. Navarrese peasants were better off than others in Spain; Basque agricultural laborers were the envy of their peninsular counterparts. The international embroilments of the Castilian rulers had little effect on Navarra's careful steps toward greater security and well-being.

THE WAR OF THE SUCCESSION

This rather complicated dispute resulted from two facts. First, Charles II of Spain died childless in 1700. In a last-minute decision, after many vacillations and under pressure from all sides, he had changed his will and designated the Bourbon prince, Philip of Anjou, grandson of Louis XIV of France, as heir to the kingdom of Spain. But (the second fact) a case could be made, and was, that Philip had no right to the throne. His grandmother, María Teresa, daughter of Spain's Philip IV, had renounced her and her descendants' claims to Spain when she married Louis XIV, in 1659.

Besides Philip of Anjou, there were two other aspirants. They were the Bavarian Prince Joseph Ferdinand, a great-grandson of that same Philip IV of Spain; and the Austrian Archduke Charles, second son of the emperor, and, like Philip of Anjou, the grandson of a Spanish princess (María, daughter of Philip III).

The European powers, scenting a threat to continental equilibrium, began disputing and pulling strings long before Charles's death. In 1698 Louis XIV proposed that the Spanish empire be divided among the three claimants. The Italian territory of Milan would go to the Archduke Charles. The remaining Italian lands and Vasconavarra (Navarra and the other Basque lands) would go to France (an indication that for Louis the Navarre Question still might have a spark of life). The rest would go to Prince Joseph of Bavaria. But the emperor, Leopold I, rejected the suggestion; and in any event one claimant, Prince Joseph, died in 1699, which altered the alignments.

After Charles's long-expected death (November 1, 1700), the situation became the pretext for a general war. Louis XIV was, perhaps apocryphally, reported to have exclaimed, in anticipation of a French victory, "Now there are no more Pyrenees!"

Austria, ignoring the will of Charles II, supported the Archduke Charles and was joined by Holland and England, and later by Portugal. All members of this Grand Alliance were anxious to curb the pretensions of France and Spain, which had formed an unusual and formidable partnership.

Philip of Anjou was crowned in Madrid in 1701. A year later, the English-Austrian-Dutch Alliance began to attack, and Spain and France responded. The War of the Spanish Succession was to go on until 1713. It was to be decided less by force of arms than by another accident of succession. When the Archduke Charles succeeded his brother Joseph as emperor, the English and Dutch were even more alarmed by the prospect of a joint Spanish-Austrian crown than they had been by the Spanish-French combination. So by a series of peace treaties among all the disputants, Philip was finally recognized by all Europe as Spain's legitimate ruler.

In Spain (only one of the many battlefields of this war), the Alliance's first assault, at Cadiz, was a failure. The next was through Portugal, where an army led by the Archduke Charles landed in 1703. Gibraltar fell in 1704. In 1705 Catalonia rose for the archduke and recognized him as Charles III. The battles ranged over Aragon, Castile, Murcia, Valencia; but did not penetrate far into Navarra.

NAVARRA IN THE WAR OF THE SPANISH SUCCESSION

Navarra was most affected by this war on its Aragon frontier along the River Ebro. Zaragoza and all Aragon had declared for the archduke in 1706. Across the river in Navarra's *ribera,*

Tudela and Corella also came out for the archduke. Cascante resisted and was twice taken. Olite, Marcilla and Villafranca were threatened.

In spite of the threat, the *Diputación* and the citizenry objected when the viceroy wanted conscripts sent into Aragon— that is, outside the kingdom. Falces, a town in the south and well within the danger zone, provided a notable example of the recalcitrance. Opposition to recruitment there was so strong that the draftees had to be locked up in the courthouse to keep them from deserting. But they could still protest; they broke up furniture and threw the pieces out the window, with some injuries to passersby below. For this rebellion they were tried and sentenced by a special military court appointed by the viceroy. The *Diputación* tried to have the judgment reversed, on the grounds that the offenders should have been tried by a regular civil court, because they were not yet formally inducted when they staged the revolt. But the viceroy refused to admit the *contrafuero,* and in fact added insult to injury by requiring the town to pay all the damages.[2]

Later (in 1706), when invasion seemed imminent, the *Diputación* had to admit that an army should be raised. Meantime, the billeting of French troops in Navarra was provoking the usual objections that arose whenever outside armies were present. The *Diputación* received at least one anonymous memorial warning of the danger of an uprising in Pamplona if the French stayed.

Still, even up to the moment of real peril for the kingdom, in 1710, the viceroy had to push and pull, cajole and threaten, to get a defensive force shaped up. Until the Austrian's armies were actually at the border, the Navarrese invoked the fuero that said they need not fight outside the kingdom.

Only when the towns on the eastern border with Aragon— Sangüesa, Lumbier, Urroz, Aioiz—had fallen, and when others in the vicinity of Olite and Tudela were occupied, and when enemy troops were intruding and pillaging to within a league of Pamplona—only then did the viceroy and his defending general, the count of Merlun, succeed in mustering a sufficient force to drive the enemy out of Navarra (January 5, 1711).

Navarra's reluctance to fight was not due to disloyalty to Philip. The people recognized him as their natural ruler, descendant of their own Albret kings who, in 1553, with the birth of

Henri de Navarre, had merged with the Bourbon line. They had welcomed him to Pamplona when he made a formal visit in 1706 to be acclaimed as king. But by all accounts, they did not see the War of the Spanish Succession as a war that threatened their own lives, liberties or property very seriously.

The only other military event that affected Navarra much during the reign of Philip V was the invasion of the kingdom that accompanied the brief war between Spain and the Quadruple Alliance (France, England, Austria and Holland) in 1719. The French invaded at Vera, in the Valley of the Bidasoa. The *Diputación* sent a force of fifteen hundred men, and Philip himself came to the front to encourage the troops. Peace was signed in 1721.

On the whole, Philip paid scant attention to his small northern kingdom. He visited only twice during his forty-six-year reign. But out of gratitude for the loyalty of Vasconavarra during the War of the Succession, he left their foral liberties strictly alone. This was the origin of the appellation "the exempt provinces."

He was not so generous in the Crown of Aragon. He abolished the fueros of Valencia and Aragon in 1707, of Mallorca in 1715, and in 1716 of rebellious Catalonia, which had not only declared for Archduke Charles, but had actually welcomed him as "Charles III." These were not simply decrees of retribution; they were steps in the process of centralization of power in Madrid. Only Navarra, in all Spain, was still called a kingdom.

However, even there the Cortes met less and less often. Meetings still depended on convocation by the king. Philip convoked the Cortes infrequently, only when he considered that some transcendent event warranted it, as in 1709, for the swearing in of his son Luis (who died in 1724); and in 1712, when he formally renounced any claim to the throne of France.

Even so, the Cortes in Navarra met oftener than did the Cortes in Madrid; eleven times for Navarra, eight for Madrid during the century. (Madrid's Cortes, after 1709, incorporated those of Castile, Aragon and Valencia.)

Another enduring institution was that of the viceroy, who still represented the monarch in Navarra and only in Navarra. In all the rest of Spain, Royal Audiences, presided over by captains general, brought Madrid to the regional capitals: Zaragoza, Valencia, Barcelona and Mallorca.

That other jealously guarded institution, the open town council, also survived throughout the Basque country, despite the trend in the rest of Spain to centralization through *ayuntamientos.*
Again, only Navarra still had its own independent judiciary in the eighteenth century. Courts in other provinces were subordinated to the two powerful Castilian chancelleries of Valladolid and Granada.
So much autonomy was not likely to endear Vasconavarra to its neighbors. For Castilian financiers the "exempt provinces" was a term of contempt. But the Basques made their accustomed reply. Though they were indeed exempt from the taxes levied on the rest of Spain, they were unique in being not only self-sufficient, making no demands on the central treasury, but indeed regularly voting the king's subsidy. The king's demands rose steadily through the 1700s and by 1801 Navarra's "donation" was more than all it had voted during the preceding century.
Nor was Navarra exempt from administrative burdens. Red tape, paperwork, and backed-up appeals clogged the governmental machinery so much that, according to Desdevizes du Dézert, interpreter of the eighteenth century, if the files of the *Consejo Real* in Pamplona had been arranged on shelves placed end to end they would have stretched nearly two miles.[3]

STABILITY AND PROSPERITY

The kingdom was more prosperous than in the preceding century. Commerce had begun to flourish. Spanish customs checkpoints, still on the French frontier in 1712, were moved to the River Ebro on Navarra's southern border in 1722. This meant there was almost completely free trade between Navarra and the Basque provinces and France. Even in time of war with France, such essentials as food, drink and fuel could pass through the mountains. Basques on both sides of the border routinely signed treaties of friendship during the century's wars, to preserve neutrality—and free trade.
In contrast with Castile, Navarra was notable for effective law enforcement and good administration during the eighteenth century. Its excellent road system got its start under the count of Gages, viceroy from 1749 to 1753, during the rather uneventful reign of Ferdinand VI, son of Philip V. It was this

viceroy who was admired by a traveling French author who wrote in 1752 that the count had succeeded in bringing to heel the Navarrese people—"the most arrogant and difficult to govern in Europe."[4]

Society, though severely stratified, was probably less so than in the rest of Spain, and was not restive. The rural agricultural population had enough to eat, sturdy homes, warm clothing; they owned their little farms and were their own masters; they lived modestly and frugally, but far better than their counterparts elsewhere. They were content.

The only really mistreated and miserable inhabitants were the *agotes*. By this century slavery had practically disappeared in Navarra. But the pariah *agotes* still existed. These outcasts of society, who may have been descended from Arian Visigoths, Muslims, Jews or some other "heretical" group, were said to smell bad and to have physical deformities and special infirmities. They were suspected of less than sincere Catholicism. They were required to live apart in their own cantons, in Basse Navarre as well as Navarra. Many made their homes in the valleys of Baztán and Roncal. Like society's rejects in other lands and times, they were not admitted to guilds or most callings. The *agotes* were mostly woodsmen or carpenters. They were few by the eighteenth century, but were not legally emancipated until the Cortes finally granted them equal rights with other citizens in 1818.[5]

At the other end of the social scale were the nobles, who constituted from five to ten percent of the Navarrese population at the end of the eighteenth century, according to one estimate.[6] This was one of the highest proportions in Spain, though the other Basque lands had even higher percentages. (In Guipúzcoa, *all* inhabitants were called noble at one time during the century.)

Between the peasantry and the nobility were the solid middle classes, who at last during this century began to occupy a position of well-being and substance, not only in their native land but also in Madrid and beyond. The ancient disinclination to get involved in peninsular affairs was giving way in the face of tempting opportunities to win fame and fortune elsewhere.

In Navarra they pursued careers as manufacturers, merchants, timber producers, governmental officials, financiers, lawyers. They acquired respectable incomes and some amassed fortunes.

Often, younger sons had to leave the kingdom in order to carve out a future for themselves. The Basques of northern Navarra and the other provinces still observed the practice of bequeathing farms and property intact to one son or daughter, usually the eldest, rather than break up family holdings for distribution among all the children. This was in contrast to customs of much of Spain, where inheritances of tiny parcels of land were the rule. It meant, in the Basque Country, that family holdings remained intact, and younger sons had to go elsewhere to find their own livelihood. Many of them did better than their brothers who stayed home. Some found a place for themselves in the lucrative trade with the Americas. Overseas, they pursued military or mercantile careers, or served the king or the church. Many Navarrese family fortunes were founded on these New World ventures.[7]

Some went to Madrid and became personages of note: served the court, did well as doctors, churchmen, men of business. There they kept in touch with each other and with Navarra through the *Real Congregación de San Fermín* (founded in Madrid in 1683). In this they followed the example of other ethnic groups in Spain's capital, where there were clubs for the Italians, Portuguese, Flemish, French and Irish. In the capital, many who gained recognition and royal favor moved from the merchant class to the nobility, perfectly possible if one had sufficient money and reputation.

Not forgetting their origins, they went home to build imposing mansions and palaces, not only in Pamplona, but also in other central and southern cities (Tudela, Sangüesa, Estella), and in the Pyrenean valley towns. Fine multistory stone homes, many displaying seigniorial arms, still attest to the material well-being and pride of birthplace of these eighteenth-century emigrés from the valleys of Baztán and Roncal, and elsewhere.

This century also marks the proliferation of splendid baroque construction throughout Navarra. Town halls and public buildings sprang up, churches and monasteries, as well as magnificent chapels and bell towers, and embellishments for existing churches and cathedrals. Pamplona's own quintessentially baroque town hall and its archepiscopal palace both date from this century.

So does the remodeling of the fifteenth-century Gothic cathedral. In the 1780s the old facade was replaced with a twin-towered, Grecian-pillared, neoclassic facade. This addition, now topped with a neon cross, prompted Michener to call the Pamplona cathedral "the ugliest beautiful church in existence."[8] Once inside, the visitor soon discovers the beauty, as in the handsomely carved tombs of Charles III of Navarra and his queen Leonora, and in the universally admired cloisters, unchanged since the fourteenth century.

Travelers through Pamplona during the second half of the eighteenth century, en route to the more animated centers of the peninsula, and usually having just left enlightened France, found it somnolent and dull. Their comments are not to be taken too seriously, being typical of tourists in a hurry to get somewhere else, but many are revealing. Pamplona was generally recognized, for example, as a clean, exemplary city in comparison with others in Spain, with attractive buildings and industrious citizens. Alert visitors recognized the cleavage between *montaña* and *ribera*. The mountain dwellers were considered frugal, of simple habits, and "with ideas as limited as their horizons." In the south, near the Ebro, on the other hand, the inhabitants were found to be addicted to cardplaying and bullfights, nocturnal carousing and fisticuffs.[9]

Casanova came through on his way to Madrid in 1767. Of his departure, he recalled that for the first twenty leagues out of Pamplona the road was fine (as good as in France), then—"I cannot say that the road became bad, but rather that I did not find a road at all."[10] The immediate worsening of the roads as soon as a traveler crosses from Navarra into other provinces was to be widely commented on well into our day.

Pamplona's population by the 1780s was about fourteen thousand. It had a reputation as a well-run city, with a body of progressive city fathers. They installed street lighting and paved the streets with flagstones just before the turn of the century. One visitor in 1783, commenting on the aqueduct, then under construction, that was to bring water from Noain to Pamplona, said: "The gentlemen of Pamplona have a genius for thinking of and carrying out projects of much importance."[11]

In spite of all this civic improvement, the Pamplona of the late 1700s was still confined within its medieval walls. The five drawbridges were still raised every night, and the city gates locked. Products of the kingdom's agriculture (wool, wine, wheat) still supported its commerce and few industries, which by now included one paper mill.

Though there were many taverns, there were also many convents. And though then, as now, the city came riotously alive during the annual San Fermín festivities, for the rest of the year it was calm and industrious, relatively unruffled by the winds of conflict that were beginning to sweep across Spain.

The irreproachable but passive Ferdinand VI, son of Philip V, was followed on the Spanish throne by the reformist Charles III. During his reign Navarra's calm prosperity continued. Then, almost coinciding with his death, the cauldron of revolution in France overflowed, threatening the equilibrium of all Europe.

THE CENTURY'S LAST WAR

The War against the Convention (1793 to 1795) was actually the first violent chapter in Spain's entry into the nineteenth century.

Spain's sympathies were, naturally, on the side of the French monarchy. After the declaration of war by the French Convention—the body that had just declared France a republic and had executed Louis XVI—the Madrid government tried to mount a "defensive attack," with mixed success.

In the western Pyrenees the French got across the border and occupied Zugarramurdi, site of caves where locals accused of witchcraft had sought refuge from the Inquisition in the sixteenth century. The French armies found no such refuge, and were driven out in short order.

The next year they were back, threatening to advance through the Valley of Baztán and from Roncesvalles on Pamplona. The Baztanese, though called on by their king to take up arms and resist, demurred. The French soon penetrated far into the Valley of the Bidasoa and also swept through and occupied most of the Basque Country's northern strongholds, including Irun, Fuenterrabia, San Sebastián, Bilbao, and even Vitoria, well to the south and in the interior of Alava.

The valleys of Roncal and Salazar to the east were also threatened. Here, resistance was enthusiastic and effective; nevertheless, the enemy occupied and burned Ochagavía at the head of the Valley of Salazar.

A year later, in 1795, Pamplona itself was in danger of siege. All men from sixteen to sixty were called up. But before an army was formed, peace was signed (July 22, 1795). The French successes on all fronts left the Spanish no other choice.

Except for the northeastern valley dwellers, not many in Navarra had been willing to take part in the war, in spite of the apparent threat to their native soil. There were two reasons: friendship with France, due to proximity and consanguinity; and a weariness with wars waged for remote causes on behalf of rulers who used their own subjects as pawns in their international political games.

But in less than fifteen years, another attack from France would elicit a diametrically opposite reaction. Navarra viewed with horror and fiercely resisted Napoleon's designs on Spain.

Not so Madrid. Charles IV, who succeeded his father in 1788, was more a placater than a fighter. He was chiefly anxious to stay on amicable terms with his wife and with his (and her) chief minister Godoy. The policy of this *monarchie à trois* toward France was one of toadying, while presenting an appearance of neutrality in the real struggle (France versus England).

By his appeasement and eventual abdication, Charles IV made inevitable the War of Independence.

XIV

Continuity in Crisis

IN THE NINETEENTH CENTURY A CONfluence of forces threatened Navarra's historical values and its very existence as a discrete state.

France was still a menace, for though the War against the Convention had temporarily repulsed foreign armies from Spain, the upheavals that the French Revolution had engendered still reverberated, on the military as well as the ideological front.

The predominantly conservative residents of Navarra felt particularly menaced by the encroachment of liberalism, republicanism and anti-clericalism, the new ideas that had penetrated Spain in spite of the best efforts of many in the government of Charles IV to insulate the country. Navarra, perhaps more than any other part of Spain, exemplified and championed the old ways that were now challenged.

But most unwelcome and dangerous was dictation from a remote Madrid where the contractual nature of Navarra's ties with her king was ignored or disdained.

To meet these threats, the kingdom's defenders drew themselves up for a last-ditch effort, which before long found its vitality and justification in the Carlist cause.

The effort failed, but without it Navarra might not have been able to achieve and hold its reputation as the most "independent" province in modern Spain.

THE WAR OF INDEPENDENCE

Chief among the institutions Navarra cherished was the monarchy. But the Spanish monarchy had degenerated from a level of respectable competence (Charles III) to utter foolishness (Charles IV). Nevertheless, Navarra remained loyal to this king who had no more sense than to put his head in the mouth of the lion Napoleon.

After Charles IV abdicated, in March 1808, and fled to France, his son Ferdinand VII succeeded, and reached a new low in kingship. He displayed not so much foolishness as perfidy, in his betrayal of his parents and his country. In spite of his servile collaboration with the French, he too was forced to abdicate, so that Napoleon could install his brother Joseph Bonaparte as Spanish ruler.

In the Madrid uprising of May 2, 1808, the Spanish people, already out of patience with the collaborationist prime minister Godoy, turned violently against the French usurpers.

The *Dos de Mayo* is as significant for Spain as the 4th of July is for the United States. It precipitated the Peninsular War or, as it is known in Spain, the War of Independence. For six years the armies of Napoleon were pitted against Spain and Portugal and their British allies.

Throughout the war the Navarrese, and many others in Spain, still called Ferdinand "El Deseado," the longed-for one. They saw him as their champion against the ministerial excesses of Godoy, and the restorer of the good old days when the monarch truly cared about his people's welfare. They kept this faith in him all during his six-year enforced absence as Napoleon's captive guest in France, from 1808 to 1814.

Navarra was occupied even before the war began, when the French General Junot's armies, which were overrunning northern Spain, headed for Lisbon.

At this point, France and Spain were officially allies; Napoleon had maneuvered the country into a treaty of alliance in 1807. So when the French reached Pamplona through Roncesvalles, in February 1808, they were admitted, but as guests and allies, not conquerors.

The French general, the wily d'Armagnac, requested that the viceroy, the marquis of Villesantoro, give lodging within the *Ciudadela,* the city's main fortress, to certain of his troops whose loyalty he pretended to doubt. The idea (he said) was to keep them shut up and out of mischief. But the viceroy refused.

D'Armagnac then devised another plan. From his lodgings in a palace nearby, he sent part of his troops to collect their daily ration of bread from the stores in the *Ciudadela.* Meantime, he had arranged for another French contingent to begin playing in the newly fallen snow that covered the ground, throwing snowballs at one another. The first group of French soldiers came back out of the *Ciudadela* and stood on the bridge as though to watch the fun—with weapons concealed under their capes. The unsuspecting Spanish garrison also paused to watch the Frenchmen frolicking in the snow. Suddenly all the French soldiers fell on the off-guard Spanish. Other French troops, who had been hiding in the palace, rushed out, overcame the *Ciudadela's* garrison, and took possession.[1]

With its fortress occupied by the French, Pamplona was in their power and remained so for most of the war. But the Navarrese resisted as vigorously as they could under the circumstances, with guerrilla activity throughout the kingdom, and with stubborn recalcitrance on the administrative front by the *Diputación.*

After the final abdication by Charles IV, and his ceding of the Spanish Crown to Joseph Bonaparte, the *Diputación* still refused to recognize Joseph as king. They alleged that this was a change of dynasty that could be acted on only by the Cortes.

Meantime, Napoleon was planning how to administer his new acquisition. The first step was to write a new constitution. Though this document abolished most institutions that permitted self-government, the fueros of the Basque provinces and Navarra were retained, though with the provision that they be "examined" and presumably modified.

Not included in the Constitution, but seriously proposed by one of the French authors, was the creation of a Basque state that would incorporate the Spanish and French Basque provinces and Navarra. The new state was even given a name: Nueva Fenicia, with the French and Spanish sections to be known as Nueva Tiro and Nueva Sidon, respectively.

Whether Napoleon took this plan seriously is unknown. But

he did intend, somehow, to segregate all Spanish lands north of the Ebro and incorporate them in the French part of his empire, rather than leave them in Spain, which he planned as an "independent" state to be ruled by his puppet Joseph.

Navarra's *Diputación* did not take kindly to the foreign presence. Feeling harassed by the French who kept intervening in their meetings and usurping their powers, the members eventually resolved to leave Pamplona. Surreptitiously, they moved to Tudela in November 1808, and issued a manifesto to all Navarra, calling the citizens to arms, in the name of fueros, church, king and country. Before leaving Pamplona the deputies had managed to avoid recognizing Joseph as king. Now they swore loyalty to Ferdinand VII, and offered loyalty to the *Junta Central*. This body was already trying to form a Spanish government in "exile"—in Cadiz—while the French continued to occupy Madrid and other major cities.

The *Diputación's* tribulations were not over. The French advance in the fall of 1808, with Napoleon himself in charge, included a march upon and the capture of Tudela, November 23. The deputies left the city and wandered through Aragon and La Rioja, seeking a safe and suitable seat for their meetings. They settled briefly in Calahorra, Rincón de Soto, and Huesca, among other places.

The bishop of Pamplona, too, suffered for his loyalty to a threatened kingdom. He refused to write a pastoral letter in favor of the new king, or to sing a Te Deum for the French armies' victories. He was then so much in disfavor that he fled to Lérida for refuge.

The response of the citizens of Navarra to their *Diputación's* call to arms was of necessity scattered and uncoordinated, but it was widespread. They quickly organized guerrillalike bands to attack the French wherever they could. The first was assembled by the parish priest of Valcarlos, just south of the Pass of Roncesvalles. The most famous of these bands was led by a young student, Francisco Javier Mina. After seven months of daring and effective attacks on the French, he was taken prisoner and removed to France. His uncle, Francisco Espoz y Mina, took up the banner and led the valiant *División de Navarra* to victory after victory against the vastly superior French forces. During the blockade, the French occupiers' reprisals against the city's inhabitants were swift and cruel, with executions and public displays of bodies.

Meantime, the Spanish armies and their English allies pressured the French. Lord Wellington, commander of the allied army, led his troops up from Portugal in pursuit of the fleeing Joseph Bonaparte. He won the final battle of the war in Vitoria in June 1813. The pursuing allied armies swept across Navarra, leaving nearly as much ruin in their wake as if they had been enemies. They besieged Pamplona, still held by the French, for four months. Finally after heroic resistance and the loss of twenty-three hundred men, the beleaguered French defenders capitulated.

By November 1813, Navarra was again free and unoccupied.

But even before the despised usurpers were expelled, Spain had begun to worry the governmental question. The absolute monarchy was considerably discredited. What, then, was the alternative?

KINGDOM OR PROVINCE

The question deeply concerned Navarra. For the next thirty years there was to be a tug-of-war between Madrid—where supporters of a strong centralized constitutional government were gaining power—and Navarra, holding out for autonomy and fueros.

Navarra was represented at the constituent Cortes that met in Cadiz in 1810 to study the matter. But the Navarrese representatives were not official, so Pamplona felt no qualms about repudiating the liberal constitution that was voted. Although the document's preamble paid tribute to the ancient fueros of the Vascongadas and Navarra, it then proceeded to abolish them. The objective was centralization. Regional autonomy had to yield to centralized constitutional unity, with appropriate limitations on the monarch's power. Such a governmental theory was anathema to the proud Basques.

Navarra could do nothing about its relegation to provincial status—except protest. The hero of the War of Independence, General Espoz y Mina, placed a copy of the despised Constitution on a chair and ordered a firing squad to shoot it.

The symbolic execution was unnecessary. The Constitution of Cadiz died a natural death without ever becoming effective. When Ferdinand VII was restored to the throne in 1814, his first act was to refuse to recognize it.

Navarra was again a kingdom, within the monarchy of Spain. Ferdinand, responding to a request from the *Diputación* that he explicitly restore the kingdom's fueros, did so in a formal decree (August 1814). Navarra rejoiced.

But Spanish liberals had not given up, and there were some even in Navarra. In 1820 liberal army officers, disillusioned with Ferdinand, forced him to accept the Constitution of Cadiz. The Spanish people, however—especially conservatives in the north —were unwilling to support such a dangerous swing to the left.

The matter was decided by the *Guerra Realista* (Royalist War), 1820 to 1823. It was Spain's first civil war.

As wars go, it was not much. Other Spanish wars of the nineteenth century overshadowed it. But in some ways it was a proving ground for the opposing viewpoints that were to clash spectacularly in the First Carlist War ten years later. On the one side were the royalists, absolutists and traditionalists. On the other were the liberals, constitutionalists (supporters of the Constitution of Cadiz), and the *afrancesados* (those who had sided with the French during the War of Independence).

The royalists' aim was to free Ferdinand, whom they saw as a prisoner of the liberals. In fact, though, he was simply following the line of least resistance in going along with the constitutionalists.

NAVARRA'S ROLE IN THE GUERRA REALISTA

In Navarra, first came civil disturbances protesting the reimposition of the Constitution and the return to provincial status that it decreed. The public was outraged at secularization of monasteries, at orders that priests must defend the Constitution in their sermons, and at the renaming of streets and plazas for it. When a battalion of national militia arrived in Pamplona in June 1821, rumors flew that it was there to "subjugate Navarra." There were frequent clashes between students and citizens of Pamplona on the one hand, and the soldiers on the other. One of the most violent, on the feast day of Saint Joseph in March 1822, ended with the townsfolk pursuing the soldiers into the Church of San Saturnino and hacking at them even in the sanctuary—a battle that left seven dead and twenty-nine wounded.[2]

Anti-Constitution feeling ran high elsewhere too: there were uprisings in Seville, Málaga, Granada, Valencia and Galicia. But actual armed guerrilla bands took the field only in the north, largely in Navarra and Catalonia. The first organized regional royalist rising was in Navarra in 1821. The *Junta Realista,* organized to spearhead royalist opposition to Madrid liberalism, urged the Navarrese to fight for religion, king and country—the same banners that would be held up before them in the Carlist wars. In 1822 armed guerrilla bands sallied down from their Pyrenean strongholds to attack towns where liberal governments were in power.

Navarra's royalists did battle outside the kingdom as well. Some troops marched off to help their allies in Catalonia, where the enemy liberal army was led by Navarra's former hero, the old warhorse Espoz y Mina. He had switched sides since the War of Independence.

Meantime, the crowned heads of Europe had been viewing with increasing uneasiness the liberals' threat to legitimate absolutism in the peninsula. At the Congress of Verona, in 1822, they considered how to deal with it. Austria, France, Russia and Prussia agreed on armed intervention to restore Ferdinand's powers.

But as it turned out, only France, where a Bourbon was again on the throne, took the field. A nephew of Louis XVIII, the duke of Angoulême led the grandiloquently named "Hundred Thousand Sons of Saint Louis" across the frontier on April 7, 1823. The Navarrese welcomed them enthusiastically, except in Pamplona. That city was officially in the liberal camp because of its Madrid-sponsored *Diputación* and the presence of liberal troops to man its fortifications. The city stood under siege for six months, yielding in September 1823.

The French army's advance southward was more a march of triumph than a campaign. It made its way to Cadiz, where the liberal government had taken Ferdinand, accepted the city's capitulation, and "liberated" the king.

The *Junta Realista de Navarra* was dissolved, after yielding its powers to the *Diputación* that had been serving in 1820 before the liberal triennium.

Ferdinand's first step, after restoration of his full powers, was to nullify all the Constitutional government's acts, and throw the liberals out. Royalists in Navarra were elated at restoration of their kingdom's sovereignty and their fueros. The victory was seen as one for "fueros, God and king."

But the king's pedestal was shaky. Ferdinand shortly demanded more money from Navarra for the royal treasury, reminding his subjects there that he had earned it by restoring their foral liberties. The *Diputación,* discouraged, sent word to the king that his faithful Navarrese saw themselves practically despoiled of all the liberties he had sworn to uphold.

"El Deseado" had lost his luster for his subjects in Navarra. But, on the eve of the Carlist wars, the institution of the monarchy had not.

THE CARLIST CAUSE

Many wars start for one cause but continue for others. The First Carlist War certainly kept altering its objectives as it went along.

The dynastic issue was the trigger. Closely linked were religious motives, the patriotic fervor that surfaced in the Vasconavarrese when they sensed a threat to their autonomy, and the romantic attraction—especially for the young—of a struggle for such lofty ideals. The presence of many trained soldiers and officers in the land—veterans of the century's two preceding wars—was also a factor; they saw a new war as a way to avoid unemployment.

Later the fueros became a lively issue, but were hardly mentioned at the outset.[3]

Though the king took third place in the Carlists' much-bruited slogan *"Dios, patria, rey"* ("God, country, king"), the kingship had top importance. Not so much how the ruler of Spain should reach the throne, but what kind of ruler: an absolute despot, or a constitutional monarch? In the early 1830s, Carlos, younger brother of Ferdinand VII, personified the former; Ferdinand, and by association his daughter, the latter. The traditionalists and royalists in the north supported Carlos initially because he seemed to promise a return to the good old days when kings were kings, their power undiluted by sharing with a legislature, an oligarchy and much of the army. The dynastic issue thus merged into the great and shifting debate of the century, with reactionaries pitted against liberals in much of Europe as well as in Spain.

But in the beginning the question was only this: Who had the true claim to succeed Ferdinand—his daughter Isabella or his younger brother Carlos?

Here is a vastly simplified account of the background of the dynastic quarrel, and how it was seen in Navarra.

Since the thirteenth century, Spain's royal succession had been in accord with the *Siete Partidas* (seven laws) of Alfonso X, which recognized the right of females to succeed.

Philip V, first Bourbon king of Spain, changed the rules with his Law of Succession. In 1713 he decreed that henceforth no woman could succeed to the throne, nor could anyone not born in Spain.

In 1789, during the reign of Philip's great grandson Charles IV, the Cortes secretly approved an annulment of Philip's Law of Succession. This act not only restored women to the line of succession, but also made it permissible for Charles (who had been born in Naples) to rule. But Charles, mysteriously, never gave the law—called the Pragmatic Sanction—the public announcement that would have made it completely legal.

In 1812 the Cortes of Cadiz came out for primogeniture, with female succession allowable in the absence of a male with a closer or more direct descent. But Ferdinand VII wiped this out, along with the whole Constitution of Cadiz, when he abrogated it upon returning to the throne in 1814.

However, Ferdinand took no specific stand on the succession laws until his third wife died, in 1829. None of his wives had given him an heir. Three things happened within ten months:

First, Ferdinand remarried, in December 1829. His fourth wife was his niece, the Princess María Cristina of Naples.

Secondly, he promulgated Charles IV's Pragmatic Sanction, to insure that should his new queen bear him a daughter, his issue would still succeed him—and his younger brother Carlos would not.

And finally, his daughter Isabella was born, in October 1830.

The king's brother Carlos made no public moves to build support for his cause during Ferdinand's few remaining years, but his supporters did. The royalists and *apostólicos* (those who would have restored the absolutism of the Hapsburg kings) were still vocal after their successes from 1820 to 1823. Now they had a rallying point for their antiliberal sentiments.

Here arises the paradox of the Carlist cause: Navarrese popular support for Carlos, in spite of Ferdinand's pains to legitimize Isabella's claim.

In Navarra respect for legality, as we have repeatedly seen, was paramount. Every king from time immemorial, once he complied with all the required formalities, commanded the unswerving loyalty of his Navarrese subjects. When Ferdinand died, in September 1833, all conditions existed for a legally justifiable recognition of Isabella. Ferdinand had gone through the proper procedures in naming her as his heir and María Cristina as his regent.

The Cortes, still functioning sporadically in Navarra, could not logically argue against Isabella's rights. Back in 1713, when Philip V had altered the laws of succession to exclude women from the throne of Spain, the new law was neither presented to nor ratified by the Cortes of Navarra. Hence the prior laws permitting women to succeed remained on the books as far as the legal minds of the northern kingdom were concerned.

Furthermore, Navarra itself had never observed the Salic Law (excluding women) and had in fact had some half dozen queens in its history as an independent kingdom.[4]

So there was both precedent and constitutional justification for the *Diputación's* proclamation of Isabella's sovereignty, in March 1834. There was also some prudence behind it; the Madrid-run garrison had the city fully in its control.

Yet outside the palace of the *Diputación* (aside from certain exceptions in Pamplona) and throughout the rural areas, anti-Isabella and pro-Carlos sentiment was open and fierce and widespread. Exceptions were from the well-to-do commercial class, and those closely associated with the central government and the army.

The explanation of this paradoxical disloyalty to the lawful monarch among most of the population must be found in the people's deep belief that their very traditions were so seriously threatened by the weak liberal government in Madrid that only a strong man could save them. So they concentrated their hopes on Carlos.

The next major issue, after the kingship, was *Dios:* the crusade to protect the ancient Catholic faith. This certainly became a major objective of the Carlists, and an understandable one, in view of the liberals' anticlericalism and the support they received from the dangerous "heretics" in France and England. For the Carlists, liberalism and Catholicism were completely imcompatible. And for the Carlists, the clergy's support went far beyond sermons and chaplainship. Many a militant priest fought in the ranks. The clergy was, in fact, almost universally on the side of Carlos, and was suspected, usually with reason, by the Cristinists of fomenting rebellion. (The Madrid government's armies were known as Cristinists during the regency of María Cristina.) The Cristinist General Rodil complained, when the war was underway, that "the most obstinate rebels are undoubtedly found among the clergy, especially in small villages, where not one remains when the queen's troops approach, and no way can be found to bring them over, though we treat them with the utmost respect."

Patria was the third cherished ideal of the Carlists. Love of country can mean many things, and has been appropriated by both sides in most wars. But for the Navarrese, in this war, it undoubtedly had a special connotation, beyond its vague reference to a Spain that Navarra did not yet feel much identity with. But *Patria,* when understood as the Kingdom of Navarra, was well worth fighting for.

As for the fueros, frequently cited as the primary Carlist war aim, they actually were not a significant issue at the beginning. Though the main Carlist strength was in the area where the ancient foral tradition was strongest (Vasconia, Navarra, Aragon, Catalonia, Valencia), the cry to defend the fueros was not raised until the war was well along. After the death of their great General Zumalacárregui, the Carlist junta had to find a new stimulant to raise recruits and money. They seized on the Basques' devotion to their regional liberties as a propaganda tool. They pointed to the presumed anti-foral intent of the Cristinist armies as a bogey when trying to drum up support among the rural and peasant populace. The other side followed suit: the Madrid government and generals periodically promised Vasconavarra that if victorious, the liberals would still conserve the fueros.

But as the Cristinist government, increasingly dominated by the more extreme or "progressive" liberals, kept protesting that it would respect the Basque fueros, the suspicious Vasconavarrese fought harder to hold onto them.

To be sure, attachment to their fueros by the citizens of Navarra may not have been totally disinterested. Only the Navarrese in all Spain handled their own finances at this time. There were no customs barriers between Navarra and France, but rather between Navarra and the rest of Spain. Only in Navarra did the Cortes, through its *Diputación,* still function. Only Navarra still had its own courts, raised its own militia. A final factor in the war was the persistent cleavage between town and country, *ribera* and *montaña.* This was particularly marked in the north and east, where conservative rural folk distrusted the cities and the disturbing innovations they stood for. Deepest, strongest support for Carlism was in the countryside, with the cities standing out as suspect islands of liberalism: Bilbao, San Sebastián, Pamplona, Barcelona.[5]

THE FIRST CARLIST WAR, 1833 TO 1840

If the ideological background of the war was tangled, its military history was almost equally so. Geographically, it was really several wars at once: one in the Basque Country, one in Aragon and one in Catalonia. There was no grand overall design on either side.

It began in September 1833, as soon as Ferdinand died. There had been two pro-Carlist gestures before: a conspiracy in Zaragoza in 1824, and a Catalan revolt in 1827. But Carlos himself was not involved in either. Then on his brother's death he assumed the title Carlos V, King of Spain, from his exile in Portugal.

In character and habits he seemed worthier of kingship than had his brother. Though lacking willpower and decisiveness, and not notably bright, Carlos was sincere and honorable and supremely conscious of his royal rights, whereas Ferdinand had been easily persuaded to trade his off. Carlos was pious and upright; Ferdinand had been boorish and immoral. Carlos did not prove a great general, but he was brave and dogged and kept his armies' loyalty. Even before the outbreak of war he had an almost fanatical following, and its vehemence may have misled him as to the breadth of his base.

In the fall of 1833 he went to the border between Spain and Portugal and was disappointed when no army appeared to conduct him in triumph to Madrid. Still hoping to gain his throne without a battle, he delayed a declaration of war until November. Meantime, all Vizcaya (including Bilbao), part of Guipúzcoa (but not San Sebastián), Vitoria, (capital of Alava), and much of Navarra (but not Pamplona) declared for Carlos. There were risings not only in Navarra, cradle of Carlism, but all around the periphery, in Catalonia, Aragon and Valencia, as well as in La Rioja and Old Castile.

All Europe was to take sides in the burgeoning conflict. On the one hand the Quadruple Alliance (1834) bound Great Britain, France, Spain and Portugal to eliminate the threats to peace in the Iberian Peninsula posed by the two pretenders: Miguel, who claimed the Portuguese throne, and Carlos. Led by Lord Palmerston of England, the four nations sought to shore up the liberal government of the queen regent, María Cristina. Recent swings in political fortune in Great Britain and France explain their stand. The Whigs had just taken over from the Tories in England. France, which had been officially proroyalist only ten years before, was now ruled by Louis Philippe, a Bourbon who depended on liberals for support.

On the other hand the old Holy Alliance (Russia, Prussia and Austria) stood for absolute monarchies everywhere and particularly in Spain. But at that moment it was not prepared to go to war for Carlos, though the Carlists in Navarra were hinting strongly in June 1834 that they would welcome such allies.

Miguel soon abandoned his hopes in Portugal and fled the country. But the cause of Carlos attracted more and more partisans. It was time for him to appear on the scene.

He finally arrived by way of London, where the English government had hoped to keep him out of the way and avoid ignition of a hot war. But he escaped, disguised as a Mexican, and came to Elizondo in Navarra's Valley of Baztán in July 1834.

He found an able Carlist general in the field, with several victories under his belt. This was Tomás Zumalacárregui. He was a native Guipúzcoan, but Navarra has appropriated him as a national hero.

Zumalacárregui had been named Carlist commander in Navarra in the fall of 1833 by the *Junta Gubernativa,* headquartered in Estella, which was to be the Carlist military capital. Later he was commander throughout the Basque Country. When Carlos arrived he had been energetically training troops and taking towns in the northern mountains for half a year. The prospects looked so encouraging that there was brave talk of a march on Madrid. But there was no money.

Carlos set up his court in the Guipúzcoan town of Oñate. His armies waged guerrilla warfare over a wide area, consolidating their hold on most of Vasconia and much of Navarra in 1834. Zumalacárregui achieved notable victories in this early period. But the big towns and the capitals were securely held by the Cristinist garrisons: Pamplona, San Sebastián, Vitoria and Bilbao. The last two had been taken away from the Carlists by General Saarsfield (of Irish descent, but a native of Spain).

It was a barbarous war, especially from 1834 on, when Quesada took command of the Cristinist armies and stepped up terroristic tactics. Both sides massacred prisoners. The Carlists, to get supplies and money, captured and tortured town officials. They tarred and feathered townswomen who helped the enemy. The cruelty of the Carlist General Ramón Cabrera, who had been trained as a priest, was legendary. His outrageous deeds in Aragon inspired corresponding reprisals by the Cristinist generals, including the shooting of Cabrera's own mother.

The veteran General Espoz y Mina, recently appointed to the Cristinist command, was no exception. He ordered the burning of an entire village (Lecároz, in the Baztán Valley) and the shooting of one in five of its male inhabitants, out of revenge for a defeat.

The English government was so alarmed at the barbarities—"Never was there a contest in which human life was so little valued"[6]—that in 1835 it sent envoys who succeeded in getting both the Cristinist command and Zumalacárregui to agree to adopt more humane practices toward prisoners and the wounded. This "Eliot Convention," however, was observed only in the Basque provinces and Navarra, and not always there.

England's Whig government was officially committed to nonintervention but actually sympathetic to the liberals and the Cristinist cause. It encouraged military assistance to the Cristinists, which took in the volunteer British Legion. France helped too, sending a four thousand-man body of the French Foreign Legion. The ten thousand-man British force, led by Colonel Delacy Evans, fought for and with the Cristinists in the north from 1835 to 1837. They were at first dumfounded by their enemies' non-English ways of waging war: "Dastardly, so like that of the American Indians (never firing a shot but from cover)!"[7] But they drilled assiduously and might have become a potent force had it not been for the miserable winter of 1835–36, when sickness wiped out nearly a fifth of their number. They saw action in and around San Sebastián, and finally retook Fuenterrabia and Irún before the end of their two-year stint. Their contribution to the Cristinist cause was not spectacular, but without them the Carlists might have managed to take and hold more in the north, perhaps even San Sebastián and Bilbao.

The latter city, Spain's third largest port, was a perennial temptation to the Carlists. Once in possession of it, they would be assured of a port to receive help from abroad and would have a tremendous boost in prestige and self-confidence.

They first tried to take Bilbao in the spring of 1835, while still encouraged by a whole string of victories: Guernica, Villafranca, Vergara, Tolosa, Estella. Against his better judgment, Zumalacárregui obeyed Carlos's orders to march on Bilbao. He was wounded in the assault and died eleven days later. The attempt was a failure. The loss of this exceptional general was a grievous blow to the Carlist cause, and marked the turning point of the war. But the Carlists still had many resources. By 1835 they had succeeded in establishing their own state within the Spanish state. They had administrative machinery: each of the Basque provinces had its *Diputación de Guerra,* and Navarra its *Junta Gubernativa.* (This body later bowed out and created a Provisional *Diputación* of Navarra, which lasted from 1838 until the end of the war.)

The Carlists had arms factories, military academies, hospitals, a university. In the three Basque provinces, they had a workable court system to deal with civil and economic cases. They had a king with a court and two capitals: Estella, the military capital, and Oñate in Guipúzcoa for show. They even had their own foreign legion, made up of foreign volunteers and deserters from the Cristinist armies and French and British foreign legions.

Even after Zumalacárregui's death, the Carlists had a fine army. He had created a durable instrument, with dedicated officers, disciplined troops, and limitless enthusiasm. But brave and daring as the Carlist soldiers were, their warfare had been largely defensive and became more so. If the Cristinist armies had ever had the Madrid government's full attention and more men, they might have mounted a concerted attack and dealt better with the dismayingly scattered guerrilla tactics of the Carlists. As it was, the entire Cristinist force was tied down in the north, yet could not dominate the enemy.

Even so, militarily it was downhill from mid-1835 for the Carlists. No succeeding general could equal Zumalacárregui, and Carlos was increasingly swayed by his unrealistic noble advisors.

AFTER ZUMALACARREGUI

Though the war seemed "languid" to one Cristinist general, it was seldom so for the Carlists. Two bold military actions and two dismaying setbacks enlivened the period from 1836 to 1837.

They made a daring feint on Madrid in the summer of 1836, which came within striking distance of the queen regent in her summer palace at La Granja. But the Basque armies, unused to such offensive tactics, were uneasy and those among them who counseled returning north with their loot while they were ahead prevailed over the would-be kidnappers of the queen.

About the same time (February to June 1836), the Carlist General Miguel Gomez was freely marching all about Spain, to Asturias and Galicia, down through Castile to Andalucia where he took Córdoba, nearly to Gibralter, then finally back to the Basque Country laden with booty. But he did not achieve his main purpose, which was to arouse enthusiasm and enlist recruits for the Carlist cause. Most Spaniards, especially in the south, were supremely apathetic about the civil war.

Carlist fortunes suffered a discouraging setback in another ill-fated attempt on Bilbao in November 1836. They besieged the city, but the Cristinists, at last, had a thoroughly able general in Baldomero Espartero. He lifted the siege, to the great encouragement of the Madrid government.

However, the Cristinists' confidence was soon severely shaken by the Battle of Oriamiendi (March 1837). They had planned an intricate but insufficiently rehearsed three-pronged attack on the Carlists in Guipúzcoa. It was to involve Evans and the British Legion, who were to march from San Sebastián to nearby Hernani; Espartero, who was to come from Bilbao; and Saarsfield, who was to lead his column from Pamplona. Two out of three never got to the battle. Espartero stopped at

Durango; Saarsfield, running into heavy rains in the mountains, returned to Pamplona. Only Evans kept to the schedule, but the opposing Navarrese battalion under the Infante Sebastián was too much for the British-Cristinist forces and they had to retreat to San Sebastián; little lost and little gained.

The Carlists' second major setback of the war's final years was the so-called Royal Expedition in the spring and summer of 1837. This was a vainglorious exercise by Carlos, influenced by a court faction that favored breaking out of the northern defenses and striking into Castile.

The expedition's pace was slow, with pauses to sing Te Deums at cathedrals along the way. The army met no resistance in Navarra, some in Aragon. It crossed the Ebro, detoured to Valencia and took it, then moved toward Madrid. Here, Carlos hoped, there might be a chance that María Cristina would come over to the Carlist cause. Since the summer of 1836, when the Sergeants' Revolt had forced her to proclaim the Constitution of 1812 and accept a Progressive ministry (more liberal than the incumbent Moderates), she had been at odds with her government, even considering a marriage between her daughter Isabel and Carlos's son.

But just about when the Carlist army appeared, the Progressive ministry fell, the Moderates came back, the queen felt less menaced, and she rejected the marriage idea.

While Carlos hesitated (still hoping God would open the hearts of his countrymen, who would then open the gates of the city), Espartero assembled a mighty army. The Carlists retreated ignominiously to Navarra without accepting the challenge.

From about this time, the Carlists, never completely in harmony, were increasingly racked by disagreement on ends and means. Two opposing factions pressed their views on Carlos: the *apostólicos,* unyielding and determined to hold out, and the "transactionists," willing to consider treating with the enemy. The former were principally Navarrese and Alavese. The transactionists included many who would make peace at any cost— even deserting Carlos—as long as the Basque liberties were guaranteed.

The most vigorous spokesman for the transactionists was General Rafael Maroto, who was named Carlist commander-in-chief in June 1838.

The Madrid government encouraged an attempt in 1838 by the notary Muñagorri to create a diversion, by raising a third army, under the slogan "peace and fueros." The aim was to divide the Carlists further and attract those willing to fight for religion and fueros but not king. With England's help, some five thousand men were raised, but the third force never really materialized.

As for the main Cristinist army, it saw very little action in 1838. It was largely ignored by the government in Madrid where the infighting by Progressives and Moderates was much more interesting.

An upsurge in cruelty on both sides during the year and a final disastrous dispute among the Carlist top command preceded the end of the war. General Maroto, violently opposed to the *apostólico* faction at the Carlist court, managed to have five of their highest officers shot, early in 1839. This fed the flames of his enemies' hatred. To save his skin—and his cause—he negotiated secretly with Espartero and the Cristinists.

Just before their agreement on terms, the Duke of Wellington was asked in London if he thought England should intervene to end the war. He replied:

> I would not give a toss up for the choice between Don Carlos and Maroto, the Queen and Espartero. They ought all to be hanged on the same tree, to avoid the injury which might be done to a second.... The Basque provinces are pretty certain of their *fueros* being secured, happen what may, if we don't interfere. I should advise all parties to leave the Spaniards to settle their own affairs.[8]

Which they shortly did. Maroto, seeing how his army's position had deteriorated, accepted Espartero's terms for an armistice, which included: recognition of Isabella (now eight years old) as legitimate queen; no loss of pay or rank for Carlist officers who joined the queen's army, or punishment for the rank and file; and a vague reference to preservation of the fueros.

The document was signed at Vergara, deep in Basque country near the Guipúzcoa-Vizcaya border, on August 29, 1839. To encourage a spirit of amity between the opposing armies drawn up to witness the ceremony, Espartero urged them to embrace each other as brothers. He set the example himself by embracing Maroto. Thus the event became known as the *Abrazo* (embrace) of Vergara, in a derogatory sense to the many Carlists who regarded it as a shameful capitulation.

Most of the dissatisfied were Navarrese and Alavese. They did not even turn up for the signing. Signatories for the Carlists were the Castilian, Guipúzcoan and Vizcayan divisions.

Navarra was the natural place for Carlos to turn to when he saw armistice as inevitable. But Navarra's die-hard Carlists alone could not reverse what they saw as a sell-out by their fellow Basques. In mid-September Carlos fled to France with hundreds of supporters. Many of them, and of the thousands of later refugees, stayed to settle in Basse Navarre.

The war went on in Aragon and Catalonia, but in July 1840 even the fierce Cabrera gave up.

So ended the six-year war, which as far as the Carlists were concerned had settled nothing. They were to resume the conflict twice more during the century, but never with as much hope of success as in the war from 1833 to 1840.

END OF A THOUSAND-YEAR CHAPTER

All wars leave scars on the countryside and the economy—scars that are slow to heal. But this war also caused permanent changes in the whole character of government, for the nation and its Basque territories.

In Spain as a whole, the monarchy lost prestige and power while the military gained influence, with veteran generals (starting with Espartero) becoming first ministers.

In Navarra, the three years that followed the peace saw the most fundamental changes in its political structure since 1512, and the final, irrevocable decree that the kingdom, born a thousand years earlier, was now to be a province.

The changes were foreshadowed by a series of assaults on Navarra's autonomy that started even before the outbreak of war. The first blow was an edict by Ferdinand in 1829, suppressing the ancient right of *sobrecarta*—the customary review by the *Diputación* of all royal orders, which right it had inherited from the Cortes. Henceforth, Navarra was to observe all royal decrees without demur or discussion, just as did the rest of Spain.

The *Diputación* objected, as was expected. It had regularly protested during the war, as Madrid kept pecking away at the fueros, in spite of the fact that its membership gradually shifted from pro-Carlist to pro-Madrid. Sympathy with the liberal government did not preclude an unwavering devotion to legality and foral liberty.

In 1833 the next blow fell. The minister of the interior ordered that Spain be divided into forty-nine provinces, a reform that would automatically wipe out Navarra's status as a kingdom. Implementation of the order was resisted and delayed.

In 1834 the queen regent promulgated a new constitution for Spain, the Royal Statute, as a gesture to appease the progressives, who had been clamoring for concrete recognition of the principles of 1812 and for a convocation of Spain's Cortes. Navarra was thereupon instructed to send *procuradores* (representatives) to this "national" Cortes, in spite of historical precedents against it. At that very moment the *Diputación* was sending one of its periodic luckless requests to Madrid that its own Cortes be convoked, which only the monarch could do.

A group of Navarrese did attend the Madrid Cortes in 1834, but less as *procuradores* than as agents of the *Diputación,* charged with getting Madrid to stop violating and threatening Navarra's fueros. The *Diputación* back in Pamplona was at one point so incensed that it threatened to resign en masse; but reconsidered when its men in Madrid sent word that the queen regent had not actually abolished the fueros—yet.

After the Sergeants' Revolt of 1836 forced María Cristina to revive the Constitution of 1812, she summoned a Constituent Cortes to enact the new liberal Constitution of 1837, which was to endure eight years.

But Navarra's foral *Diputación* finally expired even before the new constitution was promulgated. Foreseeing the inevitable, the members petitioned for dissolution, in August 1836. In October the first provincial *Diputación* was installed. Navarra's unique tribunal, the *Consejo Real,* was abolished the same year.

The new *Diputación* was no mouthpiece of Madrid, though members were selected for their liberal leanings. Almost immediately they protested vigorously, to the government and the Cortes, against the military tyranny in Navarra. Outspoken as always, the members of the *Diputación* called the continued harsh imposition of a state of war on peaceful loyal citizens a "political absurdity."[9] This and other protests and communications were written for the new *Diputación* by its secretary, the historian and antiquarian José Yanguas y Miranda. Despite his liberal sympathies, he was first a loyal citizen of Navarra. His extensive historical researches excellently qualified him to serve as watchdog of the traditional liberties.[10]

The 1837 Constitution was quickly followed by a law replacing the three Basque provinces' ancient legislatures with provincial ones, as had happened in Navarra the year before. Now all the Basques were in the same boat.

All through 1839 many Vasconavarrese hoped for the rebirth of their autonomous regimes. They were encouraged when, in August, the victorious General Espartero made a promise respecting conservation of the fueros, in the convention of Vergara, which marked the end of the First Carlist War. The reference was intentionally obscure: he said he would recommend to the government his offer to formally propose to the Cortes the "concession or modification of the fueros."

Hopes were rekindled when the Madrid Cortes, on October 25, 1839, passed a law "confirming the fueros of the provinces of Vasconia and Navarra, without prejudice to the constitutional unity of the monarchy." But a later article in the same law gave notice that as soon as possible the fueros were to be modified.

Though the Basques hailed the law as a victory, the settlement was only provisional because of the ambiguity and contradictions. The *Diputación* in Pamplona wanted to cooperate with Madrid in reaching a mutually agreeable final determination of Navarra's status. It did not, however, wish to negotiate jointly with the other Basques—and rejected Guipúzcoa's proposal to do so.

ADJUSTING TO THE INEVITABLE

The *Diputación* was prepared to yield in political matters: to give up its Cortes and to send deputies to Madrid's. But it clung to the "economic-administrative fueros" that had contributed to the kingdom's prosperity over the centuries. It began negotiating with Madrid on a pact in the spring of 1840. But the parley had to recess in August because of a governmental crisis. When the dust had settled in October, a small revolution had swept the Moderates out and the more liberal Progressives in. María Cristina resigned the regency and left Spain, but the heiress,

Isabella, was still only ten years old, so ex-Commander in Chief Espartero was named regent.

He at once deprived the three Basque provinces of their remaining autonomy. Navarra's case was next. Conversations were resumed in December 1840. The *Diputación,* after due debate, approved the Foral Pact that its emissaries had hammered out in Madrid with the government; it took effect August 16, 1841, and was henceforth the law of the land.

Navarra emerged from this ordeal with much more independence than the three Basque provinces. Its *Diputación's* willingness to give up its Cortes, viceroy and judicial system, in order to hold onto other liberties, paid off. The conclusive transfer of the customs boundary from the Ebro to the Pyrenees was an economic reverse, but was certainly no surprise; it would have happened sooner or later in the new centralized Spain. The free salt trade was replaced by a monopoly controlled from Madrid, but the sulfur and gunpowder monopoly was kept in the province.

The degree of administrative autonomy retained was and is a source of pride to the Navarrese. In effect, the provincial *Diputación* inherited from its predecessor, and from the *Consejo Real,* almost complete control over internal affairs, but its attributions were not spelled out very specifically. As a result its sphere of influence and power could—and did—adjust with the times.

Local government underwent changes too, chiefly in electoral procedures, which henceforth were to conform with the rest of Spain. Thus at last uniformity replaced the jumble of ways that town officials had been elected: sometimes by direct suffrage, sometimes—still—by *insaculación.* The towns retained much of their traditional management of their own affairs, subject to the *Diputación's* supervision.

The *pactismo* (contractual quality) of the law was very important to the Navarrese, who had always expected *quid pro quo* to be embodied in agreements with their rulers. The agreement on the provincial contribution to the national treasury was particularly significant. As we have seen, this had always been a voluntary donation, not a prescribed tax. Article 41 of the Foral Pact set Navarra's contribution at 1,800,000 pesetas annually, basing the figure on past donations. Both sides agreed, and there was no question about the amount for thirty-five years.

In contrast to Navarra's reasonableness, the other three provinces, negotiating as a separate bloc, held out for complete foral autonomy—and lost almost all.

Arturo Campión, six decades later, looked back sadly and called Navarra's settlement "an evil, but a lesser evil—less than an absolute leveling."

XV

The Long Adjustment: From Kingdom to Foral Province

THE HISTORY OF THE KINGDOM OF Navarra technically ends in 1841 with the passage of the *Ley Paccionada* (Foral Pact), the law that set up a new contractual arrangement between province and monarch. Yet for most of the nineteenth century Navarra kept on creating and pursuing many of its own policies, both external and internal. Only with the end of the militant phase of Carlism (in 1876), the cause that was more fervently supported here than anywhere else in Spain, did Navarra settle down as a province—albeit a province "more equal than others."

Two currents run through the period of adjustment. First, a largely successful running battle with the central government to insure nearly as much autonomy as Navarra had enjoyed as a kingdom. Secondly, the hopeless and tragic espousement of the Carlist cause, which, if it had succeeded, could have meant restoration of the old order, with Navarra as a kingdom within a kingdom.

On the civil front, although the new provincial *Diputación* cooperated with Madrid, it balked at any sign that the fueros so precious to its people might be in peril, winning its last major point of the century in 1893. Madrid's concessions to demands

THE LONG ADJUSTMENT 173

for local rights were largely motivated by its unwillingness to give any excuse for more Carlist uprisings.[1] Probably the two most significant examples of these nineteenth-century accommodations between Madrid and Pamplona were disentailment of municipally held lands, and the tax formula. We shall examine these before returning to the Carlist wars, tracing them and the interrelated history of Navarra to the final defeat and acceptance of the fact that the kingdom's days were at an end.

DISENTAILMENT IN NAVARRA

The first significant issue dividing the *Diputación* and Madrid after the Foral Pact was the question of whether and how the towns of Navarra were to be divested of their communal lands. Eventually the *Diputación* won the battle, fought in the halls of legislature and with letters and memoranda as weapons.

For centuries the citizens of towns and valleys in much of Spain had depended on their commonly held lands for pasture, fodder, wood supply and hunting. Also many towns owned mills, ironworks, bakeries and the like, proceeds from which went to education, charity and the clergy. All this was to be wiped out by the broad disentailing laws of 1855. Municipalities were told to divest themselves of all such property and auction it to individuals.

To Navarra this was an unthinkable *antifuero,* and the province waged a quiet but persistent fight to be exempted from the laws.

The idea of disentailment *(desamortización)* in Spain was not new. At the end of the preceding century it had been advanced in the agrarian reform theories of Jovellanos, prime minister during the reign of Charles IV, as a way to redistribute the huge landholdings of the church and the nobility, and to help the lower and middle classes to become landholders. Disentailment of ecclesiastical holdings did take place, and by the 1830s most such lands had been disposed of. Then in 1834, under pressure from the Liberals, the Queen Regent María Cristina authorized —but did not order—municipal governments throughout Spain to sell their lands.

But not until 1854 did this civil disentailment really get the go-ahead. Pascual Madoz, a native of Pamplona but no defender of the Basque fueros, was minister of the treasury in Madrid. He codified the extant disentailing laws and pushed through the Cortes an extension requiring municipalities to sell their properties through the treasury's newly established *Juntas de Ventas* (sales committees).

Navarra's deputies in the Cortes abstained from voting on the measure because even a vote against it would have implied recognition of its possible applicability to Navarra.[2] The nub of the province's opposition was the law's nonconformity with the *Ley Paccionada* (the Foral Pact of 1841)— supreme law of the land as far as the *Diputación* was concerned. The law had provided that the towns would retain control of their financial affairs, subject to supervision by the provincial *Diputación*—but certainly not subject to any organ of the Spanish state, which they rightly believed the provincial *Junta de Ventas* would be. The law established that this committee would include only one representative of Navarra's *Diputación*, with the rest of the members to be appointed from Madrid.

Still, mute opposition was not enough. The province had to take a position when disentailment became mandatory. The *Diputación* embarked on a campaign of delaying tactics through the mails. First it wrote Navarra's civil governor that, because it was not in session, it could not act on the naming of a director of the provincial *junta*. Then it did indeed appoint a director, but with the proviso that the *junta* would supervise sale of lands belonging to the state, to the military orders, and to the clergy only—not those of the municipalities.

Letters arguing these points passed back and forth between the governor and the *Diputación* from June 1855 until well into 1856. Meantime the latter permitted the towns to sell their lands, but did not require them to send the treasury twenty percent of the proceeds, as the law stipulated.

In 1856 the Moderates replaced the Progressives in Madrid, and annulled the disentailing law of May 1, 1855. The Progressives came back in 1858 and by a royal decree of October 2, 1858, reestablished it. During these shifts, Navarra did as little as possible toward disentailment. But in 1858 the Progressive ministry of the treasury reviewed Navarra's continued recalcitrance, concluded that the *Diputación* was completely out of line, and ordered it to comply. The deputies thereupon sent an eloquent plea to the queen herself.

What with this message, the *Diputación's* tenacity, the logic of its arguments, and the governor's alarm at the rising unrest in the province, the *Diputación* finally had its way, in 1859. The disentailing laws were still to apply in Navarra, but to be modified to bring them into accord with the province's foral law. And the towns could keep all proceeds from sales, and continue to use them—as they always had used the income from communal property—for good works.

The *Diputación* reached final agreement with Madrid in 1861 by acceptance of a plan to form a provincial *Junta de Ventas* that would include all its members, giving the *Diputación* a majority on the body.

It was thus able to avoid wholesale disentailment, and to accede to requests of many towns to retain their lands.

From this time on, Navarra conscientiously carried out its execution of the laws until, by 1874, the undertaking was essentially completed and the *junta* was dissolved.

Elsewhere in Spain the sale of municipally owned property was often disastrous. Town governments that put the proceeds into government bonds paying minuscule interest did not profit. Villagers and townsfolk lost their rights to use lands they had shared for centuries, where they had hunted, pastured flocks, made charcoal, cut firewood, gathered hay and fodder, and obtained lumber to build and repair their homes and farms. As for buying parcels of land, very few could afford the down payments—small though they were—when the lands were sold at public auction. Madoz's aim, to create a class of small landowners, failed.

In contrast, Navarra's towns and valleys, especially in the north, still retain far more of their communal lands than do those anywhere else in Spain. In about half the province, the income of most towns is still significantly augmented by the pastures, woodlands and forests that they administer.

All Spain had opposed disentailment, but only Navarra opposed it with success.[3]

DISPUTES ABOUT TAXES

The next major threat to Navarra's "special" status was an 1876 law (the *Concierto Económico)* that authorized the central government to exact taxes in proportion to the Basque provinces' wealth, rather than a fixed amount. Navarra had been paying 1.8 million pesetas annually, an amount set by the Foral Pact of 1841. However, the government was persuaded to restore

Navarra's privileged status, and negotiated with the *Diputación* to arrive at a new figure of 2 million pesetas annually.

But in 1893 there was a new encounter on taxes, the *gamazada,* so called after Germán Gamazo, finance minister. During the regency of María Cristina, mother of Alfonso XIII, the government again had ordered Navarra to adopt the same taxing formula as the rest of Spain. The province protested vigorously. In Pamplona, angry townspeople gathered copies of the one Madrid newspaper that supported the *gamazada* and burned them in the Plaza del Castillo, the central square.[4] More constructively, the *Diputación,* all the province's mayors, and one hundred twenty thousand male citizens signed a petition to the queen, explaining why Navarra could not comply with this *antifuero.* The queen assented and instructed Prime Minister Sagasta to arrive at an accord with "the legitimate aspirations of Navarra." The resultant agreement noted the need to "take care to conciliate the special circumstances of this province with the general interests of the nation."[5] The sense of this provision, implying the need for give-and-take on both sides, echoed the phrasing of the first major diminution of Navarra's fueros in 1839, when they were confirmed "without prejudice to the constitutional unity of the monarchy."

The agreement was hailed as a victory in Pamplona, where the citizens launched a popular subscription to erect a monument to the fueros. The impressive multifigured statue, topped with a classically garbed goddess holding aloft the revered document, still stands opposite the *Palacio de la Diputación,* as a highly visible reminder of the foral tradition. It also provides convenient perches for onlookers during the San Fermín festivities and other spectacles. The formula that it commemorates was to stand until 1927.

CARLISM REFUSES TO DIE

Meantime Navarra was still the main base for traditional monarchists and adherents of the Carlist cause, which, though quiescent after the end of the First Carlist War, was far from dead. There was no organized revival of the conflict for thirty years after the *Abrazo de Vergara* (1833). But a series of unconnected outbreaks occurred, mostly in Catalonia, from 1836 to 1839. Many historians of Carlism call this the "Matiners' War"; while others refer to it as the Second Carlist War (as we shall do).

The cast of characters included a new pretender. The old pretender, Carlos V, who had been living in comfortable captivity in Bourges, abdicated in 1845 at the age of fifty-seven and left France. His son the count of Montemolín (future Carlos VI) took his place as Carlist chief and French internee. But in 1846 he escaped to London, where he fell in love with and almost married Miss Adeline de Horsey, a beautiful English commoner. Thus distracted, he did not encourage his supporters in Spain to start anything in observation of his becoming official pretender. But some went ahead anyway.

In September 1846 several small Carlist guerrilla bands in Catalonia began raiding and swiftly retreating before government troops could catch them. In Catalan, *matiners* means "early risers"; the war may have been called the Matiners' War because these rebel chiefs were far ahead of any other Carlists in judging the time ripe for action.

Though there were some Carlist-related disturbances in Navarra in 1847, the province was more concerned with the widespread civil unrest that prevailed there in the mid-1840s. This was partly due to insecurity and unease at the new provincial status so recently imposed, partly to the disruptions that any society undergoes after a wrenching civil war. Restless young veterans of the late war were unwilling to settle down sedately. Those who had joined or remained in the government's armed forces were likely to desert, as did many from the *Guardia Civil*—Spain's national police force, created in 1844. Robbery, smuggling, homicide and beggary were problems throughout the province.

But in Catalonia the war, such as it was, went on sporadically until Montemolín, recognizing the need to harness the fighting spirit, sent orders to the veteran General Cabrera to leave France, unify the forces, and take command.

The year was 1848, when liberal revolutions were breaking out all over Europe. Cabrera obediently entered Catalonia to lead a conservative revolution. He built a ten-thousand-man army there, which fought on with some success for a year.

By now Navarra's Carlists were taking the field. But the Second Carlist War in that arena amounted to little more than isolated attacks by small bands, with no coordination, during the summer of 1848. The commanding Carlist general for Vasconavarra, Joaquín Elío, hovered over the border in France and sent heroic manifestos but never appeared. The provincial

Diputación proclaimed its disapproval of the rebels. The Isabeline general, who had a firm grip on the province, promised pardon to Carlist soldiers who turned themselves in, and many did. The insurrection in Navarra was over by August 1, 1848. Pamplona had been relatively unaffected, though the San Fermín festivities of July 1848 had to be postponed until September, and the number of bullfights reduced from six to one. The bishop of Pamplona, a man of peace but brother of the Carlist leader Elio, fled to France when faced with arrest, but was soon pardoned and allowed to return.

The war went on a little longer in Catalonia. But money, as usual, was lacking. So was the inspiring presence of Montemolín, the pretender. Cabrera begged him to come, and in 1849 Montemolín tried to cross the border from France into Catalonia, but was foiled by French customs officials and returned to England.

Cabrera soon gave up and left for France. The war in Catalonia had sputtered out by May 18, 1849. Here and there elsewhere in Spain the Montemolinist banner was raised, but the government felt assured of sufficient peace throughout the kingdom by June to grant amnesty to nearly all Carlists, at home and in exile.

The next year there was a small-scale revival of hostilities in Guipúzcoa and Navarra, limited largely to pursuits by government troops of small Carlist bands from one spot to another, with very few real confrontations.

So much for the Second Carlist War.

In 1855 Carlos V died in Trieste. Montemolín officially became Carlos VI. He issued a call to arms to celebrate the occasion. It produced a few minor uprisings in Navarra and Catalonia, but all was quiet again by April 1856.

Again in 1860 Montemolín tried to foment an insurrection by appearing in Spain. The result was the disastrous incident of San Carlos de la Rápita (on the Catalan coast south of Barcelona), where he led an expedition by sea in the misguided belief that thousands of Carlists would spring to his side as soon as he stepped ashore. Alas for his hopes. In short order the troops who accompanied him declared their loyalty to the queen. Ortega, his captain-general, was shot. Montemolín himself and his younger brother Fernando were taken prisoner. They escaped, but both died a year later.

Now the pretender was the remaining brother, the youngest son of Carlos V, Prince Juan. This unstable man was too liberal for the serious, conservative Carlists. The Carlist organ *La Esperanza* suggested, after Juan's 1860 manifesto recognizing the "progressive spirit of our times" and the need for popular participation in government, that the best place for him would be the "booby hatch."[6]

Meantime Queen Isabella's brazen immorality had outraged so many of her subjects that it was obvious she would be forced to abdicate. But who would take her place? Certainly not her son Alfonso. The Spanish were disillusioned by the whole tribe of Ferdinand VII, and were ready to consider any alternative to one of his descendants.

At last the Carlists seemed to have a viable alternative. Their movement had been gaining respectability as a legitimate parliamentary party. Juan, their current pretender, though unsuitable himself, had a son who was quite the opposite: serious, idealistic and enchanted since childhood with the idea of leading loyal Spanish legions into battle.

At a council of Carlists held in London in July 1868, 20-year-old Prince Carlos accepted the title Duke of Madrid and the role of official claimant to the Spanish throne. Then in October Juan, the pretender, agreed to abdicate in favor of his son, who was formally designated Carlos VII. The liberals, normally unenthusiastic about Carlist pretenders, were drawn to this one when he promised, if made king, to leave the choice of a constitution to a freely elected Cortes. But this remark was the first sign to some of his supporters that he might not be sufficiently conservative.[7]

Now the Carlists, with their committed young standard bearer, were in a better position than they had been for years. They decided to stand for election to the next Cortes. The chance soon came.

CARLISTS IN POLITICS

Opposition to Isabella had hardened. Army leaders, intent on creating a more liberal and centralized (and controllable) regime than she would ever consent to, engineered in September 1868 a coup d'etat that forced her into exile. This left the provisional government faced with the need to summon a Constituent

Cortes to decide on the next form of government for Spain. Under these circumstances the Carlist movement was able to take its place with the other political parties. In peace as in war, Navarra gave it hearty support; six of the seven deputies elected in Navarra were Carlists.[8] When the Cortes met in 1869, after the election, the Carlists found themselves with twenty seats.

Carlism now appealed to a broader swath of the population than ever before. Besides offering romance, victory in battle, and glory to the old martial guard, it seemed the best hope of the traditionalists, the sober rural conservatives, the devout Catholics, the country dwellers who cared less about which Bourbon king was on the throne than they did for preservation of the local status quo, curbs on the arrogant cities, and a good price for wheat.

But the party was by no means unanimous in its ideas of strategy. One faction, including most of the militants, was centered in Navarra and reached from Galicia to Catalonia. Its inclination was toward battle rather than polemics.

Southern Carlists tended more toward the philosophy of working within the system. This faction (known as Integralist or Neo-Catholic) included several powerful personalities who trumpeted their views in meetings, statements, books, and in the pages of some one hundred Carlist newspapers that had sprung up, mostly in the south.

One spokesman in particular, the novelist Navarro Villoslada, native of Viana in southwest Navarra, powerfully influenced Spanish thought with his essay "El Hombre que se Necesita" ("The Man We Need"). This was something like a "Common Sense" of its day, in manner and effect, if not in message. It was an impassioned appeal for adherence to the strong-monarch cause and to Carlos VII in particular. The ideal king of Spain, Villoslada wrote, "would say to the father of the family: You are the king of your household; to the mayor: You are the king of your municipality; to the *Diputación:* You are the king of the province; and to the Cortes: I am the King." This eloquent document was reprinted by the thousands and circulated widely.[9]

In spite of his passion, Villoslada, at this stage of his career, was in favor of a peaceful takeover of power. So was the controversial Integralist Candido Nocedal, a onetime Moderate converted to Carlism, whom Carlos VII had named chief of the party in Spain.

But the militants were not sitting quietly on the sidelines. The northern frontier of Spain, which had been almost continually agitated from 1869, grew more tense. In midsummer of that year a conspiracy centered in Pamplona had almost touched off the fuse. Ternero Garrido, a prominent Carlist, sent word to Carlos that on July 23 the Carlists would take over the city's stronghold, the *Ciudadela*, and that the citizens would then rise up and declare for their rightful king. In expectation of this event Carlos went down to the French town of Ascain, near the border. But the next news he had was of the discovery and quashing of the conspiracy. The civil governor's intelligence system had informed him of all the Carlist plans. Furthermore, there was apparently some bumbling on the part of those assigned to the takeover.

After the failure, cries of *"Viva Carlos VII!"* were still heard in Pamplona's streets, and the governor had to declare them as seditious as cries against the Constitution or the Cortes.[10]

Risings elsewhere in Spain, planned to coincide with the Pamplona event, had to be put off, though some did occur in La Mancha, León and Valencia.

Carlos and his generals still hoped to start something, perhaps in Catalonia. But promises of arms fell through and the old war hero Cabrera refused to lead the army. He had mellowed and even grown somewhat liberal, as he settled into comfortable retirement in England. His defection was a severe disappointment to the militant branch of Carlism, still at odds with the Integralists and Neo-Catholics. But at an all-Carlist conference in Vevey, Switzerland, in April 1870, the two groups patched up their differences. The Neo-Catholics took the upper hand in setting policy.

Still, throughout Navarra and the Basque provinces enthusiasm for war grew until it was almost irresistible.

Finally from exile in Paris Isabella renounced her queenship, in favor of her son Alfonso. This reinforced the Alfonsists in the Cortes, which body now had to face up to the urgency of the governmental crisis. The time for a republic had not yet come, and the consensus, as expressed in the Constitution of 1869, was for a monarchy. But who would be the monarch? The

Cortes took the novel step of inviting candidates from noble and royal houses all over Europe, then electing a king. The winner was Amadeo, duke of Aosta, second son of the king of Italy. He was crowned in Madrid in January 1871. Carlists stood for election again in 1870 and did even better than in 1868. With seventy-nine seats,[11] they and their leader Nocedal held the balance of power in a wildly divided Cortes.

THE THIRD CARLIST WAR

Navarra's last military adventure on behalf of a Carlist pretender who would restore the monarchy was the Third Carlist War, from 1872 to 1876. This conflict broke out after the Carlists failed to agree to work within the system.

In 1871, in spite of their recent electoral successes, many in the Carlist camp advocated military action. Just on the other side of Navarra's borders troops gathered in St. Jean de Luz and Bayonne, eager for the word to invade.

Carlos, to his credit, knew that the army was woefully underarmed and in September 1871 he counseled patience. Although promises of money and men for the cause were plentiful, actual deliveries were few. The pretender was pulled in opposite directions: toward war by the battle-eager army in the north, and toward temporization by the more moderate Candido Nocedal and the other Integralists. He tried to satisfy everyone: while reinforcing Candido Nocedal's authority as political leader in Spain, he kept sending encouragement and detailed battle plans to General Diaz de Rada, who was to command the general uprising expected in the eight provinces involved: four Catalan, three Vascongadas, and Navarra. The Carlist representation in the Cortes shrank to fewer than twelve members. With some justification, they charged Prime Minister Sagasta with having rigged the election.

In April Carlos sent word from Geneva that the elected deputies should not take their seats, and announced that the uprising would take place on April 21. He himself would come to Spain as soon as he could circumvent the French police.

Navarra's pent-up bellicosity exploded into a frenzy of mustering and marching. Diaz de Rada, having completed his preparations for action all along the frontier, went to Ascain in Basse Navarre with a small band, gathered a few emigrant volunteers, and led his tiny army back into Spain down the Valley of the Bidasoa, expecting to find a massive assault under way by his fellow Carlists. He was disappointed. Carlists in the field were few, mostly unarmed, and lacking in discipline. The government troops pursued them mercilessly. Nevertheless, Diaz de Rada kept moving toward Pamplona, joined by General Ollo. But he soon recognized that the situation was so desperate that Carlos must be dissuaded from his promised crossing from France. Diaz went over the mountains in search of his king, but missed connections. Carlos began his triumphal entry into Spain, unaware of the true circumstances.

His arrival at Vera de Bidasoa, on May 2, 1872, was tragically premature. Willing fighters flocked to his banners, crying "Down with the foreigner!" (Amadeo) and "Up with Spain!" But most of them were armed with sticks.

Meantime General Fulgencio Carasa and the main Carlist army in Navarra were being chased northward by the Amadeistas under Moriones. This Carlist army had heard rumors that Carlos had arrived in Spain. When, almost within sight of Guipúzcoa, they saw men in red berets atop a far-off hill, they joyfully ascertained that this was indeed the pretender's army, and the two forces joined.

But Moriones soon ferreted them out. The ensuing engagement was to prove perhaps the saddest and most memorable of the century for Navarra. Large-scale confrontations between armies were rare in the Carlist wars, especially in the north, where the Basques were masters of hit-and-run tactics. But in this case the rebels were surprised and had no choice but to fight, ill-prepared as they were.

Moriones, in the evening of May 3, 1872, fell upon the Carlists at the little mountain town of Oroquieta, in western Navarra.

Fewer than a third of the fourteen-hundred-man Carlist army had any kind of firearm. Though they outnumbered their adversaries, though Carlos himself was in the forefront, and though they resisted even after their last bullets were spent, the battle was unequal from the start. Moriones had artillery and well-armed, well-disciplined troops. He took some seven hundred prisoners, who were deported to the Canary Islands and Cuba. Carlos, practically deserted, spurred his steed toward France, with a few followers.

After this fiasco for the Carlists, Madrid followed up with divide-and-conquer maneuvers. General Serrano persuaded the Basque insurgents in Vizcaya to lay down their arms in return for a promise that their fueros would be respected (the *Convenio de Amorabieta,* May 24, 1872).

But partisans fought on independently in the Basque provinces, Castile, La Mancha, Navarra, Aragon and Catalonia. In Guipúzcoa the fierce priest Santa Cruz carried on a one-man war, characterized by almost barbaric practices. After the Basques finally gave up, the Carlists in Catalonia, without any help from other provinces, stayed in the field for seven more months.

After a very short period of recuperation the Carlists began to get ready for the next encounter. In Navarra, in December 1872, General Nicolas Ollo Vidaurreta, a veteran of the First Carlist War and of the disaster at Oroquieta, came back from France to resume the battle. He had been named commander for Navarra. He crossed the border with twenty-seven men, and a year later had a well-organized army of ten thousand volunteers. To many, Ollo seemed Zumalacárregui over again.

If the ostentatious and abortive rising of 1872 could be called the prelude to the Third Carlist War, the quiet arrival of Ollo in Navarra signals the raising of the curtain. However, political events in Spain as a whole were to determine the actual resumption of full-scale hostilities.

Amadeo resigned as king on February 11, 1873. His abdication did not arouse so much surprise as wonder that he had lasted so long: twenty-six months. His ministers had been openly hostile and uncooperative, and the Spanish people had never taken to him.

In Madrid, with the monarchy temporarily in eclipse, the Republicans had their chance, and declared the First Spanish Republic. Needless to say, Navarra's representatives were not among them: any talk of a republic was inimical to their fueros. Yet the framers of the new constitution looked favorably on the desire of the Basques for autonomy and considered creation of a federal state of Vasconia. Navarra could have been part of it.

The infant republic's hold on its armies was tenuous. It seemed a great opportunity for the Carlists to seize the initiative at last.

Carlos VII returned in July 1873 and was received in northern Spain as a conquering hero, with balls, fiestas and fireworks. He found a hard, efficient fighting force, widespread support in Vasconavarra and Catalonia, and seasoned generals in his service. These included Joaquin Elío, a native of Pamplona who was a veteran of every war since the *Guerra Realista,* and who was to achieve brilliant victories for the Carlists.

Fairly secure in Navarra, where his troops were closing in on Pamplona and where the Valley of Baztán—important route to France—was his, Carlos traveled on through the rest of the Basque Country. He was encouraged to find that nearly all Vizcaya and Guipúzcoa had fallen to or declared for the Carlists. He proceeded to Guernica to salute the holy tree of foral liberty. Taking a cue from Serrano's action the year before, he promised to respect the fueros of the Vizcayans, if they would support him. They agreed. At Christmas he was anointed king of the Basques.

Late in August the geographically and symbolically important city of Estella fell to the Carlists. Both Republicans and Carlists were obsessed with the need to take and hold this "Holy City of Carlism," second only to Pamplona in Navarra. The Carlists repulsed a Republican attempt to recapture it in November, in the famous Battle of Montejurra. Ollo with eight or nine thousand men was pitted against the sixteen thousand of the Republicans' General Moriones, who had vowed to raze the city. To celebrate their victory, the Carlists attended a Te Deum in the city, and Carlos reviewed the troops.

As 1874 opened, the vital cities that the Carlists needed but the Republicans controlled still held out: Bilbao, San Sebastián, Tolosa, Pamplona. And there was practically no coordination between Carlists in Vasconavarra and Catalonia. But otherwise Carlism seemed to be riding a wave of triumph. Money and arms poured in. The army moved with crusading zeal, telling the rosary as it marched. Religious festivals often took precedence over military operations. Carlos had captured the hearts and respect of his people. Unlike his grandfather, he lived simply, had a smaller court, and was more decisive.

The fatal attraction of Bilbao led the Carlists to a glorious defeat in 1874. They were convinced now, as they had been in the First Carlist War, that with this port they would acquire wealth, a suitable capital and, most important, the recognition of the European powers and their support in men, money and materials.

So a proposal to march on Madrid, chancy but offering great rewards, was turned down in favor of an assault on Bilbao in February 1874. The Carlist army attacked with such vigor and won so many strategic points around the city that the Republican General Moriones felt it necessary to come and break their siege. He failed utterly, and wired Madrid to send reinforcements and another general to take his place. The government there was so alarmed that Serrano, the chief minister, himself went north to take command.

The second Republican attack on the Carlist lines around Bilbao, in March, lasted for three days of fierce fighting, but again ended in defeat for the siege-breakers. Each side lost about two thousand men. The Carlists also lost two key generals, Ollo and Rada (Radica). Two months later the continuing pressure of the Republicans forced the Carlists to abandon the siege.

The third battle for Estella, in June 1874, went to the Carlists, as had the first two. The victory, again, was largely due to their skill at taking advantage of their familiar terrain. Estella, on the central plateau of Navarra, is ringed by mountains. The Carlist defenders, lodged on the heights and dominating the approaches, attacked the attackers in the passes and after three days had completely routed them.

The royal progress to celebrate the victory was an emotional occasion. First there were fireworks, and dancing and singing in the streets of the city. Then Carlos and his wife Margarita, he resplendent in his general's uniform, she in a plain black riding habit, and both wearing the red Basque beret, rode into the city on snow-white chargers, to review the victorious army of some eighteen thousand men. It seemed that all Navarra had turned out; the cheering crowds included many from Pamplona and the northern valleys. An English observer called Carlos and Margarita "de facto King and Queen of Navarre."[12]

They did indeed seem to be rulers of an actual kingdom. It encompassed nearly all of Vasconavarra except the capital cities.

As in the First Carlist War, the Carlists had set up their own administrative and war-support structure parallel to the existing civil institutions.¹³ Carlos had a minister of war, minister of state, and foreign secretary. Schools were established, including a university at Oñate. The court system had jurisdiction over Vasconavarra and that part of Castile held by the Carlists. There was again a *Diputación Foral* of the Kingdom of Navarra. It presided over civil life, and had the same attributes as the powerful provincial *Diputación* in Pamplona, which remained loyal to the Madrid government. Comparable bodies also operated in the three Basque provinces. Customs posts at the French border, and also within Navarra, assured the Carlists of income.

Rail transportation was of lively concern to the Carlist government. It proposed to the government in Madrid that the lines in the north of Spain be neutralized, available to both sides for transport of goods and civilians. Madrid refused. The Carlists later succeeded in taking over part of the lines, but they had no locomotives. In a daring action, they spirited two away from the station in Pamplona. In the spring of 1875 they set up their own railroad service through Guipúzcoa to connect with the French line at Hendaye.

Their telegraph and postal network, radiating from the Carlist capital of Estella, served all the north of Spain. They coined money at the mint in Oñate. They were well served with newspapers: from 1873, the official organ was *El Cuartel Real,* published first in Estella, then Tolosa. Later *La Cruzada Española* began publication in Bayonne.

Medical care was a serious problem. Carlos's wife Margarita, almost as assiduous as he in staying close to the armies and the action, in 1873 launched a movement called *La Caridad,* similar to the Red Cross. It was to care for the wounded of both sides. In 1874 the organization set up a fine hospital near Estella, then established others until there were eventually twenty-two in the Basque Country. But doctors were in short supply. The Carlists planned to start a school of medicine in Estella, but their final defeat came first.

THE END OF THE THIRD CARLIST WAR

The war's end was presaged by an unexpected blow that hit the Carlists in December 1874. The Spanish Republic collapsed. After the restoration of the Bourbon dynasty with the crowning of Alfonso XII in January 1875, Carlism lost what support it had had from legitimate monarchists.

Alfonso, on his accession, made conciliatory gestures toward his second cousin Carlos. But the latter rejected Alfonso's "absurd attempts at a reconciliation with the legitimate monarchy. *La legitimidad, soy yo."* (*"I* am the legitimate ruler.")

The Carlist armies took up the battle again. Withdrawing from an unsuccessful siege of Pamplona, they won a decisive victory at Lacar. Alfonso himself was nearly taken prisoner.

Carlos took advantage of a temporary lull in the fighting to go, in July 1875, to stand beneath the legendary tree of Guernica and take his oath to uphold the fueros of the Vizcayans, in the presence of two hundred representatives of the towns and villages. They acclaimed him Carlos VII, Lord of Vizcaya and King of Spain. He took the same oath at Villafranca in Guipúzcoa. But he could not repeat the performance in Alava and Navarra. Much of the former was still held by the Alfonsists, and though much of Navarra was Carlist, Pamplona was not. The Pamplona Cortes would have had to be in session for the ceremony and Carlos could not convoke it.

However, he announced that he would uphold the Alavese and Navarrese fueros just the same.

During the fall and winter of 1875, fighting was bitter. Both sides terrorized the inhabitants of towns and countryside and burned crops in their wake. Navarra was exhausted.

An Alfonsist army took possession of the Valley of Baztán in February 1876. Another, led by Fernando Primo de Rivera (uncle of the future dictator) pressed hard and finally took Estella, Carlist headquarters, later the same month. With the fall of this symbolically crucial city, Carlist resistance in the Basque Country ended. Catalonia and the central front had already capitulated.

On February 28 Alfonso came to Pamplona, passed through a specially built triumphal arch inscribed to the "Restorer of peace in Spain," and gave thanks for victory at the cathedral. The next day the war was declared officially over.

Carlos, bowing to the inevitable, crossed into France at Arneguy on February 28, 1876. As he stepped onto the international bridge, he said: "I shall come back to save Spain." But he never returned.

XVI

Into the Twentieth Century

FOR THE FOUR MIDDLE DECADES OF the nineteenth century, after the legal abolition of the old kingdom (in 1841), Navarra had evidenced a dual personality. On the one hand it was a loyal province whose officialdom supported the constitutional monarchy. On the other hand many of its citizens were part of, or sympathetic to, an activist reactionary movement dedicated to restoration of a lost order of absolutism, by force if necessary. Between these two extremes was the bulk of the population, orderly and peaceloving, but inclined to take a conservative stand in any dispute with Madrid.

With the end of the Third Carlist War, in 1876, all this changed. Carlism was still a strong force in Navarra. But its hold was far different from the sword-flourishing, banner-waving movement that had brought the citizens out to march and fight for so long. It evolved from a militant cause, determined to overthrow the existing order, to a peaceful political party. Its values shifted. As chances of seating a Carlist king on the Spanish throne receded, and threats to the Navarrese homeland lessened, devotion to the Catholic religion and defense of traditional regional liberties became the Carlist lodestars. *Dios y Fueros* remainded; *Rey y Patria* were given lip service only. For many in Navarra, Carlism was almost a religion from the late nineteenth century and into the twentieth: passed down from father to son. And it still persists, albeit as a "faith outworn." Its potency as a political party did not last so long.

As Carlism waned, ideological commitment in much of the Basque Country shifted to Basque nationalism. But Navarra did not march to the same drummer as its more industrially advanced volatile neighbors. The province remained largely rural, agricultural and preoccupied with its own concerns all through the Alfonsine reigns, through the Rivera dictatorship, and until the Civil War of 1936 to 1939.

DECLINE OF CARLISM

In exile, the pretender Carlos VII spent the last thirty-three years of his life wandering the world, from capital to capital. It was his misfortune that there were so few wars in Europe. He was perfectly fitted for soldiering and reigning, but not for much else. He did fight for Russia in the Russo-Turkish War (1877). And when Spain was faced with the loss of Cuba in 1899, Carlos, perhaps sincerely, offered his services and leadership to the country. His offer was not accepted. He died July 18, 1909, aged sixty-one, in Varese, and with him died the militant phase of Carlism. His loss was deeply felt by the Carlists, who had revered and respected him for his devotion to Spain and his bravery and leadership in battle.

Shortly after leaving Spain, Carlos had appointed Candido Nocedal the Carlist party leader. His choice was a confirmed Integrist—one whose slogan was "God and Country," and who claimed sublime indifference to such mundane matters as how to organize a government. He grew more and more extreme in his views. Later he was accused of wanting to make the Carlist party more Catholic than the pope.[1] His autocratic control alienated many Carlists.

After Nocedal's death in 1885, Carlos named the aging Navarro Villoslada as party chief—the author of the fiery "El Hombre que se Necesita," which had stirred up support for the Carlist cause just before the Third Carlist War. But in the less bellicose atmostphere of the late 1880s, Carlist leadership passed from Villoslada to a committee; then to the marquis of Cerralbo, who did much to reorganize and revitalize the party.

Meantime, the schismatic Integrist faction decided that the pretender was too liberal to be trusted, and that the party could forge ahead without a king, under the banner of "God and Country." Ramón Nocedal had succeeded his father Candido Nocedal as leader of this rightist branch. The orthodox (and majority) Carlist views were expounded eloquently in the late nineteenth century by Vázquez de Mella: regional autonomy under a traditionalist Catholic monarchy. His adherents came to be called Mellists.

After a brief period of refusing to stand for the Cortes, the Carlists came back to politics and succeeded in winning a few seats occasionally. In 1903, five of the seven deputies elected to the Cortes from Navarra were Carlists. Still later, in the 1918 elections, three from Navarra were Jaimists—that is, of that faction of the party loyal to the new pretender, Jaime I, who had succeeded his father in 1909.

The Jaimist branch became equated with the "orthodox" side of the party as a result of one of Carlism's deepest schisms, just after World War I. During the war Jaime maintained a low profile and did not publicly take sides. However, most Carlists in Spain were vociferously pro-German, and they assumed that their king was too. Many hated Britain, having been brought up on tales of how the British legion had fought against their ancestors in the 1830s. They felt more empathy with Germany, still ruled by an absolute monarch. After the war, when these Spanish Carlists learned how wide the gap really was between them and their leader, there was consternation. The party split into Jaimists and the more militant Mellists.

Navarra, bulwark and nucleus of Carlism, vacillated, but eventually a leading newspaper, *El Pensamiento Navarro,* came out in defense of the pretender.[2] Most of the clergy followed this lead. So did most of the province's Carlists, as well as those in Catalonia. The Mellist strength was in the other Basque provinces, Valencia, and other scattered points in Spain.[3]

Carlism, under whatever name, remained a political force of varying strength until 1936, but its adherents never lost their capacity to disagree. This tendency was aggravated when the goals and constituencies of Carlism became intertwined with those of the new Basque nationalist movement, as we shall see shortly.

Yet though Carlism's ability to unify the conservatives of Navarra wavered, there was one cause that continued to hold them together, regardless of party affiliation: preservation of the fueros. The staunch watchdogs of the foral tradition were not intimidated even by the repressive policies of the dictatorship that followed upon the retirement from power of Alfonso XIII in 1923.

THE DICTATORSHIP

Spain was neutral during World War I, but like much of Europe experienced social and economic unrest in the aftermath. Alfonso XIII, in 1923, under pressure from the army, made General Miguel Primo de Rivera prime minister. Both monarch and army believed a strong man could rescue the nation from its various crises: the disastrous Moroccan campaign, the breakdown of law and order, the widespread terrorism. Primo de Rivera accomplished much in these respects, but at the price of Spanish liberty and justice and self-respect.

The dictatorship persistently tried to gnaw away at the remaining powers of provincial governments. In 1924 the Municipal Statute, authorized by the finance minister José Calvo Sotelo, was announced. It aimed at replacing *ad hoc* military administrations with elected town officials. It was to give all Spanish municipalities virtual autonomy and extensive control over their own finances. Navarra's *Diputación,* until then accustomed to being sole and paternalistic supervisor of the province's towns and cities, was alarmed. The statute proposed formation of a *Consejo Foral Administrativo,* made up of representatives of town councils, which would supersede many of the *Diputación's* own administrative powers. Fortunately for the deputies' peace of mind, the statute never became completely operational and elections to the local administrative posts were never held.

The next threat to provincial power was the attempt (once more!) to alter Navarra's privileged tax structure, in 1927. As we saw in the last chapter, Navarra had survived two such attacks since the Foral Pact of 1841. Though thirty-four years had now passed since the last confrontation, the memory of the dispute was still alive.

In view of the history of Navarra's insistence on bilateral accord for any new tax formula, the civil governor in 1927 should have known better than to try to alter by decree the 1893 agreement. The *Diputación* protested with such firmness that Primo de Rivera himself came to Pamplona to see what the trouble was. As a result, he ordered his government to negotiate with the *Diputación*. The two parties eventually agreed on a new figure of six million pesetas annually. Navarra was prepared to admit that the cost of government had gone up, but wanted to be a party to any dictamen raising its contribution.

However, the new and higher figure was viewed with dismay by the press for years to come. *La Voz de Navarra* was particularly vitriolic, and in 1930 was still denouncing the dictatorship for deceiving Navarra's negotiators—and the latter for letting themselves be hoodwinked.[4]

BASQUE NATIONALISM, CARLISM AND NAVARRA

Long before these events, the political spectrum grew more kaleidoscopic with the emergence of the Basque nationalist movement. As the twentieth century progressed, the complicated politics of northern Spain saw Basque nationalists and Carlists often overlapping in their allegiances, sometimes allied, more frequently at odds.

Basque nationalism, in the broadest sense, had ancient roots, in race, culture, language and not least the Basque fueros. But toward the end of the nineteenth century it developed rapidly, especially in Vizcaya, where industrialization was altering social and economic structures. From an ethnic consciousness and desire to preserve a culture, it evolved into an impulse to organize and acquire more or even complete autonomy. This was the inevitable, if gradually realized, reaction to curbs on the Basque provinces by the centralist Spanish government since the early nineteenth century. It was also a response to what Stanley Payne calls "the intersecting of traditionalism and modernization."[5]

The spark that ignited the modern phase of the movement was struck when the Cortes, in the Constitution of 1876 after the restoration, finally implemented the 1839 laws that "modified" the fueros of the three Basque provinces and Navarra. Reaction in Vasconavarra to the new restrictions, especially those taking away their right to manage their own financial affairs, was negative. Many Basques began casting about for some way to regain their lost powers of self-government. They formed the

Partido Nacionalista Vasco (PNV) in 1894, with Sabino de Arana, a Vizcayan, as its prophet.

At first it looked as though the new party had much in common with Basque Carlism. It drew its strength from the conservative mountain dwellers of the north, from the peasantry, and from the lower middle classes of the towns. It offered alternatives to the centralizing pull of Madrid. It was devoted to Catholicism and repelled by the anticlerical tendencies displayed by the Liberals. And both parties espoused a preservation of— or return to—a degree of self-rule for the Basque provinces.[6]

It would be easy to assume that this implied an identical commitment to preservation of the fueros. It did not, because the ultimate aims of the two parties (as differentiated from their articles of faith) were not the same. The Carlists were a national party in Spain, desirous of a total military and political victory throughout the nation. The Basque Carlists supported this objective and its concomitant: preservation of regional fueros. This was imperative, so that the rights of each resulting autonomous region would be intact when it took its place within the larger federation.

But the Basque nationalists, at least in the beginning, stood for complete independence, not just some autonomy within a national framework. Therefore, preservation of the foral laws was not so pertinent to them. They took it for granted that the new Basque state would automatically draw up and respect a guarantee of its citizens' rights.

It was on this point that the Navarrese Carlists finally fell out with the Basque nationalists. But the divergences were not at once evident. For about two decades there were dialogue and occasional cooperation between the two groups, though the nationalists never succeeded in enlisting as much support in Navarra as they thought they would. Their original program had assumed the participation of all Basques. But even those in Navarra who had separatist tendencies would have preferred, if there were to be a secession from Spain, a restoration of pre-1841 Navarra (i.e., the kingdom) rather than a Navarra submerged in a seven-part state: the three Basque provinces of Spain, three of France, and Navarra.

Thus, though the Basque nationalists' natural desire to broaden their base by drawing in such a relatively prosperous member as Navarra kept them proselytizing in the province, and with some success, Basques in Navarra tended to be more concerned with preservation of their culture than with political independence. Arturo Campión, perhaps Navarra's best-known and earliest nationalist, was fervently interested in preserving the Basque language and folklore; he was less interested in political activism.

Progress for the Basque nationalists was slow, sometimes imperceptible. Still, by the eve of World War I their party, the PNV, had become mature enough to split into two factions, differing in their willingness to cooperate (or compromise) with the central Spanish government.[7] At the same time, regionalist or nationalist causes elsewhere in Spain were gaining ground or at least recognition, especially in Catalonia. But Navarra still generally resisted overtures from its Basque neighbors to join them.

Nevertheless, in the 1918 elections one of the seven deputies elected from Navarra was a Basque nationalist. But the province's true sympathies were elsewhere: as noted previously, three of the seven were Jaimists. Two were Conservatives and one was a Maurist (follower of Spain's Conservative prime minister Antonio Maura).

The PNV did better in Vizcaya that year, winning five seats. This election was an indication that at last the Basque nationalists had to be taken seriously as a political force.

The first real confrontation between Navarra's two conservative factions came in December 1918. Navarrese of many persuasions met at a Pamplona assembly to consider possible means of regaining some degree of home rule. The Basque nationalists in attendance urged an outright return to the pre-1839 system, with complete autonomy. But the nonnationalist program won. This was Carlist in spirit, Navarrese in practicality. It advocated a restoration of Navarra's foral self-government, but stipulated accommodation to the existing Spanish system.[8] The PNV, outvoted here, continued elsewhere to advocate a solution that would move the clock back a century and more for the three Basque provinces.

That same year the Madrid government set up a commission to study the case for regional autonomous governments within Spain. The impetus was the chronic unrest in Catalonia, yet the Catalan nationalists spurned the commission's meeting. Basques, however, were interested participants and put forward their proposal for an autonomous Basque state—excluding Navarra, inasmuch as Navarra had voted in Pamplona to have nothing to do with such a notion. It was an academic exercise: the government shelved the whole project.

Such a brief account of the disagreements between Basque nationalists and Carlists (or traditionalists, or foral conservatives) in Navarra might give the impression that the controversy was conducted in hushed tones and with restraint. Examination of the spoken and written words of several Navarrese public figures of the day will dispel this misconception.

We have already met Juan Vázquez de Mella, the ideological opponent of the Integrist Carlist Ramón Nocedal during the early years of the century. Mella, born in Galicia, first spread his political wings in Navarra. He was, as he himself said, a born regionalist, who urged every region in Spain to "demand an autonomy and a personality to which its history gives it the right."[9] He was a Carlist from childhood. He first served as Navarra's deputy in the Cortes in 1893 and remained there until 1916. His eloquence was legendary (one of his colleagues called him a "human volcano")—especially when directed against the liberal regime in Madrid. His passionate denunciation of the government for losing the American colonies in 1898 was so disruptive that he was expelled from the chamber.[10] Mella announced his break with moderate Carlism (Jaimism) in 1918, because he was opposed to the pretender's neutralist attitude during World War I. He devoted the rest of his life to the traditionalist faction of Carlism, which came to be known as the Mellist branch. But he was opposed to separatism. He was in favor not so much of Navarra's withdrawal from Spain, as of Spain's withdrawal from centralized liberalism.

Another notable in Navarra who was not part of the PNV but who was devoted to foral liberties was Victor Pradera Larrumbe. Born in 1873 of a Carlist family, he grew up absorbing the mystique of Carlism. In 1899 he was elected to the Cortes as deputy (Carlist) from Tolosa in Guipúzcoa. He tried to modernize Carlism. Then, disillusioned by its negativism, he became a strong traditionalist and fighter for restoration of Navarra's foral regime, while defending Spanish unity. During the Rivera dictatorship he still tried to work within the system. When the Second Republic was declared, in 1931, he rejoined the Carlists, now renamed the *Comunión Tradicionalista*. He was killed by a separatist in San Sebastián in 1936. In his best-known work, *El Estado Nuevo*, he defined the ideal nation as a "larger society of societies, not of individuals." A mark of his place in the pantheon of respected traditionalists is the fact that, when his collected works were published in 1945, the Prologue was written by Francisco Franco.[11]

However, some in Navarra spoke up just as eloquently for Basque nationalism. For example, Goicoechea Oroquieta (who wrote as Evangelista de Ibero) was a passionate supporter of an independent Basque state that would include Navarra. In his *Ami Vasco*, written in 1906, he urged a patient, unflinching struggle for Basque independence—even if it took "fifty, a hundred, or two hundred years."[12]

Circumstances bore out the need for patience. About twenty years after Evangelista de Ibero wrote those words, and shortly after Primo de Rivera assumed power, the three Basque provinces tried to persuade the dictator to grant them more autonomy—perhaps looking wistfully at Navarra's considerable degree of self-government, still greater than theirs. But the attempt failed.

As the dictatorship lumbered on, it grew more repressive of regional aspirations. This, combined with the Basque provinces' growing prosperity, worked to draw more adherents, from more strata of society, into the movement. The PNV was becoming a viable party, willing to work with others and able to command their respect in joint efforts to overthrow the dictatorship.

As Primo de Rivera's time began to run out, his periodic proposals for a new constitution were taken less and less seriously. Most Spaniards who had an opinion on the subject urged a radical change in regime, not just another piece of paper. But until 1929 a legitimizing constitution was a subject for lively debate in the press. Some in Vasconavarra saw it as a means of reviving the separation or regional autonomy issue.

The young Navarrese historian José María Lacarra, considering the various alternatives possible under a new constitution, advocated an interesting kind of federation: it would recognize the regional differences of those geographic areas that already demonstrated their awareness of their "difference"—including Catalonia, Navarra, the Vascongadas, Galicia and perhaps Asturias and Aragon. It would permit other regions, still lacking a territorial or spiritual sense of unity, to be governed for the time being by the central government "until the regional personality they seek springs forth." Then the central government could hold plebiscites every ten years to determine if these regions were ready for the degree of self-government enjoyed by their fellow provinces.[13] However, before any such proposals got beyond the speculative stage, Primo de Rivera lost the support of the two institutions that had given him power, the army and the king. He resigned in 1930. A year later Alfonso XIII also departed, after the monarchy was rejected and the way paved for the Second Republic by the municipal elections of April 1931.

XVII

The Durable Province

SINCE THE DEPARTURE OF KING ALfonso XIII from Spain in 1930, the nation has lived through four traumatic historical periods, each one involving a wrenching transition: the republic from 1931 to 1936; the Civil War, 1936 to 1939; the Franco dictatorship, 1939 to 1975; and the restoration of the monarchy with the accession of King Juan Carlos in 1975.

The way the people of Navarra responded to these four events recalls some of their reactions while a kingdom—or before—to exterior threats or invasions. The general rules: stand up for your rights and beliefs; do not be intimidated; if necessary or expedient, lie low and see what can be salvaged. And learn from experience.

When Spain embarked on its second republican experiment, in 1931, traditionalist Navarra again rose to the challenge. For the fourth time in a century, the former kingdom roused itself to defend its fueros and, perhaps, be done with republicanism for once and for all. For a time the more conservative in the province—that is, the Carlists—were tempted to join the Basque nationalists in their bid for autonomy. But they soon turned aside from that path.

When the fragile Second Republic expired, most of Navarra's rightist dissidents knew where they stood and who their allies were; they were ready to try to get along with each other in order to defeat the common enemy by open rebellion. Navarra was overwhelmingly on the Nationalist side in the Civil War. (The coalesced movements and parties of the right that rose against the Republican government in July 1936 were the Nationalists—not to be confused with Basque or Catalan nationalists.) The unanimity and potency of Navarra's support of the rebels was a phenomenon that still evokes pride in Navarrese —and incredulity in many others, who associate Basques with opposition to Franco. The war gave impetus for one more outpouring of the conservative Navarrese spirit. After the Nationalist victory, Navarra was rewarded with renewed recognition of its special fiscal autonomy.

Then came the long, seemingly calm Franco years. But it was during this period—the 1940s into the 1970s—that the seeds of change were taking root that would cause many in Navarra to question whether their familiar institutions were adequate to deal with a more industrialized economic structure and a more worldly society. Could Navarra learn from others how to profit from new economic opportunities? As we shall see, Navarra learned these lessons well.

At the same time, and increasingly in the liberated post-Franco years, Navarra has been confronted with the ever more urgent matter of to what degree it was a part of the Basque nationalist movement. How it answers this question may affect the future of the entire movement.

NAVARRA DURING THE SECOND REPUBLIC

The Republicans' mandate in 1931 was based on their strong showing in the April municipal elections. The dictator Primo de Rivera had resigned a year before; the country was poised for a return to a constitutional monarchy—or a rejection of it. Though this was not a national election, the lines were clearly drawn between the monarchists and the Republican coalition. The outcome was eagerly awaited as an indication of Spain's future direction.

Voters throughout the Basque countryside were, predictably, overwhelmingly in favor of the monarchist candidates, as was virtually all rural Spain. So was Pamplona, though the other Basque capitals were not.

But the surprising urban support for the Republican coalition served as a clear signal that the monarchy's days were numbered. Alfonso was stunned, and within three days had left the country. (Temporarily, he said, and only to avoid civil war.) And the Second Republic was born.

During the first alarms at the Republic's bold reforms and anticlericalism, the Basque nationalists and the conservative Navarrese made common cause. But their interests diverged soon after the former saw a chance to bargain with the Republic for autonomy.

The Republican Constitution of 1931 provided that if any province or provinces with common historical, cultural and economic characteristics wished to organize as an autonomous region in order to form a politico-administrative nucleus within the Spanish state, they had only to prepare a statute and present it to the Cortes. The Basque provinces jumped at the chance to at last break out of the Madrid-centered grid.

Catalonia had again set the example, having already declared itself—optimistically—an independent state in 1931. The Catalan Statute was passed a year later, but had many ups and downs.

In late May 1931, representatives of the four Vasconavarrese provinces met in Pamplona and called for an assembly of municipalities to take up the project. The large cities were mostly cool and hostile; but the towns and countryside were fervently in favor of the autonomy statute. The next conference, in Estella in June, had an attendance of some thirty thousand, and seems to have been more like a vast picnic than a caucus at which to write a political platform.[1] It attracted Basque nationalists, Navarrese Carlists, monarchists, conservative Republicans, and almost the whole spectrum of Republican Spain, except Socialists and leftists.

On September 22, 1931, a commission presented the home-rule project to the Zamora government in Madrid. In November the commission was told to prepare the statute itself and get its approval by a majority of the municipalities and by a popular referendum.

How could Navarra's Carlists, who firmly believed in an indivisible monarchy, subscribe to what was called the "Magna

Carta of separatism"? The explanation was their indignation at the assaults on Spain's religion by the Republicans. They were ready to join anyone ready to defend the Catholic faith.[2] But this one bond with the PNV (Basque Nationalist Party)—their shared devotion to Catholicism—did not prove strong enough when the time came for the real decision. When the four provinces' delegates met again in June 1932, in Pamplona, to vote on the final draft, Navarra's representatives had had second thoughts. They rejected the Statute by 123 to 109 votes. The other three provinces approved it overwhelmingly and in the subsequent plebiscites (1933) gave it, overall, an eighty-four percent favorable vote, though Alava's was only forty-six percent.[3]

Navarra's rejection, Alava's lukewarm support, and then the 1933 national elections that placed anti-regionalist Radical Republicans in control, slowed progress in Madrid. Not until October 1936 did the Cortes vote in the Basque Statute. Born after the outbreak of the Civil War, the Basque state tried bravely to reach viability, but lasted only one year. Its government went into exile. Later, Vizcaya and Guipúzcoa were punished for their resistance to the Nationalists: all their autonomy was withdrawn.

Long before then Navarra had completely removed itself from the Basque nationalist cause.

Neither for ideological nor for economic reasons did most of Navarra's citizens see any need for the statute. Their old devotion to *Dios, Patria, Rey y Fueros,* which had periodically inspired and unified the province for a century, could continue to do so. Their Catholicism, rigid and traditional, suited them very well. They saw no need to liberalize it, or to modernize their social structure. They still revered the idea of kingship.

And unlike the three Basque provinces, Navarra's material well-being was rooted in the countryside, not the cities. There was no vocal constituency of businessmen and bourgeoisie looking enviously at the economic opportunities of their northern and western European counterparts.

This is not to suggest that there was no rightist political activity in Navarra during the Republic; but it was an almost autonomous movement, unified largely by its Catholicism. The rightists in Navarra were the only ones in Spain not under the direction of the central committee in Madrid.[4]

So in spite of a historical affinity with the Basque provinces, the taint of separatism in the Basque Statute frightened the Navarrese off. As a Madrid newspaper columnist (not a Navarrese) wrote in 1934:

> Politically, there is no country in Spain so successful as Navarra. Though it is no longer called a kingdom; though it has had to get involved in the jumble of national legislative confusion; Navarra always comes through as a little, self-sufficient state, complete and perfect, ready to stand comparison with the best organized countries in Europe. Navarra does not need such new schemes as the Statute. Navarra is not concerned with those Mediterranean notions. Navarra well knows what its own traditions are, and how to live autonomously with all its personal integrity, without having to resort to the flashy games that these Irish-type malcontents play.[5]

THE CARLIST REVIVAL

The Carlists had stayed out of the political arena during the Primo de Rivera dictatorship. But they sprang back in at the birth of the Republic. Their leadership after the death of the pretender Jaime, in October 1931, was his uncle Alfonso Carlos de Borbón, the only remaining direct male descendant of the first Carlos.

This plucky eighty-two-year-old had a creditable Carlist record. In 1873, during the Third Carlist War, he had ably led an army in Catalonia to great territorial gains for the cause of his brother Carlos VII. But after a victory at Cuenca, near Madrid, in 1874, he fell out with Carlos and left Spain. Now, fifty-seven years and two pretenders later, Alfonso Carlos I agreed to act as official Carlist claimant to the Spanish crown.

His leadership, and the threat to traditional Carlist values posed by the Republic, at last healed the party's old schism, at least on the surface. Integrists and Mellists made peace with the dynastic branch. Alfonso Carlos called the revitalized party the *Comunión Tradicionalista Carlista.*

As always, its greatest strength was in Navarra, and its strength was visible in its cadres of volunteer militia, the *Requetés.*[6] The name, perhaps derived from a marching song of troops in the early Carlist wars, still honored the glorious history of Carlism while inspiring its twentieth-century activists. Young men of the 1930s, nurtured on the tales of their forefathers' exploits, joyfully donned the red beret and took up the musket.

Until 1934 the training of *Requetés* had to be clandestine, but even before the birth of the Republic, paramilitary groups began preparing to defend the old traditions—just in case. During the uncertain months before Alfonso's departure and the 1931 elections, *Requetés* were assembled and held in readiness, should the revolutionary strikes of December 1930 become a threat to provincial law and order.

For the next three years the *Requetés* organized secretly, storing up arms and supplies and drilling with wooden muskets in upstairs rooms. But by 1934 they were strong enough—and opposition to the Republic was general enough—for their leaders to bring them out into the open. In Pamplona, Viana, Villava and other towns scattered throughout Navarra, they held weekly drills in their red berets and khaki uniforms, marching about the squares and up and down the hills and valleys.

They started a weekly newspaper, *a.e.t.* (so called from the youth organization *Agrupación Escolar Tradicionalista,* parent organization of the current crop of *Requetés*). The paper flourished for half a year and reflected the views of not only the enthusiastic young, but also most Traditionalists in Navarra. Its heroes were the great Carlists of the past, and Alfonso Carlos I. It applauded the naming of Manuel Fal Conde as the pretender's delegate in Spain. Its enemies were the Socialists and their rival publication *Trabajadores!,* the Monarchists of *Renovación Española,* Communists and anyone who fostered atheism and supported the Republic.

In March 1934, *a.e.t.* told its readers that the "Marxist crooks" were getting ready to assault the country with crime and banditry. To keep Marxism's baleful shadow from engulfing the world, "We must maintain Carlism with uncompromising strength and, if necessary, unfurl the black banner of Santa Cruz." The reference was to the terrible soldier-priest of the Third Carlist War.

Gradually the opposition groups on the right drew together. In March 1934, a delegation from the *Comunión Tradicionalista,* with another from the *Renovación Española* which was as anti-Republic as were the Carlists, went to Rome to see Mussolini, and received his promise of weapons in support of their projected overthrow of the Republic.

In July four hundred young Carlists went to Italy for training in modern warfare. They included Jaime del Burgo, later the bibliographer of Carlism and historian of his Navarrese homeland. The Spanish youths, he recalled, had to conceal their identity and masquerade as Peruvian army officers who had come to familiarize themselves with Italian-made arms to be purchased by Peru.[7]

By 1935 some fifty-six hundred Navarrese *Requetés* were in fighting trim. Many of their leaders were officers who had recently been retired because of the Republic's legislation to reduce the high officer-to-nonofficer ratio in the Spanish army. Colonel Ricardo de Rada y Peral succeeded the hero of Morocco, Enrique Varela, as director of *Requeté* training.

The pretender's deputies in Spain were his nephew Prince Javier de Borbón-Parma (who became pretender after Alfonso Carlos died in 1936)[8] and Fal Conde, an Andalusian and the party secretary. At the end of 1935 the Carlists formed a military *junta* in Navarra under Prince Javier.[9]

All three rightist groups—Carlists, Monarchists, army—were now planning in earnest for a rising against the Republic. Like many others in Spain, they blamed the Popular Front government, elected in January 1936, for the accelerated church burnings and other violence.

But the dissidents had still not agreed on means, much less ends. The generals on the side of insurrection included Francisco Franco (relegated in the spring of 1936 to a post on the Canary Islands by a distrustful government), Varela, José Sanjurjo, also of Moroccan fame, and Emilio Mola, transferred in March 1936 from Morocco to Pamplona's military governorship.

Sanjurjo, born in Pamplona in 1876 of dyed-in-the-wool Carlist stock, had been the most famous soldier in Spain when he came back from his Moroccan victories, in 1927. In 1932 he led a premature rising against the Republic; he was supported by the military, Monarchists and Carlists. The count of Rodezno, leader of the Traditionalists in the Cortes, and Fal Conde were involved. But the exercise's aims were less to bring back a king than simply to overthrow the despised Republic. The two-pronged rising failed in Madrid, succeeded briefly in

Seville, then fell apart. Sanjurjo fled, was imprisoned, then was pardoned by the Cortes in 1934. Now in 1936 he was in Portugal; he kept in touch with the other plotters and sent his views on what should be the lineaments of the Spain that was to arise from the forthcoming rebellion. At one point, Sanjurjo agreed to serve as head of a provisional government, with Alfonso Carlos as king, if the Carlists engineered a successful rising on their own.

And sometimes, during that tense spring of 1936, it seemed the Carlists might decide to go it alone. Mola, chief architect of the generals' conspiracy, knew he must enlist the Carlists' battle-ready *Requetés*. But it was hard to come to terms with the Carlists. In April, from his control post in Pamplona, Mola circularized his plans. They called for Sanjurjo to fly back from Lisbon as soon as the attack was launched, and become president of a military *junta* that would "establish the law of the land." Nobody expected the rebellion to take long.

Then began negotiations on the details. Fal Conde, speaking for the Carlists, stipulated first that if their troops were to march with the rebels, the succeeding government should be a nonpolitical civilian-military directorate (headed by Sanjurjo), with the *Comunión* naming the civilian members. Mola could not promise this. Through the early summer of 1936 the haggling went on, while all Spain seethed with the unrest and disorder that unmistakably presaged civil war.

A major disagreement centered on which flag should lead the rebels into battle. The Carlists held out for the Monarchist bicolor, but Mola felt the troops should march under the tricolor of the existing government, to demonstrate the legitimacy of their protest. And he knew how little effect the Monarchist flag would have outside Navarra.[10]

Finally, Sanjurjo, Fal Conde and Mola managed to agree at least on war aims: to prepare for the return of a traditional monarchy (they did not specify which king would be called), with a nonpolitical government, at first run by the military, and to restore the old Spain by revising all the Republic's social and religious legislation.

They compromised on the flag dispute. If a body of Carlists would be operating as a separate unit they could use the Monarchist flag. But if they were in a non-Carlist battalion the whole battalion would march without any flag. (A month after the outbreak of war, at an emotional ceremony in Seville led by

THE DURABLE PROVINCE 207

General Franco, the Monarchist flag was formally adopted for all Nationalist troops.)

On July 14, 1936, Fal Conde and Prince Javier signed a document pledging the *Comunión's* support of a military uprising. On July 17 the army rebels in Morocco rose against the Republic. This was the signal for the risings on the mainland the next day.

CIVIL WAR

Into Pamplona, through the night of July 18, poured young and old Carlist volunteers, eager to join the crusade. They came by bus, by truck, by car and on foot, bringing whatever weapons they could muster, wearing whatever approximation of uniform they could manage.

By the dawn of July 19 they were assembling in the Plaze del Castillo, where Mola viewed them with amazement and some alarm. He asked a *Requetés* colonel how he was going to find arms for so many. (By now there were four thousand.) "God, who brought them here, will provide," the colonel replied.[11]

On July 20 General Sanjurjo was killed, as his plane took off from Lisbon to bring him to Burgos. But the momentum of the rebellion could not be halted even by this blow.

On July 20 the *Junta Regional Carlista de Navarra* issued, in the pages of *El Pensamiento Navarro,* its call to arms:

> This Movement is national, not solely Carlist; it involves the very survival of our country. Therefore we support it, understanding well that after our triumph we shall work with even more enthusiasm for the complete realization of our ideals, and that we shall not rest until we see our legitimate King, representative of our principles, seated on the throne of San Fernando. This is our ultimate aspiration, and we call on the conscience of the nation to judge the disinterestedness of our *Comunión,* which is ready to shed its last drop of blood for the nation, in support of a movement against the shameful government now in power, without demanding ahead of time that its doctrine be adopted.... Navarrese, think of your history, and without cowardice, obey the voice of your conscience!

Nearly everyone did. There were exceptions, for after all Pamplona had produced six thousand votes for the Popular Front that spring. And Bishop Marcelino Olaechea of Pamplona publicly deplored the outbreak of war, refusing to give the troops his unconditional blessing. But nearly all the banks, churches, governmental and administrative bodies, as well as most of the citizenry, were behind the *Alzamiento*—the Rising. On July 22 the *Diputación Foral* called on the citizens to join the national movement of liberation, on behalf of the Catholic faith, their freedom of conscience, the return of Christ to the schoolroom, material welfare, and foral liberties.

Navarra's fueros now stood the province in good stead. Thanks to its broad powers, the *Diputación* could, on its own and expeditiously, give Mola the funds he needed to launch the war.[12] By October 1936, forty thousand Navarrese—one-tenth of the province's population—had joined the Nationalist army. In this war they did not have to fight on their own soil. The red-bereted troops streamed out from Pamplona toward Aragon, to join eventually in the march on Madrid; and toward Guipúzcoa, to establish the front in the Vascongadas and cut communications with France. By September both San Sebastián and Irun, on the French border, were in Nationalist hands; in 1937, Bilbao and the entire north.

After the Nationalist victory in 1939, Navarra took its place in Franco's Spain with all the administrative and economic privileges it had tenaciously clung to since the *Ley Paccionada* of 1841. The new leaders, like many Spanish kings before them, knew how to reward their most loyal subjects.

But even before the victory, Franco paid public tribute to the province's immediate and telling support. He came to Pamplona in November 1936 and spoke from the balcony of the palace of the *Diputación*. Praising the mothers of Navarra, the blood of its heroes, and the spirit of the race, he saluted "this city of Pamplona, and Navarra, cradle of the National Movement." The climax was his addition of the laurel cross of San Fernando to the ancient shield of the Kingdom of Navarra.[13]

POSTWAR AND POST-FRANCO

After the war and during the Franco years (1939 to 1975), Navarra shared with the rest of Spain an unaccustomed stability of institutions and a surface calm that approached somnolence. Politically, there was little observable activity.

The Basque nationalists were not idle, but had to stay underground or abroad, especially during World War II, when Spain was officially neutral but clearly favored Germany. But with Franco's "rehabilitation" in international eyes in 1948, Basque nationalists lost hope that the great powers' distaste for *El Caudillo* would lead them to support a dismemberment of the Spanish state.[14] Throughout this period Navarra remained aloof from the nationalist movement. The Madrid regime's outlawing of study of the Basque language and suppression of any regionalist signals were deplored, but were not cause for demonstrations. Navarra, with Alava, still had significant freedom to tax and spend.

About 1950, Navarra's leaders set out on a new path. By now virtually all arable land was under cultivation, some of it still rather primitively to be sure. Industry was still a minor factor in the province's economy. Navarra's *Diputación,* looking at neighboring Guipúzcoa and Vizcaya, saw how the thriving manufacturing sector there was enriching the privincial coffers. The deputies set out deliberately to attract industry, and to offer tax concessions and other incentives that were hard for Spanish and foreign investors to resist. The policy was spectacularly successful, especially in the attraction of chemical, paper, iron and steel companies. Manufacturing began to replace agriculture as prime money-maker in the province, with resulting changes in the makeup of the labor force.[15] Between 1950 and 1970, the precentage of workers engaged in agriculture declined from fifty-five to twenty-six percent—which put Navarra almost where Guipúzcoa and Vizcaya had been twenty years before.[16]

The numerical increase in industrial workers was most noticeable in one urban area: Pamplona. Sangüesa, Estella and Tafalla lost population, Tudela gained slightly, but Pamplona grew astonishingly, largely because of the influx of industry in the surrounding area, with its accompanying attraction of persons to work in services. By 1978 Pamplona accounted for forty-five percent of the province's population, and sixty percent of its business enterprises.[17] Its people had long ago overflowed the old city walls, and new suburbs had sprung up all around the city. One of the first victims of urban sprawl was the massive old *Ciudadela,* the citadel built by Philip II in the sixteenth century. But to give the city fathers credit, much of its former area has been preserved as a pleasant city park, ringed by highways and apartment blocks. Most of the suburban expansion, however, took over what had been farming and grazing lands. Such growth was bound to be disruptive and to provide fertile ground for a revived political consciousness.

After the death of Franco and the restoration of the Spanish monarchy under Juan Carlos in 1975, all Spain had more questions than answers about how to deal with *apertura*—the opening up of the nation, to permit political organization, freedom of the press, and labor unionization. In the Basque provinces, agonizing questions were raised by the violence of the militant branch of the ETA ("Basque Homeland and Freedom"), which short-circuited the more measured progress of the less radical nationalists toward autonomy.

These questions obtained in Navarra too, as well as concerns about coming to terms with unaccustomed industrialization and suburbanization. It was apparent to many that the province's political orientation and its institutions had not kept pace with its economic growth. The vexing problem of Basque nationalism could not be ignored. The pressure from the other Basque provinces intensified again the moment Franco was gone. In the more dynamic societies of Guipúzcoa and Vizcaya, nationalism had long ago replaced Carlism as a rallying point for the increasingly self-conscious middle class.[18] This was partly becasue Carlism was not what it had been—a single-minded reactionary movement. It was possible, by the 1970s, even in Navarra, to call oneself a Carlist and support monarchy, communism, Basque nationalism, or atheism.[19]

Basque nationalism, too, had evolved during the Franco years. Now its adherents included many who were not even Basque, or at least did not speak the language: workers who had come to the industrial centers for jobs and who, for economic rather than ethnic reasons, espoused the cause of Basque separatism.[20] And Navarra had its share of them.

One of the first acts of the Basque nationalists after the ratification by Spain's voters of the new constitution in December 1978 was to rush through a draft of a Basque autonomy statute. For once, they got to Madrid before the Catalans with *their* proposal. However, it was two years before the Basques won approval in the Cortes.

Navarra did not participate in the drafting of the statute; not surprisingly, it had remained outside the Basque General Council that was created to manage the transition to autonomy.[21]

The same old differences between Navarra and its neighbors were aired. The Basque nationalists would have liked to include Navarra—with half the area of the Basque Country and most of its agricultural productivity. Navarra, fearful of losing its privileged status, still felt safer staying outside.

Nevertheless, there were signs that sentiment in Navarra was becoming less predictable. The *abertzale* parties (leftist and rigidly nationalist) showed unexpected strength and won nine out of the seventy seats in the provincial *Diputación* in 1979.[22] Most Navarrese could not help taking pride in the fact that, though their province was not a participant in the new provisional Basque government, provided for in the Autonomy Statute, its citizens were well represented in its leadership. And even in Navarra, *vasquismo*—literally, "Basqueness"—was the new banner for opponents of a Madrid-centered status quo, and proponents of a joining of all Basques in a new state.

On the other side were the traditional rightists (heirs, many times removed, of the Carlists), advocates of a reapproximation of the foral state that was created in 1841, and of *navarrismo*. They held that Navarra's history and destiny were quite different from those of the Basque provinces.

One solution to the confrontation between the two opposing points of view, a referendum to determine the will of the people, is advocated by some, if the extreme polarization that has occurred in Guipúzcoa and Vizcaya is to be avoided in Navarra. Those who favor a referendum see tendencies in both factions that would accept compromise.[23]

Since 1841, it has been clear that Navarra's fueros were more durable than the kingdom. Respect for *foralismo* has been so dominant for so long that it seems doubtful that even in the explosive atmosphere of the 1980s it could be entirely submerged. And if Navarra proves able to come to a peaceful and legal solution to its internal conflicts—accepting the fact that *vasquismo* can coexist with *navarrismo* and foral autonomy—the lesson might not be lost on the rest of Vasconavarra.

APPENDIX A

Rulers of the Kingdom of Navarra, 818-1512

IÑIGO IÑIGUEZ DYNASTY[1]

Iñigo Iñiguez (Iñigo Arista), 818-851
García Iñiguez, 851-860
Fortún Garcés, 860-905

JIMENO DYNASTY[2]

Sancho Garcés, 905-925
García Sánchez I, 925-970
Sancho Garcés II, 970-974
García Sánchez II (el Temblón), 974-1004
Sancho III (el Mayor), 1004-1035[3]
García, 1035-1054
Sancho IV (el de Peñalen), 1054-1076

ARAGONESE DYNASTY

Sancho Ramirez, 1076-1094
Pedro I, 1094-1104
Alfonso I (el Batallador), 1104-1134

RESTORATION OF NAVARRESE DYNASTY BY ELECTION

García Ramirez (el Restaurador), 1134-1150
Sancho VII (el Sabio), 1150-1194
Sancho VIII (el Encerrado), 1194-1234

HOUSE OF CHAMPAGNE

Teobaldo I, 1234-1253
Teobaldo II, 1253-1270
Enrique I, 1270-1274
Juana I and Felipe I (Philip IV of France), 1274-1305

CAPETIAN KINGS OF FRANCE

Luis el Hutin (Louis X), 1305–1316
Felipe II (Philip V), 1316–1322
Carlos I (el Calvo) (Charles IV, the Bold), 1322–1327

HOUSE OF EVREUX

Juana II and Felipe III (Philip of Evreux, d. 1343), 1328–1349
Carlos II (el Malo), 1349–1387
Carlos III (el Noble), 1387–1425
Blanca (d. 1441) and Juan II of Aragon, 1425–1464

HOUSE OF FOIX

Leonor and Gaston of Foix (d. 1472), 1464–1479[4]
Francisco Febo, 1479–1483

HOUSE OF LABRIT

Catalina and Juan Labrit (Catherine and Jean d'Albret), 1483–1512

APPENDIX B

The Carlist Succession to 1936*

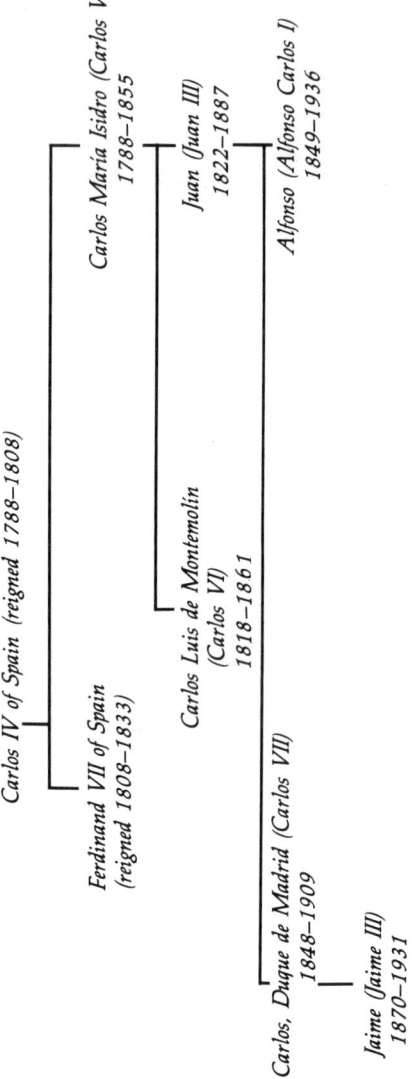

*Alfonso Carlos I (d. 1936) was the last direct male descendant of the first pretender to claim the Spanish throne. For a genealogical table showing other recent claimants, see Martin Blinkhorn, *Carlism and Crisis in Spain, 1931–1939* (Cambridge, 1975), pp. 308–11.

NOTES

NOTES TO CHAPTER I

1. The suggestion that the Basques were linked to the Scots was included in a twelfth-century guide for pilgrims to the shrine at Santiago de Compostela by Aimeric de Picaud, intended to help wayfarers to get safely through the perils along the route. See Jeanne Vielliard, ed., *Le Guide du Pélerin de Saint Jacques de Compostèle* (Maçon, 1938), pp. 13 ff.

2. For a synopsis of this and other theories, see Carlos Clavería, *Historia del Reino de Navarra* (Pamplona, 1971), pp. 11–13. The mystery has now received popular recognition, and is the subject of a book in the Robert Laffont series "Les Enigmes de l'Univers": Louis Charpentier, *Le Mystère Basque* (Paris, 1975).

3. Juan Maluquer de Motes noted new research into Basque blood-type characteristics that differentiated them from other races (*Pueblos Celtos* [Madrid, 1954], 30). Since then, a number of studies have documented the differences between Basque blood types and those of other Europeans. For example, Morton H. Levine, who conducted biological studies of Basques in two French villages in the 1960s, cites research that shows that Basques have a greater incidence of Rh-negative blood than any other people in the world ("The Basques," *Natural History*, 76 [April 1967] p. 46).

4. Julio Caro Baroja, *Los Vascos* (Madrid, 1971), pp. 379–81.

5. For a succinct description of this cave culture, see Bernardo Estornés Lasa, *Orígines de los Vascos* (San Sebastián, 1967), pp. 124 ff.

6. José Miguel de Barandiarán and Jesús Altuna, "La Cueva de Ekaín y sus Figuras Rupestres," *Munibe* (San Sebastián, 1969), pp. 333–86. Also, Ignacio Barandiarán, "Representaciones de Caballos en la Cueva de Ekaín," *Estudios de Arqueología Alavesa. Homenaje a Domingo Fernandez Medrano* (Vitoria, 1974), p. 47.

7. Julio Caro Baroja, *Los Pueblos de España. Ensayo de Etnología* (Barcelona, 1946), p. 23.

8. One of the first comprehensive compilations was by Barandiarán in 1952. He cited 300 dolmens dating from post-Magdalenian times in

the Basque Country (José Miguel de Barandiarán, *La Prehistoria en el Pireneo Vasco* [Zaragoza, 1952], maps, pp. 15 ff.). Elosegui catalogued and mapped 340 dolmens and *túmulos* (funerary monuments without a walled sepulchral chamber) in the Basque Country in 1953, with the greatest number (126) in Navarra (Jesús Elosegui, *Catálogo Dolménico del País Vasco* [Zaragoza, 1953]). Apellániz brought both these compilations up to date in his catalogue of dolmens in the Spanish Basque Country in 1973, arriving at a total of 428 (José María Apellániz, "Corpus de Materiales de las Culturas Prehistóricas con Cerámica de la Población de Carvernas del País Vasco Meridional," *Munibe*, supp. 1 [San Sebastián, 1973], pp. 147–335).

9. Juan Maluquer de Motes, *Notas sobre la Cultura Megalítica Navarra* (Pamplona, 1963), pp. 139–40.

10. Ibid., pp. 146–47.

11. José Miguel de Barandiarán, *El Hombre Prehistórico en el País Vasco* (Buenos Aires, 1953), pp. 133 and 153–55. Bosch Gimpera sees this "fluidity," with contact between the Pyrenean Basque culture and others on the Iberian Peninsula, as being marked from Paleolithic times onward, and with "crystalization" of cultural ethnic groups in the Pyrenees in the third millenium B.C. (Pedro Bosch Gimpera, "Sobre Prehistoria e Historia de los Vascos," *Munibe* [San Sebastián, 1971], pp. 419–21).

12. Jacques Blot, "Protohistoire en Pays Basque," *Bulletin de la Societé des Sciences, Lettres et Arts de Bayonne*, 129 (Bayonne, 1973), p. 22.

13. These early population centers were mostly in the northern higher regions. But there is evidence that, a little later, fairly important urban nuclei existed in the south, especially along the Ebro, which indicates that this "not very Basque" part of Navarra is as old as the north. See Julio Caro Baroja, *Los Vascos* (Madrid, 1971), p. 52.

NOTES TO CHAPTER II

1. For a reconstruction of Basque society and culture during the pre-Christian era, see Julio Caro Baroja, *Los Vascos* (Madrid, 1971), pp. 380–81.

2. The language that preceded Basque could have been introduced sometime between the Upper Paleolithic Age and the Bronze Age (ibid., p. 380). Efforts to trace the origins of the Basque language are as bewildering as, and closely related to, the search for the origins of the Basque people. Some scholars have seen similarities to other peninsular languages and have therefore asserted a racial link between Basques and Iberians. Other theories have linked Basque to western Caucasian languages, African, Egyptian, Siberian, Indo-European (including Sanskrit) and even Japanese. The problem is compounded by

NOTES 217

the fact that, until after the Middle Ages, Basque was a spoken language only. So no helpful written materials exist. Only what placenames have survived give evidence of the pre-Christian idiom. For a summary of many of the language theories, see Bernardo Estornés Lasa, *Orígines de los Vascos* (San Sebastián, 1967), pp. 245–52, 278.

3. José María Sastrústegui, *Mitos y Creencias* (San Sebastián, 1980), pp. 133 ff. See also José Miguel de Barandiarán, *Mitología Vasca* (Madrid, 1960), p. 75.

4. Barandiarán, *Mitologia*, pp. 83 ff.

5. José Miguel de Barandiarán, "Resumen de la Mitología Mariana," *Munibe,* 7 (San Sebastián, 1955), p. 262.

6. Bernardo Estornés Lasa, *Orígines,* pp. 201 and 279.

7. Vasconia, as a term synonymous with what we know as the Basque Country, has a cloudy history. As early as the first century B.C., the Romans named *vascones* those who lived in the area south of the Pyrenees to the Ebro, west to Guipúzcoa and Alava, and east to Jaca. See Germán de Pamplona, "Los Límites de la Vasconia Hispano-Romana y sus Variaciones en la Epoca Imperial," *Problemas de la Prehistoria y de la Etnología Vascas* (Pamplona, 1966), pp. 207–21. As a geographic term, Vasconia seems to have been first applied by the Romans to their lands in southwest France lying south of the Garonne and extending to, but not through, the Pyrenees. (This was the area they earlier called Novempopulania.) Later it sometimes included all the lands where *vascones* lived. Much later, as the Duchy of Vasconia acquired substance, and often extended its influence to the Basques of the Iberian Peninsula, Vasconia was understood generally to include the entire area that is now predominantly Basque.

NOTES TO CHAPTER III

1. In this central-southern area, Julio Caro Baroja has mapped more than three dozen locations where Roman vestiges have been found (*Etnografía Histórica de Navarra* [Pamplona, 1971], vol. 1, p. 56).

2. Ibid., pp. 46 and 71.

3. Lacarra, after examining many widely differing theories as to when Christianity became prevalent in the Basque Country, including some estimates as late as the eleventh century, concluded that there was a long period of coexistence of Vasco-Christians and Vasco-pagans until a "date relatively late, difficult to determine" (José María Lacarra, *Vasconia Medieval. Historia y Filología.* Conferencias 10 y 11 Enero 1956 [San Sebastián, 1957], pp. 51 and 69).

4. José María Lacarra, *Estudios de Historia Navarra* (Pamplona, 1971), p. 3.

5. William Douglass and Jon Bilbao, *Amerikanuak: Basques in the New World* (Reno, 1975), p. 36.

6. Quoted from a fourteenth-century Arab manuscript that included a history of the Muslim presence in Spain from 708 to 1287 (Evariste Lévi-Provençal, *Le Péninsule Ibérique au Moyen Age, d'après le Kitab-Arrawd Al-mitar* [Leiden, 1938], p. 70).

7. Religious zeal may have accounted partly for the Muslims' march into France, but the expectation of plunder in Tours was the immediate aim (W. Montgomery Watt and Pierre Cachia, *A History of Islamic Spain* [New York, 1967], pp. 16 and 18).

8. Arturo Campión, *Nabarra en su Vida Histórica* (Pamplona, 1925), p. 104.

9. Douglass and Bilbao, *Amerikanuak,* p. 34.

NOTES TO CHAPTER IV

1. As translated by Ralph Giesey in his examination of the Oath of Sobrarbe, *If Not, Not* (Princeton, 1968), p. 46.

2. José María Lacarra, *Historia Política del Reino de Navarra,* vol. 1. (Pamplona, 1972), p. 68.

3. Justo Pérez de Urbel and Ricardo del Arco y Garay, "España Cristiana: Comienzo de la Reconquista (711–1038)," *Historia de España,* Ramón Menéndez Pidal, ed. (Madrid, 1964), vol. 6, pp. 306–7.

4. Ibid.

5. See note 1, ch. 1.

6. Felipe Mateu y Llopis, "El Hallazgo de 'Pennies' Ingleses en Roncesvalles," *Príncipe de Viana,* 40–41 (Pamplona, 1950), pp. 201–10. For more on effects of the pilgrim traffic, see José María Lacarra, *Historia del Reino de Navarra* (Pamplona, 1972), vol. 1, pp. 340–41.

7. Sancho the Great, influenced by what he observed in Europe, did introduce some feudal practices. But for a discussion of Navarra's society, and why it developed with a less feudalistic pattern than the rest of Europe in the medieval period, see Georges Desdevises du Dézert, *Don Carlos d'Aragon, Prince de Viane: Etude sur l'Espagne du Nord au XVe Siècle* (Paris, 1889), p. 33.

8. The first king to reign over a land known as Navarra was Sancho Abarca, who ruled from 970 to 974 (Julio Caro Baroja, *Materiales para una Historia de la Lengua Vasca en su Relación con la Latina* [Salamanca, 1945], p. 221, n. 39). The name may date back to the eighth century (Julio Caro Baroja, *Etnografía Histórica de Navarra* [Pamplona, 1971], vol. 1, pp. 121–22 and footnote 34, p. 121). For a presentation of the river theory, see Manuel de Lecuona, "Etimología de la Voz 'Navarra,'" *Munibe* (1962), pp. 532–37.

NOTES TO CHAPTER V

1. Chronology and interpretation of Sancho's reign are drawn largely from Fr. Justo Pérez de Urbel, *Sancho el Mayor de Navarra* (Madrid, 1950).
2. Ibid., pp. 268–69 and 297–320, for background on Sancho's relations with the church and the Cluniac reform. See also Lacarra, who points out that Sancho's directive to the Cluniac monks to reform the monasteries may have been meant in the literal sense: to restore and rebuild monasteries that had been damaged or ruined by wars (José María Lacarra, *Estudios de Historia Navarra* [Pamplona, 1971], pp. 220–22).
3. This is the traditional explanation of Navarra's disintegration after Sancho's death (see Pérez de Urbel, *Sancho el Mayor,* p. 262). However, recent interpretations maintain that Sancho did not divide his kingdom, but left it all to García. The brothers' subsequent jealous ambition and enmity, not Sancho's will, led to the partition of his realm (Antonio Ubieto de Arteta, "Estudios en Torno a la División del Reino por Sancho el Mayor," *Príncipe de Viana* [Pamplona, 1960], pp. 12–13.
4. Jaime Vicens Vives, *Approaches to the History of Spain* (Berkeley, 1967), p. 50.
5. Only the pope held out for compliance with Alfonso's will. Papal references to García Ramírez, who became king of Navarra, and to his son Sancho el Sabio used the term duke instead of king. But when the third in line, Sancho el Fuerte, became king the pope gave him the royal title, as an inducement to enlist him in the holy wars against the Muslims (Angel J. Martín Duque, "La Restauración de la Monarquía Navarra y Las Ordenes Militares [1134–1194]," *Homenaje a Lacarra* [Zaragoza, 1977], p. 322.
6. John Gillingham, *Richard the Lionheart* (New York, 1978), p. 220.
7. Fausto Arocena Arregui, *Guipúzcoa en la Historia* (Madrid, 1964), p. 76.
8. Luis del Campo Jesús, *Dos Esculturas de Sancho el Fuerte* (Pamplona, 1976), pp. 27–28.

NOTES TO CHAPTER VI

1. There may have been only 300 to 400 families of Jews in Navarra in the thirteenth century, mostly in Pamplona and Tudela. See J. N. Hillgarth, *The Spanish Kingdoms: 1250–1516,* vol. 1, *1250–1410: Precarious Balance* (Oxford, 1976), pp. 31–32.
2. Fritz Yitzhak Baer, *History of the Jews in Christian Spain* (Philadelphia, 1961), vol. 1, p. 18.

3. This reference to *el pueblo de la tierra* supported Campión's theory that the primitive Navarrese monarchy was a "pure" monarchy, and that its base was the people, as distinguished from feudal monarchies founded on relationships involving personal loyalties and homage between vassals and lords (Arturo Campión, *Gacetilla de la Historia de Nabarra. Mosaico Histórico* [Pamplona, 1923], pp. 144–45).

4. Georges Desdevises du Dézert, *Don Carlos d'Aragon: Etude sur l'Espagne du Nord au XVe Siècle* (Paris, 1889), p. 39.

5. But because of Navarra's shifting boundaries and old ties with French dioceses, ecclesiastical jurisdiction was blurred. The bishops of Dax and Bayonne, in Gascony, had or claimed to have authority over the northern parts of the country. See P. E. Russell, "Navarre," *Encyclopedia Britannica,* 1968, vol. 16, p. 137.

6. Carlos Clavería, *Historia del Reino de Navarra* (Pamplona, 1971), p. 114.

7. Jaime del Burgo, *Navarra* (Madrid, 1972), p. 116.

8. For a compilation of 164 municipal fueros and charters granted during the medieval period in these kingdoms, see Tomás Muñoz y Romero, *Colección de Fueros Municipales y Cartas Pueblas de Castilla, León, Corona de Aragon y Navarra* (Madrid, 1847). Yanguas y Miranda's *Diccionarios* also include some analysis and commentary on municipal fueros. More recently, Lacarra began classifying the fueros in "families" (José María Lacarra, "Notas para la Formación de las Familias de Fueros Navarros," *Anuario de Historia del Derecho Español,* 10 [1933], pp. 203–72).

9. José María Lacarra and Angel J. Martín Duque, *Fueros de Navarra, 1. Fueros derivados de Jaca: 2, Pamplona* (Pamplona, 1975), p. 21.

10. Lacarra dates the granting of this fuero to San Sebastián at about 1180, not the more frequently cited 1150 (José María Lacarra and Angel J. Martín Duque, Fueros de Navarra, 1. Fueros derivados de Jaca: 1, Estella-San Sebastián [Pamplona, 1969], pp. 28–29.

11. J. N. Hillgarth, *The Spanish Kingdoms,* p. 11.

12. William A. Douglass and Jon Bilbao, *Amerikanuak: Basques in the New World* (Reno, 1975), p. 78.

13. José Moret and François Aleson, *Anales del Reino de Navarra* (Tolosa, 1890–1892), vol. 3/4, pp. 235–36.

14. The theory that the *Fuero General* dates from the twelfth century is based on one clue: that both its prologue and the fuero of Tudela refer to the elusive Fuero of Sobrarbe. Alfonso the Warrior in his fuero of Tudela said: "I give and concede to all the people of Tudela . . . those good fueros of Sobrarbe, that they should have them just as [do] the better *infanzones* of my whole kingdom" (Ralph E. Giesey, *If Not, Not* [Princeton, 1968], p. 36). Other than this, a few exemptions and privileges were set down in Alfonso's document, but the main body of the

fuero is assumed to be found in the Sobrarbe fuero—not reproduced in Tudela's. Lacarra believes the fueros of Sobrarbe were applicable to the higher nobility only: note Alfonso's use of the word *infanzones* (José María Lacarra, "Notas," p. 211).

15. The first evidence of Basque as a written language appeared at the end of the early medieval period, but it was never an official language. No surviving documents of any of the four Basque provinces are written in Basque. See Julio Caro Baroja, *Los Vascos* (Madrid, 1971), p. 515; Maximiano García Venero, *Historia del Nacionalismo Vasco* (Madrid, 1945), pp. 318–19.

16. All quotations from the *Fuero General* are the author's translation, based on the 1964 edition published by Editorial Aranzadi of Pamplona under the direction of the Diputación Foral de Navarra. This is a reissue of the 1869 edition, which was edited by Pablo Ilarregui and Segundo Lapuerta. They worked from the earliest version in the Archivo de Comptos in Pamplona, dating from the late thirteenth or early fourteenth century. For an examination of data relating to the actual date of the manuscript, see Hortensia Viñes Rueda, *Estudio Filológico del Manuscrito No. 1 del Archivo General de Navarra* (Pamplona, 1975), p. 18.

17. Pelayo, who had been in Rodrigo's army, took refuge in Asturias and continued the fight against the Muslims, becoming the first Asturian monarch (718 to 737). See Jaime Vicens Vives, *Approaches to the History of Spain* p. 32, note. (Berkeley, 1967).

18. Arturo Campión, *Gacetilla*, pp. 144–45.

19. Here too there may have been a derivation from Visigothic law and the *Liber Judiciorum*. The seventh-century preface to this Visigothic code included a warning to new monarchs:

King you will be if you do what is right.
If you do not do so, you will not be king.

See Rachel Bard, *The Medieval Fueros of Navarre* (Seattle, 1971), p. 24.

20. Jean-Auguste Brutails, *Documents des Archives de la Chambre de Comptes de Navarre* (Paris, 1890), pp. 3–4.

21. The fine for murder of a *franco*, Jew, Muslim or *vilano* was 500 sueldos. For commodity price data in Navarra in the fourteenth and fifteenth centuries, basis for the calculation of equivalents in livestock, see Earl Hamilton, *Money, Prices and Wages in Valencia, Aragon and Navarra, 1351–1500* (Cambridge, 1936), pp. 228–30. José Yanguas y Miranda also compiled scattered price data for the period: *Diccionario de Antigüedades* (Pamplona, 1964), vol. 3, pp. 333 ff.

22. José Yanguas y Miranda, *Diccionario*, vol. 5, pp. 293–94.

NOTES TO CHAPTER VII

1. The Crown of Aragon acquired Valencia and the Balearics; León-Castile annexed great portions of Andalucia; Portugal almost doubled in size. See J. N. Hillgarth, *The Spanish Kingdoms, 1250–1516, I: 1250–1410, Precarious Balance* (Oxford, 1976), pp. 17–18.
2. Pierre Narbaitz, *Nabarra, ou quand les Basques Avaient des Rois* (Bayonne, 1978), p. 218.
3. For music and verses of 45 of his songs, see Higinio Anglés, *Las Canciones del Rey Teobaldo* (Pamplona, 1973).
4. Carlos Clavería, *Historia del Reino de Navarra* (Pamplona, 1971), p. 112.
5. Translation by the author of verses quoted by Carlos Clavería, note 4, above.
6. Eulogio Zudaire Huarte, *Teobaldo I, Rey Trovador* (Pamplona, 1973), p. 14.
7. Ibid., p. 9.
8. Hillgarth, *Spanish Kingdoms*, p. 19.
9. Narbaitz, *Nabarra*, p. 230.
10. Fausto Arocena Arregui, *Guipúzcoa en la Historia* (Madrid, 1964), p. 57.
11. Narbaitz, *Nabarra*, p. 233.
12. Ibid., p. 239.
13. A son of Louis, Jean, was born after his father's death but lived only a week or so. Six years later he was posthumously recognized as having been a legitimate king by the Cortes, and most chronological lists of the kings of Navarra include him as Juan el de Pocos Dias (John of the Few Days).
14. Clavería, *Historia*, p. 155.
15. Narbaitz, *Nabarra*, p. 290.
16. Javier Zabalo Zabalegui, *La Administración del Reino de Navarra en el Siglo XIV* (Pamplona, 1973), pp. 158, 210 ff.
17. Clavería, *Historia*, p. 156.

NOTES TO CHAPTER VIII

1. Javier Zabalo Zabalegui, "Algunos Datos sobre la Regresión Demográfica Causada por la Peste en la Navarra del Siglo XIV," *Miscelánea Ofrecida a José María Lacarra* (Zaragoza, 1968), p. 490.
2. Barbara Tuchman, *A Distant Mirror* (New York, 1978), p. 132.
3. Javier Zabalo Zabalegui, *La Administración del Reino de Navarra en el Siglo XIV* (Pamplona, 1973), p. 41.
4. Desmond Seward, *The Hundred Years War: The English in France, 1337–1453* (New York, 1978), p. 83.

NOTES

5. Carlos Clavería, *Los Vascos en el Mar* (Pamplona, 1966), p. 348. Clavería describes the river traffic and Tudela's centuries as a great river port (pp. 347–51).

6. José María Lacarra, *Historia Política del Reino de Navarra* (Pamplona, 1972), p. 155.

7. Jaime Vicens Vives has explored the fact that Juan was the second son of a second son and its effect on his character, psyche and ambitions, in his *Juan II de Aragon (1398–1479): Monarquía y Revolución en la España del Siglo XV* (Barcelona, 1953), pp. 18 ff.

8. The life of Carlos, prince of Viana, has been well documented, especially by Manuel Iribarren in *El Príncipe de Viana (un Destino Frustrado)* (Barcelona, 1947). His name also lives on in the Diputación Foral de Navarra's distinguished Institución Príncipe de Viana.

9. José Moret and François Aleson, *Anales del Reino de Navarra* (Tolosa, 1890–1892), vol. 7, p. 44.

10. Sarah Bradford, *Cesare Borgia* (New York, 1976), p. 287.

11. José Yanguas y Miranda, *Diccionario de Antigüedades del Reino de Navarra* (Pamplona, 1964), vol. 1, p. 496.

NOTES TO CHAPTER IX

1. For a detailed history of the first part of this complex period (1512–1518), see Prosper Boissonade, *Histoire de la Réunion de la Navarre à la Castile* (Paris, 1893); Spanish translation by Tomas Yoldi Mina, *La Conquista de Nabarra en el Panorama Europea* (Buenos Aires, 1956–1961).

2. Prosper Boissonade, *Histoire de la Réunion*, p. 398.

3. Campión cites a 1516 letter from Cardinal Cisneros to Lopez de Ayala concerning these demolitions, undertaken because "there is hardly a person in the kingdom we can trust" (Arturo Campión, *Gacetilla de la Historia. Mosaico Histórico* [Pamplona, 1923], p. 436).

4. Tomás Yoldi Mina, tr., *La Conquista,* vol. 3, pp. 411–12.

5. Authenticity of the papal bull excommunicating the Albrets is still in dispute. For a synopsis of the bibliography on the subject, see José María Lacarra, *Historia del Reino de Navarra* (Pamplona, 1972), p. 432, n. 190.

6. Boissonade, *Histoire de la Réunion,* p. 455.

7. Tomás Yoldi Mina, *La Conquista,* vol. 4, p. 236.

8. Ibid, p. 385.

NOTES TO CHAPTER X

1. After Charles's death, in 1558, what with one thing and another, Philip was not officially recognized as king by Navarra until 1561. The

Cortes felt that the kingdom, in view of its special status within the Spanish nation, should receive its own specially prepared copy of Charles's abdication proclamation. Finally, after repeated petitions to Castile, the document arrived in 1561, and Philip officially became King of Navarra. See Carlos Clavería, *Historia del Reino de Navarra* (Pamplona, 1971), p. 375.

2. Florencio Idoate, "Las Fortificaciones de Pamplona a Partir de la Conquista de Navarra," *Príncipe de Viana,* 1954, pp. 57–109.

3. Rachel Bard, "The Decline of a Basque State in France: Basse Navarre, 1512–1789," *Essays in Honor of Jon Bilbao* (Reno, 1977), p. 86.

4. "Bayona," *Enciclopedia General Ilustrada del País Vasco. Cuerpo A.* (San Sebastián, 1973), vol. 4, pp. 274 and 294.

NOTES TO CHAPTER XI

1. For data on the maturing of the institutions of Navarra, see María Puy Huici Goñi, *Las Cortes de Navarra durante la Edad Moderna* (Madrid, 1963); Joaquín José Salcedo Izu, *El Consejo Real de Navarra en el Siglo XVI* (Pamplona, 1964), and *La Diputación del Reino de Navarra* (Pamplona, 1969).

2. Joaquín José Salcedo Izu, *El Consejo Real de Navarra en el Siglo XVI* (Pamplona, 1964), p. 270.

3. Ibid., p. 271.

4. Ibid., p. 243.

5. Arturo Campión, *Nabarra en su Vida Histórica* (Pamplona, 1929), p. 212.

6. This procedure, formally outlined by the Cortes in 1765, described the steps necessary to achieve a seat from the sixteenth century onwards. See María Puy Huici Goñi, *Las Cortes de Navarra,* pp. 63 ff.

7. Ibid., p. 162.

8. Ibid., pp. 211, 243.

9. Joaquín José Salcedo Izu, *La Diputación,* p. 184.

NOTES TO CHAPTER XII

1. John Lynch, *Spain under the Habsburgs* (Oxford, 1969), p. 126.

2. José Luis Comellas, *Historia de España Moderna y Contemporanea* (Madrid, 1968), p. 243.

3. María Puy Huici Goñi, *Las Cortes de Navarra durante la Edad Moderna* (Madrid, 1963), p. 293.

4. Florencio Idoate, *Notas para el Estudio de la Economía Navarra y su Contribución a la Real Hacienda (1500–1650)* (Pamplona, 1960), p. 13.

5. Lynch, *Spain,* p. 126.

NOTES 225

6. Huici Goñi, *Las Cortes*, p. 324. See also José Yanguas y Miranda, "Pechas," *Diccionario de Antigüedades del Reino de Navarra* (Pamplona, 1964), vol. 2, pp. 325 ff.
7. Idoate, *Notas*, p. 95. Idoate's *Notas* are the source for much of the data on the Navarrese economy in the seventeenth century.
8. Ibid., p. 50.

NOTES TO CHAPTER XIII

1. Julio Caro Baroja, *La Hora Navarra del XVIII (Personas, Familias, Negocios e Ideas)* (Pamplona, 1969), p. 15.
2. This episode is related, along with other descriptions of the impact of the War of the Succession on Navarra, by Florencio Idoate in "La Defenestración de Falces" in his *Rincones de la Historia de Navarra* (Pamplona, 1954), vol. 1, pp. 120–22.
3. Georges Desdevises du Dézert, *L'Espagne de l'Ancien Régime*, vol. 2, *Les Institutions* (Paris, 1899), p. 147.
4. José María Iribarren, *Pamplona y los Viajeros de Otros Siglos* (Pamplona, 1957), p. 78.
5. Antonio Dominguez Ortiz, *La Sociedad Española en el Siglo XVIII* (Madrid, 1955), pp. 235–36. See also Idoate, "Más sobre Agotes," *Rincones*, p. 162.
6. Dominguez Ortiz, *La Sociedad*, p. 70.
7. Caro Baroja, *La Hora Navarra*, p. 33 ff. For more on Basque emigration to and success in the New World, see William A. Douglass and Jon Bilbao, *Amerikanuak: Basques in the New World* (Reno, 1975), pp. 67 ff.
8. James Michener, *Iberia* (Greenwich, 1968), p. 581.
9. Iribarren, *Pamplona*, pp. 102 ff.
10. Ibid., p. 93.
11. Ibid., p. 97.

NOTES TO CHAPTER XIV

1. Carlos Clavería, *Historia del Reino de Navarra* (Pamplona, 1971), p. 405.
2. Rafael Gambra Ciudad, *Guerra Realista* (Pamplona, 1972), p. 12.
3. Raymond Carr, *Spain 1808–1939* (Oxford, 1966), p. 186.
4. The six queens of Navarra were: Toda (queen-regent, 925–938); Juana I (1274–1305); Juana II (1329–1349); Blanca I (1425–1441); Leonor I (1479); and Catalina (Catherine) I (1483–1517).
5. Raymond Carr points out that the rural character of Carlism was what defeated it in the long run, because it could not draw on the resources of the cities (*Spain 1808–1939*, p. 187).

6. According to Lord Eliot, one of the emissaries sent by England to persuade the combatants to wage a more civilized war. See Edgar Holt, *The Carlist Wars in Spain* (London, 1967), p. 72.
7. Ibid., p. 99.
8. Ibid., p. 188.
9. Rodrigo Rodriguez Garraza, *Navarra de Reino a Provincia (1828–1841)* (Pamplona, 1968), pp. 257–58.
10. Yanguas had been named archivist in Pamplona in 1830. By the time he became secretary to the *Diputación* (1834) he had written his dictionary of the fueros of Navarra and his history of the kingdom. His monumental four-volume dictionary of antiquities was to appear in 1840. For a complete account of his life, see José Ramón Castro, *Yanguas y Miranda: Una Vida Fecunda al Vaivén de la Política* (Pamplona, 1963).

NOTES TO CHAPTER XV

1. Idoia Estornés Zubizarreta, *Carlismo y Abolición Foral* (San Sebastián, 1976), p. 143.
2. Rafael Gomez Chaparro, *La Desamortización Civil en Navarra* (Pamplona, 1967), pp. 60 ff.
3. Gomez Chaparro attributes this unique success in Navarra to the energetic and intelligent mediation of the *Diputación* between the treasury and the town councils, without which the municipally owned lands would now be as nonexistent as the customs posts on the Ebro (ibid., p. 170).
4. Ana María Calzada, *La Prensa Navarra a Fines del Siglo XIX* (Pamplona, 1964), p. 27.
5. Maximiano García Venero, *Historia del Nacionalismo Vasco, 1793–1936* (Madrid, 1945), p. 240. For more documentation of this era, see Francisco-Javier de Arvizu y Aguado, *Elementos de Historia de Navarra y su Regimen Foral* (Pamplona, 1953), ch. 8.
6. Jaime del Burgo, *Antecedentes de la 3a Guerra Carlista* (Pamplona, 1974), p. 5.
7. Edgar Holt, *The Carlist Wars in Spain* (London, 1967), p. 234.
8. Carlism was an overwhelming popular choice in the rest of the Basque Country too. See Estornés Zubizarreta, *Carlismo,* p. 149.
9. Santiago Galindo Herrero, *Breve Historia del Tradicionalismo Español* (Madrid, 1956), p. 178.
10. Del Burgo, *Antecedentes,* p. 13.
11. Estornés Zubizarreta, *Carlismo,* p. 155.
12. Holt, *The Carlist Wars,* p. 258.
13. The civil administration of the Carlists is described by Jaime del Burgo (3a Guerra Carlista [Pamplona, 1974], pp. 16–20).

NOTES TO CHAPTER XVI

1. Idoia Estornés Zubizarreta, *Carlismo y Abolición Foral* (San Sebastián, 1976), p. 194.
2. *El Pensamiento Navarro* is the only newspaper in the province that has been published continuously since the last century. It began as a strongly anti-liberal paper, *La Lealtad Navarra,* but in 1897 took its present name. For an analysis of the press of Navarra in the late nineteenth century, see Ana María Calzada, *La Prensa Navarra a Fines del Siglo XIX* (Pamplona, 1964).
3. Román Oyarzun, *Historia del Carlismo* (Madrid, 1965), p. 410.
4. *La Voz de Navarra* (Pamplona), Sept. 22, 1930. For more on the press reaction, see the Goñi clipping collection, *Administración Foral, 1917-1931,* in the Basque Collection, University of Nevada Library.
5. Stanley H. Payne's *Basque Nationalism* (Reno, 1975) is the most up-to-date and comprehensive study of Basque nationalism, starting with the conjectural prehistoric era and continuing to the twilight of the Franco period.
6. For a summary of the early similarities of the two parties, see Stanley Payne, "Carlism—Basque or 'Spanish' Traditionalism," in *Anglo-American Contributions to Basque Studies* (Reno, 1977), p. 122.
7. Payne, *Basque Nationalism,* p. 95.
8. Maximiano García Venero, *Historia del Nacionalismo Vasco, 1793-1936* (Madrid, 1945), pp. 373-86. The debate on the proposition, reproduced by García Venero in its entirety, exemplifies the opposing points of view and the oratory they inspired.
9. Juan Vázquez de Mella, *Regionalismo y Monarquía* (Madrid, 1957), p. 180.
10. Santiago Galindo Herrero, *Pensadores Tradicionalistas* (Madrid, 1955), p. 21.
11. Victor Pradera, *Obra Completa* (Madrid, 1965), p. 410.
12. Payne, *Basque Nationalism,* p. 88.
13. *La Voz de Navarra* (Pamplona), June 6, 1929.

NOTES TO CHAPTER XVII

1. José Antonio de Aguirre y Lekube, *Entre la Libertad y la Revolución, 1930-1935* (Bilbao, 1976), pp. 66-68.
2. Joaquín Arrarás, *Historia de la Segunda República Española* (Madrid, 1964), vol. 1, ch. 7.
3. Stanley Payne, *Basque Nationalism* (Reno, 1975), pp. 129 and 134.

4. "Un Examen Minuciosa de las Fuerzas Políticas en Cada Una de las Provincias," *Ahora* (Madrid), February 16, 1934.

5. José María Salavierría in *ABC*, January 11, 1934, quoted in Francisco-Javier de Arvizu y Aguado, *Elementos de Historia de Navarra y su Regimen Foral* (Pamplona, 1953), p. 115 (author's translation).

6. A personal memoir and history of this period, basis for much of this section, are found in Jaime del Burgo, *Conspiración y Guerra Civil* (Madrid, 1970). See also the same author's *Requetés en Navarra antes del Alzamiento* (San Sebastián, 1939), pp. 95–105.

7. Jaime del Burgo, one of the "Peruvians," pretended to be from Cuzco and had to master its history and geography in a great hurry (*Conspiración y Guerra Civil*, pp. 519–20).

8. For brief biographies of all the pretenders through the 1960s, see Idoia Estornés Zubizarreta, *Carlismo y Abolición Foral* (San Sebastián, 1976), Appendix 3, pp. 200–203.

9. For more on Javier de Borbón Parma and his son Carlos Hugo, see Martin Blinkhorn, *Carlism and Crisis in Spain, 1931–1939* (Cambridge, 1975), pp. 223 ff.; see also his genealogical table, pp. 310–11.

10. Luis Romero, *Tres Días de Julio* (Barcelona, 1972), p. 378.

11. Ibid., p. 376.

12. Arvizu y Aguado, *Elementos*, p. 121.

13. Ibid., p. 122.

14. Payne, *Basque Nationalism*, pp. 228–29.

15. In 1962,the share of agriculture and food production in Navarra's gross national product was 45 percent; industry, 30 percent. In 1975, agriculture accounted for 14 percent; industry, 44 percent. See Jesús Bueno Asín, "Problemática de la Economía Navarra," *Navarra desde Navarra* (reprinted from *Jakin*) (Bilbao, 1978), pp. 93 ff.

16. Robert P. Clark, *The Basques: The Franco Years and Beyond* (Reno, 1979), pp. 8–9.

17. Asín, *Problemática*, p. 101.

18. Stanley Payne, "Carlism—Basque or 'Spanish' Traditionalism" in *Anglo-American Contributions to Basque Studies: Essays in Honor of Jon Bilbao* (Reno, 1977), p. 121.

19. Blinkhorn, *Carlism and Crisis*, p. 306.

20. For background on the apparent decline in the coincidence of Basque-speaking with the strength of the Basque Nationalist Party, see Robert P. Clark, "Language and Politics in Spain's Basque Provinces," *West European Politics* (London, January 1981), pp. 85–103.

21. Clark, *The Basques*, pp. 340–42.

22. Ibid., p. 391.

23. Juan Pablo Fusi Aizpúrua, "Sobre Navarra," *Cuenta y Razón* (Winter 1981), p. 78.

NOTES TO APPENDIX A

1. Chronology until 905 is based on Pérez de Urbel's account of the birth of the Navarrese kingdom, covering the period 718 to 905. The first dynasty stemmed from a Navarrese family, of the same stock as the Banu Qasi, who were leaders in Pamplona's resistance to the French. The second dynasty was descended from Jimeno, who had been governor of Pamplona for the French in 816 but who subsequently led the successful rebellion against them (Fr. Justo Pérez de Urbel, "Lo Viejo y lo Nuevo Sobre el Origen del Reino de Pamplona," *al-Andalus,* 19 [1954], pp. 1–42.)

2. General authority for chronology from 905 is the genealogical table in Soldevila's history, which was prepared by Antonio Ubieto and revised by José M. Lacarra (Fernando Soldevila Zubirubu, *Historia de España,* vol. 3 [Barcelona: Ediciones Ariel, 1962], p. 128).

3. Sancho's date of accession is usually given as 1005. His biographer, Pérez de Urbel, places it at 1004 (Fr. Justo Pérez de Urbel, *Sancho el Mayor de Navarra* [Madrid: Institución Príncipe de Viana, 1950], p. 14).

4. Juan II was the real ruler during Leonor's nominal reign, except for 21 days in 1479, the year of his death.

BIBLIOGRAPHY

Aguado Bleye, Pedro. *Manual de Historia de España.* 9th ed. 3 vols. Madrid: Espasa-Calpe, 1964.

Aguirre y Lekube, José Antonio de. *Entre la Libertad y la Revolución, 1930–1935.* Bilboa: Ed. Geu, 1976.

Angles, Higinio. *Las Canciones del Rey Teobaldo.* Pamplona: Diputación Foral de Navarra, 1973.

Apellániz, José María. "Corpus de Materiales de las Culturas Prehistóricas con Cerámica de la Población de Cavernas del País Vasco Meridional," *Munibe* (1973) Supplement 1.

Arazuri, José Joaquin. *El Municipio Pamplonés en Tiempos de Felipe II.* Pamplona: Ed. Aranzadi, 1973.

Arbeloa, Joaquin. *Los Orígines del Reino de Navarra.* 3 vols. San Sebastián: Ed. Auñamendi, 1969.

Arocena Arregui, Fausto. *Guipúzcoa en la Historia.* Madrid: Ed. Minotauro, 1964.

Arrarás, Joaquin. *Historia de la Segunda República Española.* 4 vols. Madrid: Ed. Nacional, 1964 (1st ed., 1956).

Arribas, Antonio. *The Iberians.* Ancient People and Places Series, Glyn Daniel, ed. Vol. 36. New York: Praeger, 1964.

Arvizu y Aguado, Francisco-Javier de. *Elementos de Historia de Navarra y su Regimen Foral.* Pamplona: Diputación Foral, Ed. Aramburu, 1953.

Asín, Jesús Bueno. "Problemática de la Economía Navarra," *Navarra desde Navarra.* Bilbao, 1978.

Aulestia, Gorka. "Euskal Herria et les Romantiques Français," unpublished manuscript based on M.A. thesis "Le Pays Basque vu par les Romantiques Français." Reno: University of Nevada, 1978.

Baer, Yitshak. *A History of the Jews in Christian Spain.* Translated from the Hebrew by Louis Schoffman. 2 vols. Philadelphia: Jewish Publication Society of America, 1966.

Ballesteros y Beretta, Antonio. *Historia de España y su Influencia en la Historia Universal.* 2nd ed. 11 vols. Barcelona: P. Salvat, 1948.

Balparda y las Herrerías, Gregorio de. *Historia Crítica de Vizcaya y de sus Fueros.* 3 vols. Madrid: Artes de la Ilustración, 1924–1945.

Barandiarán, Ignacio. "Representaciones de Caballos en la Cueva de Ekain," *Estudios de Arqueología Alavesa. Homenaje a Domingo Fernandez Medrano.* Vitoria: Diputación Foral de Alava, 1974.

Barandiarán, José Miguel de. *El Hombre Prehistórico en al País Vasco.* Buenos Aires: Ed. Vasca Ekin, 1953.

―――. *El Hombre Primitivo en el País Vasco.* Zarauz: Ed. Itxaropena, 1934.

―――. *Mitología Vasca.* Madrid: Ed. Minotauro, 1960.

―――. *La Prehistoria en el Pirineo Vasco: Estado Actual de su Estudio.* Zaragoza: Primer Congreso Internacional del Pirineo del Instituto de Estudios Pirinaicos, 1952.

―――. "Resumen de la Mitología Mariana," *Munibe,* 7 (1955) 262–64; 8 (1956) 66–75.

――― and Jesús Altuna. "La Cueva de Ekain y sus Figuras Rupestres," *Munibe* (1969), p. 333.

Bard, Rachel. "The Decline of a Basque State in France: Basse Navarre, 1512–1789," *Anglo-American Contributions to Basque Studies: Essays in Honor of Jon Bilbao.* William A. Douglass, Richard W. Etulain, and William Jacobsen, Jr., eds. Reno: Desert Research Institute, 1977.

―――. "The Medieval Fueros of Navarra." Seattle: M.A. thesis, University of Washington, 1971.

Barrau-Dihigo, L. "Les Origines du Royaume de Navarre d'après une Théorie Récente," *Revue Hispanique,* 7 (1900) 141–505.

Blinkhorn, Martin. *Carlism and Crisis in Spain, 1931–1939.* Cambridge: Cambridge University Press, 1975.

Blot, Jacques. "Protohistoire en Pays Basque," *Bulletin de la Societé des Sciences, Lettres et Arts de Bayonne,* 129 (1973) 17–45.

Boissonade, Prosper. *Histoire de la Réunion de la Navarre à la Castile: Essai sur les Relations des Princes de Foix-Albret avec la France et l'Espagne (1479–1521).* Paris: Alphonse Picard et Fils, 1893.

―――. *La Conquista de Nabarra en el Panorama Europea.* Translated from the French, with notes, by Tomas Yoldi Mina. 4 vols. Buenos Aires: Ed. Vasca Ekin, 1956–1961.

Bosch Gimpera, Pedro. "Sobre Prehistoria e Historia de los Vascos," *Munibe* (1971), pp. 419–21.

Bradford, Sarah. *Cesare Borgia.* New York: Macmillan, 1976.

Brutails, Jean-Auguste, ed. *Documents des Archives de la Chambre des Comptes de Navarre, 1196–1384.* Paris: E. Bouillon, 1890.

Burgo, Jaime del. *Antecedentes de la Tercera Guerra Carlista.* Temas de Cultura Popular de Navarra No. 188. Pamplona: Diputación Foral de Navarra, 1974.

———. *Navarra.* Madrid: Ed. Alfaguara, 1972.

———. *Primera Guerra Carlista.* Temas de Cultura Popular de Navarra No. 156. Pamplona: Diputación Foral de Navarra, 1973.

———. *Requetés en Navarra antes del Alzamiento.* San Sebastián: Ed. Española, 1939.

———. *Segunda Guerra Carlista.* Temas de Cultura Popular de Navarra No. 167. Pamplona: Diputación Foral de Navarra, 1973.

———. *Tercera Guerra Carlista.* Temas de Cultura Popular de Navarra No. 194. Pamplona: Diputación Foral de Navarra, 1974.

Burgo, Jaime Ignacio del. *Historia del Fuero.* Temas de Cultura Popular de Navarra No. 8. Pamplona: Diputación Foral de Navarra, 1968.

Camino y Orella, Joaquín Antonio de. *Historia Civil, Diplomática, Antigua y Moderna de la Ciudad de San Sebastián.* Vol. 1. Madrid: Biblioteca de Historia Vasca, 1923.

Campión, Arturo. "La Constitución de la Primitiva Monarquía y el Origen y Desenvolvimiento de las Cortes de Navarra," *Euskariana,* 5th series, *Algo de Historia,* vol. 3 (October 1915), pp. 152–67.

———. *Gacetilla de la Historia de Navarra. Mosaico Histórico.* Pamplona, 1923.

———. *Navarra en su Vida Histórica.* 2d ed. Pamplona: J. García, 1929.

Campo Jesús, Luis del. *Sancho el Fuerte de Navarra.* Pamplona: La Acción Social, 1960.

Caro Baroja, Julio. *España Primitiva y Romana.* Historia de la Cultura Española Series. Barcelona: Ed. Seix Barral, 1957.

———. *Etnografía Histórica de Navarra.* 3 vols. Pamplona: Ed. Aranzadi, 1971–1972.

———. *La Hora Navarra del XVIII (Personas, Familias, Negocios y Ideas).* Pamplona: Institución Príncipe de Viana, Diputación Foral de Navarra, 1969.

———. *Materiales para una Historia de la Lengua Vasca en su Relación a la Latina.* Salamanca: Universidad de Salamanca, 1945.

———. *Los Pueblos de España. Ensayo de Etnología.* Barcelona: Ed. Barna, 1946.

———. *Los Vascos.* 3d ed. Madrid: Ed. Istmo, 1971.

Carr, Raymond. *Spain 1808–1939.* Oxford: Clarendon Press, 1966.

——— and Juan Pablo Fusi Aizpúrua. *Spain: Dictatorship to Democracy.* London: Allen & Unwin, 1979.

Carroquino, Julio and Angel Ximénez de Embún. *Compendio Histórico de Navarra*. Zaragoza: M. Embid, 1932.

Castro, José Ramón. *Carlos II el Malo*. Temas de Cultura Popular No. 241. Pamplona: Institución Príncipe de Viana, Diputación Foral de Navarra, 1975.

―――. *Carlos III el Noble, Rey de Navarra*. Pamplona: Institución Príncipe de Viana, Diputación Foral de Navarra, 1967.

―――. *Yanguas y Miranda: Una Vida Fecunda al Vaiven de la Política*. Pamplona: Ed. Gomez, 1963.

Charles, Prince of Viana. *Crónica de los Reyes de Navarra, por d. Carlos Príncipe de Viana*. José Yanguas y Miranda, ed. Pamplona: Teodoro Ochoa, 1843 (1st ed., 1454).

Charpentier, Louis. *Le Mystère Basque*. Paris: Ed. Robert Laffont, 1975.

Clark, Robert. *The Basques: The Franco Years and Beyond*. Reno: University of Nevada Press, 1979.

―――. "Language and Politics in Spain's Basque Provinces," *West European Politics* (January 1981), p. 85.

Clavería, Carlos. *Historia del Reino de Navarra*. Pamplona: Ed. Gomez, 1971.

―――. *Los Vascos en el Mar*. Pamplona: Ed. Aramburu, 1966.

Comellas, José Luis. *Historia de España Moderna y Contemporanea (1474–1965)*. 2d ed. Madrid: Ed. Rialp, 1968.

Correa, Luis. *Historia de la Conquista del Reino de Navarra por el Duque de Alba en 1512*. José Yanguas y Miranda, ed. Pamplona: Langas y Ripa, 1843. (First published as *La Conquista del Reyno de Navarra*, Toledo, 1513.)

Davant, Jean-Louis. *Histoire du Pays Basque*. Bayonne: Ed. Goiztiri, 1972.

Desdevises du Dézert, Georges Nicolas. *Don Carlos d'Aragon: Etude sur l'Espagne du Nord au XVe Siècle*. Paris: Armand Colin, 1889.

―――. *L'Espagne de l'Ancien Régime*. 2 vols. Paris: Societé Française d'Imprimerie et de Librairie, 1899.

Domínguez Arévalo, Tomás. *Los Teobaldos de Navarra*. Madrid: San Francisco de Sales, 1909.

Domínguez Ortiz, Antonio. *La Sociedad Española en el Siglo XVIII*. Madrid: Institución Balmes de Sociología, Consejo Superior de Investigaciones Scientíficas, 1955.

Douglass, William A. and Jon Bilbao. *Amerikanuak: Basques in the New World*. Reno: University of Nevada Press, 1975.

Douglass, William A., Richard Etulain and William H. Jacobsen Jr., eds. *Anglo-American Contributions to Basque Studies: Essays in Honor* of Jon Bilbao. Publications on the Social Sciences No. 13. Reno: Desert Research Institute, 1977.

Elizondo, Miguel de. *Compendio de los Cinco Tomos de los Annales de Navarra.* Pamplona: Pedro J. Esquerro, 1732.

Elliott, J. H. *Imperial Spain, 1469–1716.* New York: New American Library, 1963.

Elosegui, Jesús. *Catálogo Dolménico del País Vasco.* Zaragoza: Real Sociedad de los Amigos del País, 1953.

Enciclopedia Ilustrada del País Vasco. San Sebastián: Ed. Auñamendi, 1971.

Enciclopedia Universal Ilustrada Europeo-Americana. 70 vols. Barcelona: Hijos de J. Espasa, 1905–1930. (Also known as *Enciclopedia Espasa.* Vols. 51–70 published by Espasa-Calpe.)

Epton, Nina Consuelo. *Navarre: The Flea between Two Monkeys.* London: Cassell, 1957.

Estornés Lasa, Bernardo. *Historia del País Vasco.* Zarauz: Ed. Vasca, 1933.

———. *El Ducado de Vasconia.* Zarauz, 1959.

———. *Orígines de los Vascos.* 4 vols. San Sebastián, 1967.

Forondo y Aguilera, Manuel de. *Estancias y Viajes del Emperador Carlos V.* 1914 (ejemplar especial).

"Fuero," *Enciclopedia Universal Ilustrada Europeo-Americana.* Vol. 24. Barcelona: Espasa-Calpe, 1924.

Fuero General de Navarra. Pablo Ilarregui and Segundo Lapuerta, eds. Based on the original in the Archivo de Comptos. 2d ed. Pamplona: Ed. Aranzadi, for Biblioteca del Derecho Foral, 1964 (1st ed., 1869).

Fusi Aizpúrua, Juan Pablo. "Sobre Navarra," *Cuenta y Razón* (Winter 1981), p. 78.

Galindo Herrero, Santiago. *Breve Historia del Tradicionalismo Español.* Madrid: Publicaciones Españolas, 1956.

———. *Pensadores Tradicionalistas.* Temas Españolas No. 191. Madrid: Publicaciones Españolas, 1955.

———. *Segunda Guerra Carlista.* Temas Españolas No. 111. Madrid: Publicaciones Españolas, 1954.

Gallop, Rodney. *A Book of the Basques.* Reno: University of Nevada Press, 1970 (1st ed., London: Macmillan, 1930).

Gambra Ciudad, Rafael. *Guerra Realista.* Temas de Cultura Popular No. 137. Pamplona: Diputación Foral de Navarra, 1972.

———. *La Primera Guerra Civil de España (1821–23).* Madrid: Escelicer, 1950.

García Gallo, Alfonso. *Manual de Historia del Derecho Español: El Origen y la Evolución del Derecho.* 3rd ed. Madrid: Artes Gráficos y Ediciones, 1967.

García Valdeavellano, Luis. *Curso de Historia de las Instituciones Españolas: De los Orígines al Final de la Edad Media.* Madrid: Revista de Occidente, 1968.

―――. *Historia de España.* 3d ed. 2 vols. Madrid: Revista de Occidente, 1963.

García Venero, Maximiano. *Historia del Nacionalismo Vasco, 1793–1936.* Madrid: Gráficas Uguina, Ed. Nacional, 1945.

Garran y Moso, Justo. *El Sistema Foral de Navarra y Provincias Vascongadas.* Pamplona: Ed. Aramburu, 1935.

Giesey, Ralph E. *If Not, Not: The Oath of the Aragonese and the Legendary Laws of Sobrarbe.* Princeton: Princeton University Press, 1968.

Gillingham, John. *Richard the Lionheart.* New York: Times Books, 1978.

Gomez Chaparro, Rafael. *La Desamortización Civil en Navarra.* Pamplona: University of Navarra, Institución Príncipe de Viana, 1967.

Hamilton, Earl J. *Money, Prices and Wages in Valencia, Aragon and Navarra, 1351–1500.* Vol. 51 of Harvard Economic Studies. Cambridge: Harvard University Press, 1936.

Henningsen, C. F. *The Most Striking Events of a 12-months Campaign with Zumalacárregui, in Navarre and the Basque Provinces.* 2 vols. London: John Murray, 1836.

Hillgarth, J. N. *The Spanish Kingdoms: 1250–1516.* Vol. I. *1250–1410. Precarious Balance.* Oxford: Clarendon Press, 1976.

Holt, Edgar. *The Carlist Wars in Spain.* London: Putnam, 1967.

Huarte, Eulogio Zudaire. *Teobaldo I, Rey Trovador.* Temas de Cultura Popular No. 155. Pamplona: Diputación Foral de Navarra, 1973.

Huici Goñi, María Puy. *Las Cortes de Navarra durante la Edad Moderna.* Madrid: Ed. Rialp, 1963.

Idoate, Florencio. "Las Fortificaciones de Pamplona a Partir de la Conquista de Navarra," *Príncipe de Viana,* 15 (1954) 57–109.

―――. *Notas para el Estudio de la Economía Navarra y su Contribución a la Real Hacienda (1500–1650).* Pamplona: Diputación Foral de Navarra, 1960.

―――. *Rincones de la Historia de Navarra.* 3 vols. Pamplona: Ed. Gomez, 1956–1966.

Iribarren, José María. *Historias y Costumbres.* Pamplona: Ed. Gomez, 1956.

―――. *Pamplona y los Viajeros de Otros Siglos.* Pamplona: Institución Príncipe de Viana, Diputación Foral de Navarra, 1957.

Iribarren, Manuel. *El Príncipe de Viana (un Destino Frustrado)*. Barcelona: Montaner y Simon, 1947.

Irujo, Manuel de. *Inglaterra y los Vascos*. Buenos Aires: Ed. Vasca Ekin, 1945.

Lacarra y de Miguel, José María. "El Desarollo Urbano de Navarra y Aragon en la Edad Media," *Pireneos*, 6 (1950) 5–34.

──────. *Estudios de Historia Navarra*. Pamplona: Colección Diario de Navarra, 1971.

──────. *Guía del Archivo General de Navarra*. Pamplona: Diputación Foral de Navarra, 1953.

──────. *Historia Política del Reino de Navarra*. 3 vols. Pamplona: Ed. Aranzadi, 1972.

──────. "Notas para la Formación de las Familias de Fueros Navarros," Anuario de Historia del Derecho Español, 10 (1933) 203–72.

──────. *Vasconia Medieval. Historia y Filología*. San Sebastián: Seminario Julio de Urquijo, 1957.

────── and Angel J. Martín Duque. *Fueros de Navarra. 1. Fueros Derivados de Jaca. 1. Estella-San Sebastián*. Pamplona: Diputación Foral de Navarra, Institución Príncipe de Viana, 1969.

──────. *Fueros de Navarra. 1. Fueros Derivados de Jaca. 2. Pamplona*. Pamplona: Diputación Foral de Navarra, Institución Príncipe de Viana, 1975.

Lambert, Elie. "Les Routes des Pyrenees Atlantiques et leur Emploi au Cours des Ages," *Pireneos*, 7 (1951) 335–82.

Lecuona, Manuel de. "Etimología de la Voz 'Navarra'," *Munibe* (1962), pp. 532–37.

Lévi Provençal, Evariste. "Du Nouveau sur le Royaume de Pampelune au IXe Siècle," *Bulletin Hispanique*, 55 (1953) 5–22.

──────. *La Peninsule Ibérique au Moyen Age, d'après le Kitab Ar-rawd Al-mitar*. Leiden: E. J. Brill, 1938.

Levine, Morton H. "The Basques," *Natural History*, 76 (April 1967) 44–50.

Livermore, Harold. *A History of Spain*. Minerva Press, 1968 (1st ed., London: Allen and Unwin, 1958).

López y Mendizabal, Isaac. *Breve Historia del País Vasco*. Biblioteca de Cultura Vasca, vol. 21. Buenos Aires: Ed. Vasca Ekin, 1945.

Lynch, John. *Spain under the Habsburgs*. Vol. 2: *Spain and America, 1598–1700*. Oxford: Basil Blackwell, 1969.

Madrazo, Pedro de. *Navarra—sus Monumentos y Artes. Su Naturaleza e Historia. Usos, Costumbres y Fueros*. San Sebastián: Auñamendi, 1972 (1st ed., 1886).

Maluquer de Motes, Juan. "Consideraciones sobre el Problema de la Formación de los Vascos," *Problemas de la Prehistoria y de la Etnología Vascas*. Pamplona: Institución Príncipe de Viana, 1966.

―――. "Notas sobre la Cultura Megalítica Navarra," *Príncipe de Viana*, 92–93 (1963) 93–147.

―――. *Pueblos Celtos*. Madrid: Espasa Calpe, 1954.

Martín Duque, Angel J. "La Restauración de la Monarquía Navarra y las Ordenes Militares (1134–1194)," *Homenaje a don José María Lacarra. Estudios Medievales. I*. Zaragoza: Anubar, 1977.

Martinez Erro, José R. *Olite, Corte de Reyes*. Tafalla: Eugenio Orive Casave, 1946.

Mateu y Llopis, Felipe. "El Hallazgo de 'Pennies' Ingleses en Roncesvalles," *Príncipe de Viana*, 40–41 (1950) 201–10.

Mayer, Ernst. *Historia de las Instituciones Sociales y Políticas de España y Portugal durante los Siglos V a XIV*. 2 vols. Madrid: Anaurio de Historia del Derecho Español, 1926.

Mella, Juan Vázquez de. *Regionalismo y Monarquía*. Madrid: Ed. Rialp, 1957.

Merriman, Roger Bigelow. *The Rise of the Spanish Empire in the Old World and the New*. 4 vols. New York: Cooper Square Publ., 1962 (1st ed., 1918).

Michener, James. *Iberia; Spanish Travels and Reflections*. Greenwich: Fawcett-Crest, 1968.

Moret, Padre José de. *Congressiones Apologéticas sobra la Verdad de las Investigaciones Históricas de las Antigüedades del Reyno de Navarra*. Pamplona: M. G. de Zabala, 1678.

―――. *Empeños de Valor y Bizarros Desempeños, o Sitio de Fuenterrabia*. Translated from the Latin by Manuel Silvestre de Arlegui. Pamplona: 1763 (?).

―――― and François Aleson. *Anales del Reino de Navarra*. 7 vols. Tolosa: Eusebio Lopez, 1891 (1st ed., Pamplona, 1684–1709).

Muñoz y Romero, Tomas, ed. *Colección de Fueros Municipales y Cartas Pueblas de Castilla, León, Corona de Aragon y Navarra*. Madrid: José María Alonso, 1847.

Narbaitz, Pierre. *Navarra, ou Quand les Basques Avaient des Rois*. Bayonne: Diffusion Zabal, 1978.

"Navarra," *Enciclopedia Universal Ilustrada Europeo-Americana*. Vol. 37. Barcelona: Espasa-Calpe, 1929.

Ochoa de Alda, Teodoro. *Diccionario Geográfico-histórico de Navarra*. 2d ed. Pamplona: Ochoa de Alda, 1852 (1st ed., 1842).

Oyarzun, Román. *Historia del Carlismo.* Madrid: Ed. Fe, 1939.

Pamplona, Padre Germán de. "Los Límites de la Vasconia Hispano-Romana y sus Variaciones en la Epoca Imperial," *Problemas de la Prehistoria y de la Etnología Vascas.* Pamplona: Institución Príncipe de Viana, 1966.

Payne, Stanley G. *Basque Nationalism.* Reno: University of Nevada Press, 1975.

———. "Carlism—Basque or 'Spanish' Traditionalism," *Anglo-American Contributions to Basque Studies: Essays in Honor of Jon Bilbao.* William A. Douglass, Richard W. Etulain and William H. Jacobsen Jr., eds. Reno: Desert Research Institute, Publications on the Social Sciences No. 13, 1977.

Pérez de Urbel, Fr. Justo. "Lo Viejo y lo Nuevo sobre el Origen del Reino de Pamplona," *al-Andalus: Revista de las Escuelas de Estudios Arabes de Madrid y Granada,* 19 (1954) 1–42.

———. *Sancho el Mayor de Navarra.* Madrid: Institución Príncipe de Viana, Consejo de Cultura de Navarra, 1950.

——— and Ricardo del Arco y Garay. *España Cristiana: Comienzo de la Reconquista (711–1038).* Vol. 6 in "Historia de España." Ramón Menéndez Pidal, ed. 2nd ed. Madrid: Espasa-Calpe, 1964.

Pericot García, Luis. *Historia de España.* 6 vols. Barcelona: Instituto Gallach de Liberia y Ediciones, 1943.

Pradera, Victor. *Obra Completa.* 2 vols. Madrid: Instituto de Estudios Políticos, 1945.

Ramos, Demetrio. *Historia de las Cortes Tradicionales de España.* Burgos: Ed. Aldecoa, 1944.

Reglá, Juan, José María Jover, and Carlos Seco. *España Moderna y Contemporánea.* Appendix by Emilio Giralt y Raventos. Barcelona: Ed. Tiede, 1963.

Robertson, William. *The History of the Reign of the Emperor Charles V.* 3 vols. Boston: Phillips, Sampson, 1857.

Rodriguez Garraza, Rodrigo. *Navarra de Reino a Provincia (1828–1841).* Pamplona: University of Navarra, 1968.

Roelker, Nancy Lyman. *Queen of Navarre, Jeanne d'Albret, 1528–1572.* Cambridge: Belknap Press of Harvard University Press, 1968.

Romero, Luis. *Tres Días de Julio.* 3rd ed. Barcelona: Ed. Ariel, 1972.

Russell, Peter Edward. *The English Intervention in Spain and Portugal in the Time of Edward III and Richard II.* Oxford: Clarendon Press, 1955.

———. "Navarre," *Encyclopedia Britannica,* 1968, vol. 16, pp. 137–38.

Sainz de Varanda, Ramón. *La Ley Paccionada de Navarra y la Vigencia de las Norma Forales sobre Succesión Intestada.* (dissertation) Zaragoza: Institución Fernando el Católico, 1914.

Salcedo Izu, Joaquín José. *El Consejo Real de Navarra en el Siglo XVI.* Pamplona: University of Navarra, Institución Príncipe de Viana, 1964.

―――――. *La Diputación del Reino de Navarra.* Pamplona: Institución Príncipe de Viana, 1969.

Sánchez-Albornoz, Claudio. *Despoblación y Repoblación del Valle del Duero.* Buenos Aires: Instituto de Historia de España, 1966.

―――――. *Vascos y Navarros en su Primer Historia.* Madrid: Ed. del Centro, 1974.

Sánchez Alonso, Benito. *Fuentes de la Historia Española e Hispano-Americana.* 3rd ed. 3 vols. Madrid: Consejo Superior de Investigaciones Científicas, Instituto Miguel de Cervantes, 1952.

Satrústegui, José María. *Mitos y Creencias.* San Sebastián: Ed. Txertoa, 1980.

Schulten, Adolf. *Geografía y Etnografía Antiguas de la Peninsula Ibérica.* Translated from the German by H. Schlunk and Luis Vasquez de Parga. Vol. 1. Madrid: Consejo Superior de Investigaciones Científicas, Instituto Rodrigo Caro de Arqueología, 1959.

Seward, Desmond. *The Hundred Years War: the English in France, 1337–1453.* New York: Atheneum, 1978.

Soldevila Zubirubu, Fernando. *Historia de España.* 2nd ed. 4 vols. Barcelona: Ed. Ariel, 1962.

Trevor Davies, R. *Spain in Decline 1621–1700.* London: Macmillan, 1965.

Tuchman, Barbara. *A Distant Mirror.* New York: Ballantine, 1978.

Ubieto Arteta, Antonio. "Estudios en Torno a la División del Reino por Sancho el Mayor de Navarra," *Príncipe de Viana,* 78–81 (1960), pp. 5–237.

―――――. "La Participación Navarro-Aragonesa en la Primera Cruzada," *Príncipe de Viana,* 28 (1947) 357–83.

"Vasconia," *Enciclopedia Universal Ilustrada Europeo-Americana.* Vol. 67. Barcelona: Espasa-Calpe, 1929.

Vera Idoate, Padre Gregorio. *Navarra en las Cruzadas.* Pamplona: Ed. Aramburu, 1931.

Vicens Vives, Jaime. *Approaches to the History of Spain.* Translated by Joan Connelly Ullman, ed. Berkeley: University of California Press, 1967.

———. *Atlas de Historia de España.* 5th ed. Barcelona: Ed. Tiede, 1965.

———. *Juan II de Aragón (1398–1479). Monarquía y Revolución en la España del Siglo XV.* Barcelona: Ed. Tiede, 1953.

Vielliard, Jeanne, ed. *Le Guide du Pélerin de Saint-Jacques de Compostéle.* Maçon: I. Protat Frères, 1938.

Viñes Rueda, Hortensia. *Estudio Filológico del Manuscrito N° 1 del Archivo General de Navarra. Extracto.* Pamplona: Ed. Gomez, 1975.

Watt, W. Montgomery and Pierre Cachia. *A History of Islamic Spain.* New York: Anchor Books, Doubleday, 1967.

Yanguas y Miranda, José. *Diccionario de Antigüedades del Reino de Navarra.* 3 vols. Pamplona: Diputación Foral de Navarra, Institución Príncipe de Viana, 1964 (1st ed., 1840).

———. *Diccionarios de los Fueros del Reino de Navarra, y de las Leyes Vigentes Promulgadas hasta las Cortes de los Años 1817 y 1818 inclusivo.* San Sebastián: I. Ramon Baroja, 1828.

———. *Historia Compendiada del Reino de Navarra.* San Sebastián: Ignacio Ramón Baroja, 1832.

Yoldi Mina, Tomás, trans. *La Conquista de Nabarra en el Panorama Europeo.* 4 vols. Buenos Aires: Ed. Vasca Ekin, 1956–1961. Translation of Prosper Boissonade, *Histoire de la Réunion de la Navarre à la Castile* (q.v.).

Zabala, Federico de. *Historia del País Vasco.* San Sebastián: Ed. Auñamendi, 1971.

Zabalo Zabalegui, Javier. *La Administración del Reino de Navarra en el Siglo XIV.* Pamplona: University of Navarra, 1973.

———. *Algunos Datos sobre la Regresión Demográfica causada por la Peste en la Navara del Siglo XIV.* Zaragoza: Miscelanea Ofrecida a José María Lacarra y de Miguel, 1968.

Zubizarreta, I. E. "Baja Navarra," *Enciclopedia Ilustrada del País Vasco,* 1971, vol. 3, pp. 559–87.

———. *Carlismo y Abolición Foral: en Torno a un Centenario, 1876–1976.* San Sebastián: Ed. Auñamendi Argitaldaria, 1976.

INDEX

Abd-al-Rahman, 21
Abd-al-Rahman III, 24–25
a.e.t., newspaper of *Agrupación Escolar Tradicionalista*, 204
Agotes, 144
Agramontés faction, 78, 80, 91
Agriculture, 4, 5, 15, 46, 146, 209, 228 n. 15
Aioiz, 141
al-Andalus. *See* Muslims
Alava, 1, 13, 18, 24, 73; during reign of Sancho the Great, 30; absence from Vergara, 167; at end of Third Carlist War, 188
Alba, duke of, 82, 85, 86
Albania, 73, 74
Albrets: first armed attempt to regain Navarra, 85–86; second attempt, 86; excommunication of, 88, 223 n. 5 (Ch. IX); third armed attempt to regain Navarra, 90–91; fourth attempt, 94–96; merge with Bourbon line, 142. *See also* Catherine de Foix; Jean d'Albret; Henri d'Albret
Alcabala, 133
Alfonso I the Warrior, king of Aragon and Navarra, 37, 43, 45, 51, 220 n. 14
Alfonso II, king of Asturias, 26
Alfonso III, king of Asturias, 17
Alfonso V, king of Aragon, 77, 79

Alfonso VI, king of Castile, 36, 49
Alfonso VII, king of Castile, 109
Alfonso VIII, king of Castile, 38, 63
Alfonso X, king of Castile, 63
Alfonso XII, king of Spain, 187, 188
Alfonso XIII, king of Spain, 192, 198, 199
Alfonso Carlos de Borbón (Alfonso Carlos I), 203, 205, 206, 214
al-Hakam II, 25
Almansur, 25, 28, 37
Almohads, 42
Almoravids, 37, 42
Alsasua, 22
Altamira, cave of, 2
Alvaro de Luna, 78
Amadeo, duke of Aosta and king of Spain, 182, 184
Andalucia, 128, 222 n. 1 (Ch. VII)
Anelier, 62, 64
Antoine de Bourbon, 102
Apostólicos, 157, 165, 166
Aquitaine, 16, 27, 38, 63, 72
Aragon, 18, 25, 32, 47, 62, 124, 222 n. 1 (Ch. VII); relations with Navarra in seventeenth century, 131; in Carlist Wars, 160–61

Aragonese dynasty of Navarra, 37, 212
Arana, Sabino de, 194
Asparros. *See* Lesparre
Asturias, 17, 19, 20, 23
Asturias-León, 18
Autrigones, inhabitants of Vizcaya, 13

Baja Navarra. *See* Basse Navarre
Balearic Islands, 222 n. 1 (Ch. VII)
Banu Qasi, 20–21; relations with Pamplona, 22, 23; influence on Basques, 25
Barcelona: city, 160; county, 33, 34
Basque Country, xi; in Carlist Wars, 160, 188. *See also* Basque provinces; Vasconavarra; Vasconia
Basque language, 7, 11, 51, 195, 209, 216 n. 2, 221 n. 15, 228 n. 20
Basque nationalism, 190, 193, 194, 195, 208, 210; and Carlism, 193–96
Basque Nationalist Party. *See* Partido Nacionalista Vasco
Basque provinces: in First Carlist War, 163–64, 167; provincial legislatures, 169; loss of autonomy, 171; modification of fueros, 193; violence in, 210
Basque Statute, 202, 203
Basques: origins, 1–5, 215 n. 2; prehistoric, 4–5, 216 n. 11; in Navarra, 14; and Franks, 16; and pilgrims, 26; prowess as warriors, 64; as voyagers, 73–74; volunteers in Castilian army, 95; nobility, 144; inheritance practices, 145; devotion to fueros, 159, 211; blood types, 215 n. 3; emigration to New World, 145, 225 n. 7 (Ch. XIII)
Basques, French, 102. *See also* Basse Navarre
Basse Navarre, 1, 34, 38, 54, 64, 83, 85, 87, 88, 94, 103, 167, 182; Estates (Cortes) of, 88; disclaimed by Charles V, 102
Bayonne, 85, 103
Baztán, Valley of, 86, 87, 161, 162, 188
Béarn, 83, 85, 91, 103
Beaumontés faction, 78, 79, 80, 81, 91, 95
Berbers, 15, 37
Berenguela, daughter of Sancho the Wise, 38
Berenguer, count of Barcelona, 33
Bermeo: fuero of, 50
Biaix, Pierre de, 92
Bidasoa River, 38, 129, 131
Bigorre, 22, 85
Bilbao, 160, 162, 164, 185, 186
Black Death, 71, 135
Black Prince. *See* Edward, Prince of Wales
Blanca, daughter of Blanca of Navarra and Juan II of Aragon: marries Enrique IV of Castile, 78; dies, possibly by poison, 80
Blanca, queen of Navarra, 76–77; death and will of, 78
Blanche, sister of Sancho the Strong and countess of Champagne, 59–60
Bonaparte, Joseph, 150, 151, 152
British Legion, 162, 164
Burgo, Jaime del, 205

INDEX

Caballeros, 44; exempt from taxes, 69
Cámara de Comptos, 104–5
Campión, Arturo, 16, 74, 110, 171, 195
Capetian kings of France and Navarra, 213
Caristios, inhabitants of Alava, 13
Carlism, 149, 172, 210; as political party, 180, 182, 189, 191, 194; and Basque nationalism, 193–196; revival of, 203–7; rural nature of, 225 n. 5 (Ch. XIV)
Carlist succession, 214, 228 n. 9
Carlist War, First, 154, 156–67; dynastic issue, 156–57; religious issue, 157; clergy in, 159; patriotic issue, 159; foral issue, 159–60; Quadruple Alliance and, 161; Holy Alliance and, 161; Carlos V arrives in Navarra, 161; barbarity in, 162, 166; death of Zumalacárregui, 163; attempts on Bilbao, 163, 164; feint on Madrid, 164; Royal Expedition, 165; disagreements among Carlists, 166; peace of Vergara, 166–67; Alavese and Navarrese absence from peace signing, 167
Carlist War, Second, 176–78; called "Matiners' War," 176, 177; outbreak in Catalonia, 177; Carlists of Navarra take field, 177; Diputación disapproves, 178; effects on Pamplona, 178
Carlist War, Third, 182–188;

Carlists retreat from politics, 182; war preparations in Navarra, 182–83; Carlos VII arrives, 183; defeat at Oroquieta, 183; *Convenio de Amorabieta,* 184; Ollo rebuilds army, 184; Carlist victories at Estella, 185, 186; failure at Bilbao, 185–86; most of Vasconavarra in Carlist hands, 186; military administration, 186–87; railroads, 187; *La Caridad,* 187; Carlos rejects Alfonso overtures, 188; siege of Pamplona, 188; Estella falls to Primo de Rivera, 188
Carlist wars. *See* Carlist War, First; Carlist War, Second; Carlist War, Third
Carlos I (Charles IV of France), king of Navarra, 67
Carlos II *el Malo,* king of Navarra, 69, 70–73
Carlos III *el Noble,* king of Navarra, 55, 74–77; as patron of the arts, 74–75
Carlos, duque de Madrid (Carlos VII), 179, 180, 181, 182, 183, 185, 188, 190, 214; leader in Third Carlist War, 182–88; anointed king of Basques, 185; proclaimed king of Spain, 188; goes to France, 188
Carlos Hugo, Carlist pretender, 228 n. 9
Carlos Luis de Montemolín (Carlos VI), 177, 178, 214
Carlos María Isidro (Carlos V), 156, 164, 165, 177, 178, 214; claim to throne, 157; character, 160; arrival at

Elizondo, 161; flees to France, 167
Carlos, prince of Viana, 77; marries Ines of Cleves, 78; enmity of Juan II, 78–79; death of, 79; commemorated, 223 n. 8 (Ch. VIII)
Caro Baroja, Julio, 2, 28, 139
Carolingian Empire, 20, 32
Carthaginians, 7, 11
Casanova, 146
Cascante, 141
Castile, 18, 30–32, 47, 62, 72, 124; as leader of the Reconquest, 36; vs. France, 77
Catalina, queen of Navarra. *See* Catherine de Foix
Catalonia, 18, 62; Cluniac monks in, 27; Sancho the Great and, 33–34; supports Carlos, Prince of Viana, 79; in Carlist wars, 160–61, 177–78, 184, 188; declares independence, 201
Catherine de Foix, queen of Navarra, 80, 82, 83, 91, 92. *See also* Albrets
Catholic Church. *See* Catholicism
Catholicism, 44, 158, 189, 194, 202, 220 n. 5
Catholic monarchs, 81. *See also* Ferdinand II of Aragon; Isabella I of Castile
Caves, 2–3
Celts, in Spain, 6
Cerralbo, marquis of, 190
Cesar Borgia, 81
Champagne, House of, 59–85, 212. *See also* Teobaldo I; Teobaldo II
Charlemagne: attempts conquest of Zaragoza, 16–17; demolishes walls of Pamplona, 17; ambushed by Basques, 17; creates Carolingian Empire, 20
Charles, archduke of Austria, 139–40
Charles II, king of Spain, 125, 130, 139
Charles III, king of Spain, 147
Charles IV, king of France. *See* Carlos II
Charles IV, king of Spain, 148, 149, 150
Charles V, Holy Roman Emperor and king of Spain, 87, 89, 90, 91, 92, 96, 98, 99, 112; visits Navarra, 99; second visit, 100; abdicates and dies, 100; will of, 100–102
Charles V, king of France, 72
Charles VII, king of France, 74
Charles Martel, 15
Chièvres, chief minister to Charles V, 90, 91
Christianity: religion of Romans, 11; in Vasconia, 13, 14, 15, 217 n. 3; in Navarra, 27
Cisneros, Cardinal, 87, 90, 91, 92, 223 n. 3
Ciudadela, 102, 106, 134, 151, 209
Clergy, 44–45; exempt from taxes, 69; in Cortes, 110, 112; in Carlist wars, 159
Cluniac reform, 26, 27–28, 35, 219 n. 2
Cluny. *See* Cluniac reform
Cofradía de Arriaga, 24
Compostela. *See* Santiago de Compostela
Comuneros uprising, 93, 94, 95
Comunión Tradicionalista, 196, 203, 204
Concierto Económico, 175

Consejo Real, 90, 104, 105, 107–8, 143; abolished, 168
Constitution of 1812. See Constitution of Cadiz
Constitutions: of Cadiz, 153, 154, 157, 165, 168; of 1837, 168, 169; of 1876, 193; of 1931, 201; of 1978, 210
Contrafueros, 112, 116
Córdoba, 37, 164
Corella, 141
Correa, Luis, 86
Corte Mayor, 107
Cortes of Cadiz, 153, 157
Cortes of Castile, 90, 92, 109
Cortes of Navarra, 45, 66, 67, 79, 80, 91, 100, 104, 109–11, 112–13, 115–19, 125, 133, 158; first Cortes, 110; longevity of institution, 121–22; in eighteenth century, 142; procedure for acquiring seat, 111, 224 n. 6
Cortes of Spain, 104, 109, 168
Cristinists, defined, 159
Cuarteles, 133

de Horsey, Adeline, 177
de Ibero, Evangelista. See Oroquieta, Goicoechea
Desdevizes du Dézert, Georges, 143
Diaz de Rada, General, 182, 183
Diputación, 104, 105, 119–20, 141, 161, 167, 168, 169, 192, 208; loyal to Ferdinand VII, 152; in liberal camp, 155; recognizes Isabella II, 158; dissolved and replaced by provincial Diputación, 168; surviving powers, 170; and disentailment, 173–75; of Carlists, 187; encouragement of industry, 209

Disentailment, 173–75, 226 n. 3
Dolmens, 3, 215 n. 8
Dorset, marquis of, 82, 85
Dos de Mayo, 150
Duero River Valley, 18
du Guesclin, 71

Ebro River, 74, 95, 146; customs posts, 143, 170
Echauri, 5
Edward, Prince of Wales (the Black Prince), 71, 72, 73
Edward I, king of England, 65
Edward III, king of England, 67, 69, 71, 72
"El deseado." See Ferdinand VII
Ekaín, cave of, 3
Eleanor of Aquitaine, 38, 39, 60, 72
Election procedures, 113–15, 170
Elections: of 1870, 182; of 1903, 191; of 1918, 191, 195; of 1931, 198, 200; of 1978, 210; of 1979, 211
Elio, General Joaquín, 177, 185
Eliot Convention, 162
El Pensamiento Navarro, 191, 227 n. 2 (Ch. XVI)
"El Restaurador." See García Ramírez
England: European involvement, 72; and First Carlist War, 162
Enrique I, king of Navarra, 64
Espartero, General Baldomero, 164, 165, 166, 167, 169, 170
Estella, 73, 85, 95, 186, 209; fuero of, 49; representatives in Cortes of Navarra, 113; as Carlist military capital, 161, 185; falls to Alfonsists, 188; 1931 autonomy conference, 201
ETA, 210
Ethelred II, king of England, 27

Evans, Colonel DeLacy, 162, 164–65
Evreux, House of, 67–78; 106, 213

Falces: resistance to fighting outside kingdom, 141
Felipe II (Philip V of France), king of Navarra, 66–67, 110
Felipe III. *See* Philip of Evreux
Ferdinand of Trastámara, 77
Ferdinand I, king of Aragon, 76, 77
Ferdinand II, king of Aragon, 81–90; conquers Navarra, xi, 82; marries Isabella of Castile, 79; alliance with Henry VIII, 82; sends army into Navarra, 85; consolidates position, 87; dies, 90; and Cortes of Navarra, 115
Ferdinand VI, king of Spain, 143, 147
Ferdinand VII, king of Spain: accedes to throne and abdicates, 150; restored to throne, 153; restores Navarra's fueros, 154; accepts Constitution of Cadiz, 154; nullifies Constitution of Cadiz, 155; question of successor, 156–57; dies, 158; decree abolishing *sobrecarta*, 167; unpopularity of heirs, 179
Fernando, count of Castile, 32, 33, 36
Fernando III, king of Castile, 72
Fernán González, count of Castile, 18, 24
Feudalism, 53–54, 218 n. 7, 220 n. 3
Foix, House of, 76, 213
Foix-Albret dynasty, 80–83, 106

Foralismo, 211
Foral Pact of 1841, 170, 174
Fortifications. *See* Navarra, fortifications in
Fortún Garcés, king of Pamplona, 23, 25
Francis I, king of France, 86, 89, 90, 91, 93, 96
Francisco Febo, king of Navarra, 80
Franco, Francisco, 197, 199, 200, 205, 207, 208, 210
Francos, 28, 42, 45–46, 75
Franks: drive Visigoths from Gaul, 12; as allies of Basques, 16; influence on young kingdom, 20; as enemies, 21–22
French Foreign Legion, 162
French Revolution, 149
Fuenterrabia, 39, 63, 96, 97, 162
Fuero General, 66, 71, 113; prologue to, 19, 52; origins of, 50–51, 220 n. 14, 221 n. 16; analysis of, 52–58; *Amejoramiento* by Philip of Evreux, 68; amendments by Carlos III, 76
Fueros, xi, 29, 76; of Aragon and Navarra, 25; proliferation of in twelfth century, 47; compilation of in *Fuero General,* 50–51; cited by Pamplonese in 1512, 83; of Vasconavarra retained in Napoleon's constitution, 151; given lip service in Constitution of Cadiz, 153; as issue in Carlist wars, 159; hopes for conservation of, 169; monument to, 176; and Carlists and Basque nationalists, 194; durability of, 211

INDEX

Fueros de población, 47. See also individual city names
Fueros municipales, 47, 220 n. 8. See also individual city names
Galicia, 17; Romans reach, 11
Gallop, Rodney, xiii
Gamazada. See Gamazo, Germán
Gamazo, Germán, 176
García, count of Castile, 30
García, king of Navarra, 36, 219 n. 3
García Iñiguez, king of Pamplona, 23
García Ramírez, king of Navarra, 37–38
Gascony, 63, 65, 72, 85
Gascony, Duchy of. See Vasconia, Duchy of
Germaine de Foix, 88, 89
Godoy, Manuel, 148, 150
Gomez, General Miguel, 164
Gonzalo (son of Sancho the Great), king of Sobrarbe and Ribagorza, 36
Granada, 62, 81
Greece, Navarrese in, 73–74
Gregory IX, 61
Guernica, 185, 188
Guerra Realista, 154–55
Guipúzcoa, 1, 13, 18, 24, 73, 86; during reign of Sancho the Great, 30; English army in, 85; relations with Navarra in seventeenth century, 131; nationalism replaces Carlism, 210
Guyenne, 82, 85

Hapsburgs, 98–103
Henri d'Albret, 92, 93, 94, 96, 97
Henri de Navarre (Henry IV), king of France, 142
Henry, duke of Lancaster, 71

Henry II (Henry of Trastámara), king of Castile
Henry II, king of England, 38, 39, 63, 72
Henry VIII, king of England, 82, 85, 93, 96
Hidalguía, 44; exempt from taxes, 69
Hisham II, 25
Hospitalers, 37
Huarte: fuero of, 49
"Hundred Thousand Sons of Saint Louis," 155
Hundred Years' War, 67, 72, 82

Infanzones, 44
Infanzones de Obanos, 110
Iñigo Arista, first king of Pamplona, 20, 21; origins of family, 22
Iñigo Arista (Iñíguez) dynasty, 22–23, 212
Inquisition, 81–82
Insaculación. See Election procedures
Institución Príncipe de Viana, 223 n. 8 (Ch. VIII)
Integrists, 180, 181, 191
Irache, monastery of, 15, 45
Isabelle, wife of Teobaldo II, 63
Isabella I of Castile, 79, 89
Isabella II, queen of Spain, 156, 157, 158, 166, 170, 179, 181
Islam, faith of the Muslims, 14
Iturbie, truce of, 88

Jaca, 48; fuero of, 47–48, 49, 50
Jaime I, king of Aragon, 40, 60, 63, 72
Jaime III, Carlist pretender, 191, 214
Javier de Borbón-Parma, Carlist pretender, 205, 228 n. 9
Javier Mina, Francisco, 152

Jean d'Albret, consort of
  Catherine de Foix, 80, 82, 83,
  86, 88, 90; dies, 91
Jeanne d'Albret, 101, 102
Jesuits, 95
Jews, 42–43, 55, 68, 219 n. 1
  (Ch. VI)
Jimeno dynasty, 212
Jimeno el Fuerte, 22, 23
Jovellanos, Melchor, 173
Juan II, king of Aragon, 70,
  76–79, 229 n. 4; marries
  Blanca, 76; assumes title King
  of Navarra, 78; marries Juana,
  79; dies, 80; psychological
  analysis of, 223 n. 7
Juan II, king of Castile, 78
Juan III, Carlist pretender, 179,
  214
Juan Carlos, king of Spain, 199,
  210
Juan "el de Pocos Días," 222 n.
  13
Juana of Castile, daughter of
  Ferdinand and Isabella, 89,
  90, 91
Juana I, queen of Navarra, 65,
  66
Juana II, queen of Navarra, 66,
  67, 69, 72
Junta Gubernativa, 163
Junta Realista de Navarra, 155
Juntas de Ventas, 174–75

Kings of Navarra. *See* Rulers of
  Navarra

Labourd, 1, 32, 126
Labrit, House of, 213. *See also*
  Albrets; Catherine de Foix;
  Jean d'Albret
Lacarra, José María, 197
La Lealtad Navarra. See El
  Pensamiento Navarro

La Navarrería, 48, 65, 66, 75;
  fuero of, 48
La Palice, General de, 86, 94
La Rioja, 73; acquired by
  Sancho the Great, 30; lost to
  Castile, 37; won from Castile,
  37; in Carlist Wars, 161
Lascaux, cave of, 2
Las Navas de Tolosa, 39
La Voz de Navarra, 193
Lecároz, 162
León, 18, 33, 47, 222 n. 1 (Ch.
  VII)
Leonor, queen of Navarra:
  marries Gaston de Foix, 78;
  declared heir to Navarra, 79;
  reigns briefly, 80, 229 n.4
Lesparre, Seigneur de, 94, 95, 96
Ley Paccionada. See Foral Pact
Leyre, monastery of, 15, 45
Liber Judicorum. See Visigoths,
  law of
Logroño, 73, 95–96; fuero of, 49
Los Arcos, 95
Louis IX (Saint Louis), king of
  France, 61, 63, 64, 67
Louis X, king of France. *See*
  Luis I
Louis XII, king of France, 82,
  86, 88
Louis XIV, king of France, 129,
  139, 140
Louis the Pious, 21, 22
Loyola, Iñigo de, 95
Luis, brother of Carlos II of
  Navarra, 73–74
Luis I (Louis X of France), king
  of Navarra, 66
Lumbier, 11, 126, 141

Madoz, Pascual, 173, 175
Magdalenian culture, 2
Magna Carta, 51
Marcilla, 141

INDEX

Margarita, wife of Carlos VII, 186, 187
Marguerite of Bourbon, mother of Teobaldo II, 63
Marguerite of Valois, sister of Francis I, marries Henri d'Albret, 97
Mari, 8
María Cristina of Hapsburg, queen regent of Spain, 176
María Cristina of Naples, queen regent of Spain, 157, 161, 164, 165, 168, 169, 173
María Teresa of Spain, 130, 139
Maroto, General Rafael, 165, 166
"Matiners' War." See Carlist War, Second
Maximilian, Holy Roman Emperor, 87, 93
Maya, 95, 96
Mella, Juan Vázquez de, 191, 196
Michener, James, 146
Miguel, Portuguese pretender, 161
Mola, Emilio, 205, 206, 207
Monasteries, 15, 27, 35, 45
Money. See Prices
Monreal, fuero of, 49
Montaña vs. *ribera*, 4, 132, 146, 160
Montejurra, battle of, 185
Moret, Padre José de, 50, 126
Moriones, General, 183, 186
Moriscos, expelled from Spain, 125
Mozarabs, 43
Mudejares, 43
Muñagorri, 166
Munia "La Mayor," wife of Sancho the Great, 30, 31
Musa, 15
Musa ibn Musa, 21

Muslims: in Basque Country, 14, 15, 25, 28; expedition to France, 15, 218 n. 7; in Spain, 16, 37, 62, 218 n. 6; as threat to Pamplona, 21–22, 24; internal quarrels of, 25; cultural influence of, 25; defeated at Las Navas de Tolosa, 39, 62; in cities of Navarra, 43; references to in *Fuero General*, 55, 68
Mussolini, Benito, 204

Nájera, 73
Napoleon, 147, 150
Naturaleza, 112
Navarra: formation of kingdom, 10, 14, 18, 28; geography of, 8; first use of name, 28, 218 n. 8; Europeanization of under Sancho the Great, 35; ties with England, 38; loses outlet to sea, 39, 49; relations with Guipúzcoa, 39, 131; coat of arms, 39, 208; urbanization from twelfth century, 42; class distinctions, 43–44, 54–55; medieval judicial system, 57; ruled by French monarchs, 65–67; anti-Semitism in, 68, 71; effects of Black Death, 71; civil war, 79–90; conquered by Ferdinand, xi, 83; fortifications in, 87, 102, 151, 223 n. 3; united with Castile, 90; taken by Lesparre, 94; reconquered by Castile, 96; acceptance of Charles V, 99; institutions of, 104–122; in Thirty Years' War, 127; secessionist attempt in 1648, 129; attacked by France, 130; relations with Aragon, 131;

with Castile, 131; contributions to national treasury, 133, 143, 170; economy in seventeenth century, 136–37; under the Bourbons, 138–39; roads, 143, 146; classes in eighteenth century, 144; provincial status imposed, 153; removed, 153–54; reimposed, 154; Ferdinand restores fueros, 155; support for Carlists, 157–58, 167, 180, 181, 182; final decree imposing provincial status, 167, 168; Jaimist sentiment in, 191; and Basque nationalism, 194–95; rejects Basque Statute, 202; in Civil War, 207–8; postwar economy, 209–210; *vasquismo* and *navarrismo,* 211; as "pure" monarchy, 220 n. 3; monarchs of, 212–13

Navarre Question, 84, 87, 89, 91, 92, 96, 100, 103, 126, 129

Navarrismo, 211

Neo-Catholics. *See* Integrists

Newspapers, 193; of Carlists, 187, 204; reaction to tax increase of 1927, 193. *See also El Pensamiento Navarro; La Voz de Navarra*

Noain, 96; aqueduct of, 146

Nobility, 44; in Cortes, 110–11. *See also Caballeros; Hidalguía; Ricos hombres*

Nocedal, Candido, 180, 182, 190

Nocedal, Ramón, 191

Noyon, Conference of, 91, 92, 94

Nueva Fenicia, 151

Nuevo Vizcaya, fuero of, 50

Oliva, bishop of Vich, 34

Olivares, conde duque de, 126, 127, 128

Ollo Vidaurreta, General Nicolás, 183, 184, 186

Oñate, 162, 163, 187

Ordoño II of Asturias, 18, 23

Orduña, fuero of, 50

Oriamiendi, battle of, 164–65

Oroquieta, 183

Oroquieta, Goicoechea (Evangelista de Ibero), 197

Ostabat, 64

Pallars, County of, 18, 33, 62

Pamplona: capital of Navarra, 8; founded, 11; occupied by Visigoths, 12; Muslim opinion of, 15; occupied by Muslims, 16; ravaged by Charlemagne, 17; ruled by Franks, 17; kingdom of, 18, 19, 22, 28; bishops vs. nobility and kings, 44–45, 67; *burgos* of, 48, 65, 75; Castillo of, 66, 95, 100; cathedral, 75, 118, 145; capitulates to Ferdinand, 83; welcomes Lesparre, 94; fortifications strengthened by Philip II, 102; representatives in Cortes of Navarra, 113; relations with other cities, 134; threatened by armies of Archduke Charles, 141; baroque buildings in , 145; population, eighteenth century, 146; threatened during war against the Convention, 147; French admitted in 1808, 150; besieged, 153; on liberal side during Carlist wars, 160; abortive Carlist rising of

INDEX 251

1869, 181; controlled by
  Republicans, 185; Alfonsist in
  Third Carlist War, 188;
  conservative assembly in
  1918, 195; assembly to
  consider autonomy, 201;
  population growth, 209
Partido Nacionalista Vasco
  (PNV), 194, 195, 196, 197,
  202, 228 n. 20
Pasajes, 132
Pass of Roncesvalles. *See*
  Roncesvalles
Paterno, abbot of San Juan de la
  Peña, 35
Payne, Stanley, 193
Peace of the Pyrenees, 129, 130
Pecha, 69
Pedro I, king of Aragon and
  Navarra, 37
Pedro IV the Ceremonious, king
  of Aragon, 71
Pedro the Cruel, king of Castile,
  71, 72
Pelayo, king of Asturias, 221 n.
  17; victory over Muslims, 17;
  mentioned in Prologue to
  Fuero General, 20, 52, 53
Peru, 205
Pesquisas, 109
Philip, archduke of Austria, 89
Philip II, king of Spain, 98, 100;
  and Protestantism, 101, 103;
  and Cortes of Navarra, 116;
  recognized as king of
  Navarra, 223–24 n. 1
Philip III, king of France, 65
Philip III, king of Spain, 124–26;
  and the Navarre Question,
  126
Philip IV, king of Spain, 126–30
Philip IV the Fair, king of
  France, 65
Philip V, king of France. *See*
  Felipe II

Philip V, king of Spain, 140,
  141, 142; promulgates Law of
  Succession, 157
Philip VI, king of France, 67,
  69, 72
Philip of Evreux, consort of
  Juana II, 67, 69; on crusade,
  69
Pilgrims: route to Santiago de
  Compostela, 26–27; influence
  on Navarra, 27; guidebook,
  26, 215 n. 1
PNV. *See* Partido Nacionalista
  Vasco
Pompey, founds Pamplona, 11
Portugal, 124, 128, 160, 161, 222
  n. 1 (Ch. VII)
Pradera, Victor, 196–197
Pragmatic Sanction, 157
Prices in medieval Navarra, 221
  n. 21
Primo de Rivera, Fernando, 188
Primo de Rivera, Miguel, 192,
  193, 197, 198, 200
Puente la Reina, 26; fuero of,
  49
Pyrenees: Indo-European
  invasion through, 6; as border
  between France and Spain,
  129, 140; customs posts at,
  170

Queens of Navarra, 158,
  212–13, 225 n. 4 (Ch. XIV)

Ramiro (son of Sancho the
  Great), king of Aragon, 35–36
Ratonera, 118
Real Congregación de San Fermín,
  145
Reccared, Visigothic king,
  conversion of, 13
Reconquest, 14, 24, 36, 62
Rentería, 132

Republic, Spanish: First (1873–74), 184, 187; Second (1931–36), 196, 199, 200, 201
Requetés, 203–4, 205, 206
Residencias, 109
Ribagorza, County of, 18, 33, 62
Ribera. See *Montaña* vs. *ribera*
Richard I, king of England, 38, 39
Richelieu, Cardinal, 127
Ricos hombres, 44, 45; exempt from taxes, 69
Romans: in Basque Country, 9, 11, 217 n. 1; in Spain, 10, 11, 12
Roncal, Valley of, 85, 86, 87, 91
Roncesvalles: monastery of, 15; Pass of, 15, 17, 22, 26, 91, 94
Roncevaux. *See* Roncesvalles
Royal Expedition, 165
Rulers of Navarra, 212–13, 229 n. 1 and n. 2. *See also* Queens of Navarra

St. Jean Pied de Port, 64, 85, 87, 91, 94
St. Michel de Cize, 64
Salazar Valley, 22
Salic Law, 66, 158
Salvatierra, 73
San Cernín, 65, 75
Sancho III the Great, king of Navarra, 27, 29–36; prosperity under, 29; and Castile, 30–32; territorial gains, 30–34; and León, 33–34; and the Muslims, 34; and the church, 35; division of kingdom, 35–36, 56, 219 n. 3; and feudalism, 54; date of accession, 229 n. 3
Sancho IV, king of Navarra, 37
Sancho VII the Wise, king of Navarra, 38, 54
Sancho VIII the Strong, king of Navarra, 38, 39–40; as *El Encerrado,* 39, 59; effigy of, 40
Sancho Garcés (Sancho Abarca), fourth king of Pamplona, 23, 24
Sancho García, count of Castile, 30
Sancho Guillermo, duke of Gascony, 33, 34
Sancho Ramírez, king of Aragon and Navarra, 36, 37, 47
San Fermín, 13; patron saint of Pamplona, 135; festival of, 178
Sangüesa, 11, 95, 141, 209; fuero of, 49
San Juan de la Peña, 35
Sanjurjo, José, 205, 206, 207
San Nicolás, 75
San Salvador de Leyre. *See* Leyre, monastery of
San Saturnino, 48; Church of, 154
San Sebastián, 45, 63, 87, 132, 160, 162, 185; fuero of, 49, 220 n. 10
Santa Cruz (priest), 184, 204
Santiago de Compostela, 26
Santimamine, cave of, 2
Septimania, 17
Servicios, 69, 99, 109, 116, 133
Sevilla, 62
Siete Partidas, 157
Simancas, battle of, 24
Slaves, 55, 143
Sobrarbe, 18, 19, 25, 32, 62; fuero of, 51, 220 n. 14
Sobrecarta, 119, 167
Soule, 1
Spanish Civil War, 199, 200, 207; Navarra in, 207–8
Spanish March, 27, 34, 62

Tafalla, 209

INDEX

Taxes, 69, 175–76, 192–93. *See also Alcabala; Cuarteles*
Templars, 37
Teobaldo I, king of Navarra, 40, 45, 50; accession, 59; as songwriter, 60–61; on crusade, 61
Teobaldo II, king of Navarra, 63, 72; and Eighth Crusade, 64; dies, 64
Teobaldo III, 65
Thibaut of Champagne. *See* Teobaldo I
Thirty Years' War, 123, 127
Toda, queen regent of Pamplona, 24, 25
Toledo: as Visigothic capital, 12; regained from Muslims, 36
Tolosa, 185
Toulouse: as Visigothic capital, 12
Transactionists, 165
Transhumance, 4
Truce of Iturbie. *See* Iturbie, truce of
Tuchman, Barbara, 71
Tudela, 25, 49, 73, 81, 85, 95, 100, 134, 141, 209; representatives in Cortes of Navarra, 113; fuero of, 220 n. 14; as river port, 223 n. 5
Tunisia, 64

Ultrapuertos. *See* Basse Navarre
Universidades, 112
Urroz, 141

Valencia, 62, 222 n. 1 (Ch. VI); in Carlist Wars, 161, 165
Vardulos, inhabitants of Guipúzcoa, 13
Vasconavarra, 1, 139, 186, 193; "exempt provinces," 142, 143
Vascones, 217 n. 7

Vasconia, 9, 11, 12, 15, 38; Romans in, 11; Duchy of, 10, 16, 32, 34; synonymous with Basque Country, 217 n.7
Vasquismo, 211
Vecindad, 57
Velasco, governor of Pamplona, 21
Vélez, Marqués de los, 127
Vera de Bidasoa, 142, 183
Vergara, 166; *Abrazo de,* 167, 176
Vermudo, king of Leon, 33
Viana, 49
Viceroys, 105, 117; in Navarra under Hapsburgs, 106–7; in eighteenth century, 142
Vikings, 23, 32
Vilanos, 46
Villafranca, 144
Villalva (Castilian general), 91
Villoslada, Navarro, 180, 190
Visigoths: in Spain, 12–13; resistance to by Basques, 12; and religion in Basque Country, 13–14; linked with *Fuero General,* 52; law of, 221 n. 19
Visits, 108–9
Vitoria, 50, 73, 160
Vizcaya, 1, 13, 18, 24; during reign of Sancho the Great, 30; salt tax and stamp tax revolts, 128; fueros sworn to by Carlos VII, 188; nationalism replaces Carlism, 210

War against the Convention, 147–48
War of Independence, 148, 150–53
War of the Succession, 139–41
Wellington, duke of, 153, 166
William, duke of Aquitaine, 35

William the Pious, duke of
  Aquitaine, 27
Witchcraft, 147

Yanguas y Miranda, José, 81,
  113, 169, 226 n. 10 (Ch. XIV)

Yusef I, 37

Zaragoza, 36
Zugarramurdi, 147
Zumalacárregui, General Tomás,
  159, 161, 162, 163